CW00329027

FIFTY YEARS
AMONG THE
BEES

C. C. MILLER

DOVER PUBLICATIONS, INC.
MINEOLA, NEW YORK

Bibliographical Note

This Dover edition, first published in 2006, is an unabridged republication of the work originally published by The A. I. Root Company, Medina, Ohio, in 1915.

International Standard Book Number: 0-486-44728-6

Manufactured in the United States of America
Dover Publications, Inc., 31 East 2nd Street, Mineola, N.Y. 11501

FIFTY YEARS
AMONG THE
BEES

Cordially Yours,
C. C. Miller.

TRIBUTES TO DR. MILLER

BY E. R. ROOT.

[Dr. C. C. Miller died Sept. 4, 1920. The following tribute was paid him in the October (1920) Gleanings in Bee Culture by his old-time friend and close acquaintance, Editor E. R. Root. This tribute tells of Dr. Miller's contributions to beekeeping rather more exactly and with less modesty than Dr. Miller has told of them himself.]

A great voice has been stilled; but those bright and breezy sayings from the Sage of Marengo, always labeled with smiles, will live after. Such a life can not die; but all that is earthly of Dr. C. C. Miller passed away on Sept. 4, 1920, in his nine-tieth year.

When he was obliged to give up his department of Stray Straws in Gleanings in Bee Culture some months ago, on ac-count of severe sickness and his advanced age, there came a feeling over me that I must see him once more before he passed from the scenes of earth, feel his handshake, and see that face so beaming with smiles.

As I was scheduled to be present at a Chautauqua held at Madison, Wis., on Aug. 16 to 20, I decided that on my return I would pay Dr. Miller a visit between trains. On arriving at the Chautauqua I told Dr. E. F. Phillips that I purposed to go and see the man who wrote Stray Straws, and asked him if it would not be possible for him and Mr. Geo. S. Demuth to go along with me. Precisely that thought was in the minds of both of these men, and we were not long in making up a little party to motor from Madison to Marengo. This party was made up of Dr. E. F. Phillips, Geo. S. Demuth, H. F. Wilson, and the writer.

We had expected to see Dr. Miller showing his age, and the once virile face and form infirm with years; but we were agreeably surprised to see apparently the same man with the same vigor of body and mind that I had seen 35 years earlier. He seemed to be at his very best, and the members of our party all agreed that his mind was as alert and keen as ever. He appeared to be a man of 60 or 70 years rather than 90.

That wonderful smile that betokened the happy nature within must have camouflaged whatever of bodily infirmity there might have been. And surely there was some, because he died just two weeks to a day after our visit. I said, "Doctor, I'd give 20 cents for a picture or two of you;" and instantly he came back with a laugh, saying: "Beg pardon. I'll have to charge you 35 cents this year." At this the camera clicked, and the result is shown in the accompanying photo, showing him in laughing mood at 90 years of age.

I had told him I had come to convey the best wishes of my dear old father, and it gave me pleasure to tell the Doctor of the joy that his letter of Aug. 7 gave to A. I. Root. I further added that father wanted to pay him a visit, and hoped that he might yet do so. I shall never forget how that smile seemed to fade a little, and then how it came back with its wonted sweetness in these words:

"I should dearly love to see your father again, for he and I are about the only ones left of the old group. But tell him he must come soon, as sometimes I think I have not many days to live. If I do not see him on this side, I surely shall on the other side."

The grand old man of beedom never claimed to be an inventor. He never claimed he had any secrets, for he had none. His great service to the bee world was not in discovering new things but in discovering practical methods for producing more and better honey with the appliances that the beekeeper already has. One would never find anything in the Doctor's apiary but standard hives, standard Langstroth frames, and standard equipment sold by every supply dealer in the country. While he did not invent, he did pick out of the mass of crudities inventions that he approved. Tho Dr. Miller did not claim to be an inventor, there are some things that bear his name, for instance the Miller feeder and the Miller introducing cage.

There is hardly a standard article sold by manufacturers, and accepted by the beekeeping public today, that was not passed upon by Dr. Miller before it went on the market. For example, the eight and ten frame dovetailed hives were submitted to Dr. Miller before being introduced to the public. In the same way brood-frames, self-spacing frames, bee-escapes, and introducing-cages were passed before the critical

eyes of Dr. Miller. If he pronounced them good the manufacturers made them and they went to the public. The fact
that these things have been in use for 20 and even 30 years
by practical beekeepers all over the United States shows how
nearly Dr. Miller was right.

Perhaps the biggest thing the Doctor ever did for bee
culture was to show to the world the real nature of European
foul brood. He blazed the way in perfecting a new cure for
that disease—a cure that is accepted today. E. W. Alexander
furnished the basis for the treatment, and S. D. House, Camil-
lus, N. Y., showed that the period of queenlessness could be
reduced. He also showed that a resistant stock of Italians
would go a long way in curing the disease and keeping it out
of the apiary. But the ideas advanced above by Alexander
and House were so revolutionary that there were but very few
who took any stock in them. Only too well do I remember
how I was criticised for publishing these "false" doctrines.
But it was not until Dr. Miller had tried them out and had
proved that they were along right lines that the beekeeping
world began to take notice. The good Doctor went further
than either Alexander or House in showing the true nature of
the disease, and, possibly, how it spreads. When, therefore,
Dr. Miller introduced these new methods of treatment the
whole of beedom turned right about face. Later work by Dr.
Phillips and his assistants proved the soundness of Dr. Miller's views.

Dr. Miller, later on, brought out, if he did not invent, a
plan for uniting bees with a sheet of newspaper. The plan
is very simple and effective. He moved the weaker of the two
colonies to be united and placed it on top of the stronger one.
Between the two stories was placed a sheet of newspaper
(with or without a small hole punched in it). The bees would
gradually unite thru this paper; and because the uniting was
so gradual there would be no fighting and less returning of the
moved bees to their old stand.

Dr. Miller would have been great in any line of work or
profession. Had he stayed in music his fame would have gone
over the world, I verily believe; and if he had kept on in the
practice of medicine he would have advanced the profession

materially. Even in the early days he said people did not
need medicine so much as they needed common sense in treating their bodies. Fifty years ago he believed that hygiene,
plenty of water inside and out, rest, and temperance in eating, are far more important than drugs. Our best doctors
today would testify that he was fifty years ahead of his time.
The modern schools of medicine are advocating less drugs and
more hygiene, plenty of good air and water. When Dr. Miller was going thru college he did not know that he could
overwork, but soon found that he was burning the candle at
both ends. He came out of college a full-fledged graduate
with several hundred dollars to the good, but with health
broken. All his life he had to be careful what he ate, as a
consequence. He was always obliged rigidly to deny himself,
but the result was that he kept himself active in mind and
body. He was not only a great teacher but a great healer.

This little sketch would be incomplete, were I not to refer
to a very admirable and dominant characteristic in Dr.
Miller—that temperament or quality in his nature that makes
the world delightful and everything lovely—so much so that
it showed out not only in his face but in his writings. I
think some of the happiest times of my life have been spent
in Dr. Miller's home. Not only did he carry optimism thru
the printed page, but we found it at the breakfast-table and
all thru the day without a break. He went further. His con-
versation was one ripple of merriment thruout. He never
ridiculed, but he could see the funny things of life, and sometimes I have come away from his table sore from laughter. He
had the habit of taking one by conversational surprise, and
would have him holding his sides almost before he knew it.

I said to him 30 years ago: "Doctor, I wish there were
some way by which you might reproduce those breezy remarks
you make at conventions and in your home—those little side-
lines that are so helpful and seem like a drink of cold water
on a hot day. Is it not possible that you could send Gleanings
a page or two of short items of general comment each month?
and I would suggest the name 'Kernels of Wheat,' as we already have a department, 'Heads of Grain.'"

He liked the idea; but for a title he suggested that "Stray

Straws" would be much more appropriate. That would be more in line with his ability, he said. Our older and younger readers know how well he succeeded in giving us "Stray Straws." They were really kernels of wheat. Dr. Miller's paragraphs of five to a dozen lines were worth whole articles; and almost every one of those paragraphs was replete with smiles.

Years ago at some of the conventions there was more or less strife; and well do I remember that Dr. Miller, in his quiet way, with a smile that was more persuasive than a policeman's club, would smooth out all the difficulties, leaving a good feeling all around. In this respect he and Prof. Cook were without a peer. I remember one day he came to me, in the history of the National Beekeepers' Association, when there seemed to be a bitter fight on. He said to a group of us: "You have asked me to pour oil on the troubled waters. The job is too big for me, boys. But I will try my best if you will offer a prayer that only good may prevail"—and it did.

This brings me to another important side of Dr. Miller's character—an abiding faith in 'God. Come what might, with him all was well. There came a time when, thru some mismanagement on the part of others, he lost a considerable part of his savings. With a sweet spirit of resignation he wrote: "I have not lost all. I have my good wife and my sister. I have a few years of vigorous life left to me yet. I have in prospect a good crop of honey. The Lord has always taken care of me, and I am not worried over the future."

E. R. Root.

BY DR. E. F. PHILLIPS.

[The following tribute to Dr. Miller was written by Dr. E. F. Phillips, in charge of Bee Culture Investigations, U. S. Dept. of Agriculture, Washington, D. C., and printed in Gleanings in Bee Culture for November, 1920. Dr. Miller and Dr. Phillips were close and cherished friends to each other.]

The life and work of Dr. C. C. Miller were a benefit to the beekeeping of America and of the whole world which can be measured accurately only in after years. Those of us who have had the pleasure of laboring in this field while he was making his contributions to the science and art of beekeeping know well that in many ways we are indebted to him, but it will take time for the proper weighing of his life in terms of helpfulness to fellow beekeepers. One can now do no more than to express feebly a sense of personal loss and to tell a few of the more outstanding benefits from his work. One thing is clear: there has been no beekeeper of the past half century who was his superior.

Beginning in 1861 and until his death, Doctor Miller was interested in bees, a record of prolonged activity in this vocation rarely if ever equalled. Since 1878 it was his sole business. Naturally his earliest beekeeping was unimportant, but in 1870 he made his first contribution to the beekeeping press and for fifty years his writings have formed an important part of our literature. Even the editors of the bee journals have not contributed more to the current literature than did he, and probably he wrote he wrote more "copy" than did any other writer of the time. His writings are distinguished by accurate diction, clarity, humor, and sympathy.

To discuss in detail the investigations that Doctor Miller carried on in beekeeping would virtually be to write a history of beekeeping of the past half century, for there have been no important discoveries or events of that period in which he did not play some part. He began beekeeping before the days of the comb-honey section and lived until the time when extracted honey largely replaced comb honey. The period of comb-honey production brought forth the keenest work in beekeeping practices of any period in beekeeping, for all the problems are greatly intensified in comb-honey production. Naturally we do not give to Doctor Miller credit for all the brilliant work of this period, but all must admit that no man of the time made more important contributions to comb-honey production than he did.

In his first book, "A Year Among the Bees," he recognizes the two great problems of that and of the present day as follows: "If I were to meet a man perfect in the entire science and art of beekeeping, and were allowed from him an answer to just one question, I would hesitate somewhat whether to ask him about swarming or wintering. I think, however, I would finally ask for the best and easiest way to prevent swarming, for one who is anxious to secure the largest crop of comb honey." His later books contain almost the same phrasing, except that he omits mention of the winter problem, indicating clearly that during the comb-honey period swarm control stood out above all other problems in importance. In the brilliant work on this subject he had no superior and to his work we go for the methods which finally won out. However, comb-honey production, and the small colonies incident to the beekeeping methods of that period, brought on the wintering problem acutely, and in this work also he excelled. A careful study of his writings reveals a knowledge of the needs of the bees during the winter, and his results were better than those of most other beekeepers of the time.

Altho comb honey is passing, until recently Doctor Miller continued to produce it, and as late as 1913 (at the age of 83) he broke all records of per colony production of sections. But even at his advanced age he did not stick tenaciously to his old methods, for during the past few years, altho reducing the size of his apiary, he took up the production of extracted honey. We can not paint an adequate picture of the character of the man, but we get an illuminating sidelight in the fact that he took up this new line, not to make his work easier, not because others were producing extracted honey, but because he might thereby help to make honey a more freely used food on the table of the average family.

The more recent changes in beekeeping methods in no way reduced the importance of Doctor Miller's work and influence. One of the most important, if not the most important, contributions of his life came late in his experience. In 1909 (one is tempted to say fortunately—for beekeepers) European foul brood broke out virulently in his apiary. Up to that time various methods had been advocated for its control, but there was no agreement on the subject and virtually no progress was being made. Doctor Miller's location is not one in which this disease would continuously do serious damage, but thru a total failure in the white-clover honey crop that year his apiary became heavily infected, giving him abundant experimental material. The work which he did that summer and the careful record which he month by month laid before the beekeepers thru the journals form the basis for the first real progress in the control of the disease, which has caused and is still causing losses of thousands of dollars annually. The point which deserves special emphasis in an appreciation of the man is the fact that the disease was virtually absent from his apiary the following year, and from that time on he was not seriously troubled by it, for in one season he had solved the problem of European foulbrood control. To the work he took an accurate knowledge of the efforts and mistakes of others, an appreciation of the nature of the disease and, above all, a keen scientific mind. His work on this disease is his greatest monument.

To have led beekeepers in investigations of better methods was an accomplishment, but perhaps as great a service lay in his efforts to prevent mistakes. The comb-honey era was replete with bad methods, proposed in the effort to solve the serious problems of the time, and no beekeeper outdid Doctor Miller in pointing out the errors arising from incorrect or too scant observations and from faulty conclusions. He was at all times tolerant, yet he could in his finished style lay bare in a few words the foibles of the upstart or the vicious advice of the unscrupulous. He was tender with those who erred thru lack of information, and it sometimes takes a close observer to detect his glee in the slaughter of the ungodly.

We can continue to point out the good things that Doctor Miller did, and beekeepers will continue so to do for many years, so long as beekeeping is carried on. These things serve to make clear the admiration and respect in which he is held by his fellow beekeepers. Such statements fail, and fail utterly, to make clear the affection and love in which he was held by beekeepers everywhere thruout the country. I have had the opportunity to speak before groups of beekeepers in most parts of the country, and it has rarely been possible or desirable to close a talk on bees without telling of something that Doctor Miller did for the industry. Reference to his work and to him invariably brings forth a warm smile of appreciation. A few years ago I took some photographs of him in the apiary and these have been used all over the country as lantern slides; never have they been shown that they did not call forth applause. How may we account for this high esteem in which he is held by all his fellow workers?

The outstanding characteristic of Doctor Miller's life, and the thing for which he is most loved, was his keen interest in "things," as he expressed it. Two weeks to the day before his death five beekeepers visited him, and of those present at that happy meeting no one was younger in mind than he. He told us then that he had always supposed that as one grows old his interest in things would fade away, but that on the contrary he found himself more and more interested as the years passed. The youthful spirit of the man is illustrated by the fact that when over eighty years of age he took up a new line of work, the growing of gladioli. Always a lover of flowers, he began this work at this age as a specialty. He grew corms for sale by the thousands. The flowers were not for sale, however, for aside from the dozens of cuttings in his home his best "customer," as he expressed it, was a children's hospital in Chicago, to which the cut flowers were sent daily. Not only was he growing these flowers on a commercial scale, but at his advanced age he carried out experiments in cross-pollination. Recently he made several hundred crosses and grew the resulting seedlings, and of the number he saved out for further work over a hundred of some promise. Of these he finally selected over twenty of the best and he told us that he hoped from these to get six or eight varieties worthy of perpetuation and naming. It takes perhaps ten years to secure enough corms to offer a variety for sale, but this seemed not in the least to decrease his eagerness for new forms, which he could scarcely hope to use commercially. His interest in these flowers was so keen that he hesitated to let us, uninitiated in gladioli, to find out how "crazy" he was about them, and he refused to tell us what he had paid for certain rare and valuable corms. This at the age of ninety years! Such a man is one for whom a person a half century younger in years can feel the same friendship and affection as for one of his own age. His mind was as young as ever; only his body was old.

To explain the heartfelt affection in which he was held by beekeepers generally would be a foolish task for any but a master writer. In essential respects I have an advantage over the master writers, for I knew Doctor Miller, and, too, I know how beekeepers feel. I know that his death brings to all of us a feeling of great and irreparable loss. Yet at the same time our feeling can not be that only of sorrow, for his death was but the closing of a finished life. He had finished his work, permitted to him by the worn body that served as a vehicle for his young mind, and our feeling at this time can scarcely be other than one of thankfulness that he lived so long and that we were privileged to know him, to learn from him and to imitate him in his all-embracing desire to help those with whom he had contact.

To put these thoughts in words is not an easy task, nor would it now be attempted were it not for an assurance that the readers of these comments will charitably say that here are stated feebly what we all think: in the death of Doctor Miller we have lost a dear and close friend, but we are better beekeepers because of his work and better men because of his life.

Washington, D. C.

PREFACE.

In the year 1886 there was published a little book written by me entitled "A Year Among the Bees." In 1902 it was enlarged, and appeared under the title "Forty Years Among the Bees. In preparation for the present edition I undertook the revision with little thought of the number of changes to be made or the number of pages to be added in order to bring it fully up to date (about one-eighth being new matter), but it is hoped that the changes and additions may make it of more value to the reader. As I began beekeeping in 1861, fifty years ago, the present name seems appropriate.

However much some personal friends may like the brief biographical sketch that occupies the first few pages, others may think that the space could have been better occupied. There remains, however, the privilege of skipping those few pages.

Most of the pictures are from photographs taken by myself or under my immediate supervision, at least so far as concerns "touching the button." The Eastman Kodak Co. "did the rest."

Marengo, Ill., 1911.   C. C. MILLER.

INTRODUCTION.

One morning, five or six of us, who had occupied the same bedroom the previous night during the North American Convention at Cincinnati, in 1882, were dressing preparatory to another day's work. Among the rest were Bingham, of smoker fame, and Vandervort, the foundation-mill man. I think it was Prof. Cook who was chaffing these inventors, saying something to the effect that they were always at work studying how to get up something different from anybody else, and, if they needed an implement, would spend a dollar and a day's time to get up one "of their own make," rather than pay 25 cents for a better one ready-made. Vandervort, who sat contemplatively rubbing his shins, dryly replied: "But they take a world of comfort in it," I think all beekeepers are possessed of more or less of the same spirit. Their own inventions and plans seem best to them, and in many cases they are right, to the extent that two of them, having almost opposite plans, would be losers to exchange plans.

In visiting and talking with other beekeepers I am generally prejudiced enough to think my plans are, on the whole, better than theirs; and yet I am always very much interested to know just how they manage, especially as to the little details of common operations, and occasionally I find something so manifestly better than my own way, that I am compelled to throw aside my prejudice and adopt their better way. I suppose there are a good many like myself; so I think there may be those who will be interested in these bee-talks, wherein, besides talking something of the past, I shall try to tell honestly just how I do, talking in a familiar manner, without feeling obliged to say "we" when I mean "I." Indeed, I shall claim the privilege of putting in the pronoun of the first person as often as I please; and if the printer runs out of big I's toward the last of the book, he can put in little i's.

Moreover, I don't mean to undertake to lay down a methodical system of beekeeping, whereby one with no knowledge of the business can learn in "twelve short lessons" all about it, but will just talk about some of the things that I think would interest you, if we were sitting down together for a familiar chat. I take it you are familiar with the good books and periodicals that we as beekeepers are blest with, and in some things, if not most, you are a better beekeeper than I; so you have my full permission, as you go from page to page, to make such remarks as, "Oh, how foolish!" "I know a good deal better way than that," etc., but I hope some may find a hint here and there that may prove useful.

I have no expectation nor desire to write a complete treatise on beekeeping. Many important matters connected with the art I do not mention at all, because they have not come within my own experience. Others that have come within my experience I do not mention, because I suppose the reader to be already familiar with them. I merely try to talk about such things as I think a brother beekeeper would be most interested in if he should remain with me during the year,

FIFTY YEARS AMONG THE BEES.

BIOGRAPHICAL—BOYHOOD DAYS.

Fifty miles east of Pittsburg lies the little village of Ligonier, Pa., where I was born June 10, 1831. Twenty miles away, across the mountains, lies the ill-fated city of Johnstown, where my family lived later on. The scenery about Ligonier is of such a charming character that in recent years it has become a summer resort, a branch railroad terminating at that point. Looking down upon the town from the south is a hill so steep that one wonders how it is possible to cultivate it, while between it and the town flows a little stream called the Loyalhanna, with a milldam upon whose broad bosom I spent many a happy winter hour gliding over the icy surface on the glittering steel; and in the hot and lazy summer days, with trouser-legs rolled up to the highest, I waded all about the dam, the bubbles from its oozy bed running up my legs in a creepy way, while I watched with keen eyes for the breathing-hole of some snapping turtle hidden beneath the mud, then cautiously felt my way to its tail, lifted it and held it at arm's length for fear of its vicious jaws, and with no little effort carried it snapping and struggling to the shore. Ever in sight was the mountain, abounding in chestnuts, rattlesnakes, and huckleberries, and I distinctly recall how strange it seemed, when all was still about me, to hear the roar of the wind in the tree-tops on the mountain eight or ten miles away.

EARLY EDUCATION.

My earliest opportunities for education were not of the best. Public schools were not then what they are today, for they were just coming into existence. I recall that we children, upon hearing of a free school in a neighboring village, decided that it must be a very fine thing, for what else could a free

school be than one in which the scholars were free to whisper
to their hearts' content. The teachers, in too many cases,
seemed to be chosen because of their lack of fitness for any
other calling. The one concerning whom I have perhaps the
earliest recollection was a man who *distinguished* himself by
having a large family of boys named in order after the presidents, as far as the United States had at that time progressed
in the matter of presidents, and who *extinguished* himself by
falling into a well one day while he was drunk.

But with the advent of free schools came rapid improvement, and I made fair progress in the rudiments, even though
the advancement of each pupil was entirely independent of
that of every other. Indeed, there was no such thing as a *class*
in arithmetic. Each one did his "sums" on his slate, and submitted them to the "master" for approval, the master doing
such sums as were beyond the ability of the pupil, in some
cases a more advanced pupil doing this work in place of the
teacher. Tom Cole was a beneficiary of mine, and every time
I did a sum for him he gave me an apple. I do not recall that
I lacked the apples, and apples then and there were worth 12½
cents a bushel.

PARENTS.

When ten years old I suffered a loss in the death of my
father, the greatness of which loss I was at that time too young
fully to realize. He was an elder in the Presbyterian church,
but for one of those days very tolerant of the views of others.
He was most lovable in character, and the wish has been with
me all through my life that I might be as good a man as my
father. I think he was chiefly of English extraction, although
his ancestry had for many generations lived in this country.
His father had tried to make a tailor of him, but he did not
take kindly to that business, and became a physician.

My mother was a German, her father and mother having
both come from the fatherland. Like many others at that day,
her education never went beyond the ability to read, and I am
not sure that her reading ever went outside of the Bible. Possibly confining her reading to so good a book was one reason
why she was a woman of remarkably good judgment, and to

her credit be it said that she spared no pains to carry out the dying wish of my father that the children should be allowed to secure an education. She was a faithful Methodist; and, although belonging to the two different churches, my parents usually went to church together, first to one church and then to the other.

When my mother married the second time, she married a Methodist, and as the children came to years of discretion they

Fig. 1—Home of the Author (from the Southwest).

were impartially divided between the two denominations, three to each (there were six of us—myself and five sisters).

Two years were taken out of my school life to clerk in a country store three miles away. For the first year I got twenty-four dollars and board, my mother doing my washing. The second year 1 was advanced to fifty dollars.

BEGINS STUDY OF MEDICINE.

Then I undertook the study of medicine under the tutelage of the leading—I am not sure but he was the only—village physician. The Latin terms met in my reading tripped me badly, and by some means I got it into my head that if I could spend three months at the village academy I might be so good a Latin scholar that my trouble would be overcome. Dr. Cummins was very insistent that it was vital for my strength of character that having begun to read medicine I should not be weak enough to be dissuaded from my purpose by a little thing like the lack of Latin, and if I must have the Latin I could work half time at it, spending the other half in his office. Possibly he needed an office boy.

ATTENDS ACADEMY.

But I was equally insistent that I must have one uninterrupted term at the academy, and at it I went, taking up other studies as well as Latin. When the term was completed I felt pretty certain that two or more terms were needed to make a complete scholar of me, and by the time I had finished the two more terms I had settled into the determination that I would not stop short of a college course. A college course, however, took money, little of which I had. At my father's death it was supposed he had left a fair property, but it was in the hands of others, and by some means it soon melted away. I kept on at the academy, taking part of my college course there.

ENTERS COLLEGE.

While yet in my teens I taught school at Shellsburg, and afterward in Johnstown. I entered Jefferson College at Canonsburg, Pa., which college was afterward united with Washington College, and from there went to Union College, at Schenectady, N. Y. This last undertaking was a bit reckless, for when I arrived at Schenectady I had only about thirty dollars, with nothing to rely on except what I might pick up by the way to help me to finish up my last two years in college. I had a horror of being in debt, and so was on the alert for any work, no matter what its nature, so it was honest, by which I could earn something to help carry me through.

WORKS WAY THROUGH COLLEGE.

I had learned just enough of ornamental penmanship to be able to write German text, and so got $44.00 for filling in

the names in 88 diplomas at the two commencements. I taught
a singing school; I worked in Prof. Jackson's garden at seven
and a half cents an hour; raised a crop of potatoes; clerked at
a town election; peddled maps; rang one of the college bells;
and, as it was optional with the students whether they taught
or studied during the third term senior, I got $100.00 for
teaching during that term at an academy at Delhi, N. Y.
Neither were my studies slighted during my course, which was
shown by my taking the highest honor attainable, Phi Beta
Kappa, which, however, was equally taken by a number of my
class.

Fig. 2—Peabody Honey-Extractor.

I secured my diploma, allowing me to write A.B. after my
name, and left college with fifty dollars more in my pocket than
when I arrived there. It was not, however, so much what I
earned as what I didn't spend that helped me through. I kept
a strict cash account, and if I paid three cents postage on a
letter or one cent for a steel pen or two blocks of matches, it
was carefully entered, and probably a good many cents were
saved because I knew if I spent them I must put it down in
black ink.

CHEAP BOARD-BILLS.

The item that gave me the greatest chance for economy was my board-bill. I boarded myself all the time I was in college. My board cost me thirty-five cents a week or less most of the time. The use of wheat helped to keep down the bill. A bushel of whole wheat thoroughly boiled will do a lot of filling up. The last ten weeks, with less horror of debt before me, I became extravagant, and my board cost me sixty-six and a half cents a week.

In the long run, however, I paid dear enough for my board, for its quality, together with a lack of exercise, so affected my health that I never fully recovered from it. Strange to say, I was so ignorant that I did not know exercise was essential to health. That was before the day of athletics in college.

STUDY AND PRACTICE OF MEDICINE.

After teaching a term in Geneseo (N. Y.) Academy, I took up the study of medicine in Johnstown, Pa., attended lectures in Michigan University, at Ann Arbor, Mich., and received the degree of M.D. I practiced medicine a short time in Earlville, Ill., and went to Marengo, Ill., for the same purpose, in July, 1856.

It did not take more than a year for me to find out that I had not a sufficient stock of health myself to take care of that of others, especially as I was morbidly anxious lest some lack of judgment on my part should prove a serious matter with some one under my care. So with much regret I gave up my chosen profession.

TEACHES AND TRAVELS.

In 1857 I abandoned a life of single blessedness, marrying Mrs. Helen M. White. I spent some years in teaching vocal and instrumental music, and was for several years principal of the Marengo public school. Before devoting my entire time to beekeeping, I was for one year principal of the Woodstock school, most of the time driving there thirteen miles each morning, and returning to Marengo at night.

I traveled two years for the music house of Root & Cady, making a specialty of introducing the teaching of singing in public schools. In 1872 I went to Cincinnati, where I spent six months helping to get up the first of May musical festivals under the direction of Theodore Thomas. At the close of the festival I began work for the Mason & Hamlin Organ Co. at their Chicago house.

FIRST BEES.

To go back. July 5, 1861—I was in Chicago at the time —a swarm of bees passing over Marengo took in their line of march the house where my wife was. She was a woman of remarkable energy and executive ability, generally accomplishing whatever she undertook, and she undertook to stop that swarm. Whether the water and dirt she threw among them had any effect on the bees I do not know, but I know she got the bees, hiving them in a full-sized sugar-barrel.

In her eagerness to have the bees properly housed—or barreled—she could not wait the slow motion of the bees, but taking them up by double handfuls she threw them where she wanted them to go. In so doing she received five or six stings on her hands, which swelled up and were so painful as to make it a sick-abed affair. This was a matter much to be regretted, for ever after a sting was much the same as a case of erysipelas, preventing her from having anything whatever to do with handling bees except in a case of extremity.

Previous to that time I had not been interested to any great extent in bees. When a small boy I had captured a bumblebees' nest and put it in a little box, but I do not recall that there was a remarkable drop in the price of honey on account of there being thrown upon the market a large amount of honey produced by those bumblebees.

BEE PALACE.

When I was a little older I remember helping my stepfather carry home, one night, a colony of bees in a box hive (movable-comb hives were not yet invented), the colony being intended to stock a "bee palace." This bee palace was a rather imposing structure. I think it cost ten dollars. It was large enough to contain about four colonies and was raised about two feet high on four legs. On the top was a hole over which the box hive was placed, with the expectation that the bees would build down and occupy the entire space. The bottom was made very steep, so that wax-worms falling upon it would, however unwillingly, be obliged to roll out! When a nice piece of honey was wanted for the table, all that was necessary was to take a plate and knife and cut it out, a door for that pur-

Fig. 3—Wide Frame.

pose being in one side of the palace. The plate and knife were never called into requisition, the magnitude of the task of filling that palace being so great that the bees concluded to die rather than to undertake it. Many years after, I saw at the home of an intelligent farmer near Marengo the exact counterpart of that bee palace, which an oily-tongued vender had just induced him to purchase.

BEES IN BARREL.

Notwithstanding my utter ignorance of bees, I began to feel some immediate interest in the bees my wife caught. I put them in the cellar, and at some time in the winter I went to a beekeeping neighbor, James F. Lester, and with no little anxiety told him that some disease had appeared among my bees, for I found under them a considerable quantity of matter much resembling coarsely ground coffee. He quieted my fears by telling me it was all right, and nothing more than the cappings that the bees had gnawed away to get at the honey in the sealed combs.

In the spring I sawed away that portion of the barrel not occupied by the bees, and when the time for surplus arrived I bored holes in the top of the hive and put a good-sized box over. There were holes in the bottom of the box to correspond with the holes in the hive. I made three box hives, after the Quinby pattern, with special arrangement for surplus boxes, and they were well made.

"TAKING UP" BEES.

When the bees swarmed I hived them in one of the new hives, and later on "took up" the bees in the barrel. Altogether I got 93 pounds of honey from the barrel and am a little surprised to find it set down at 12½ cents a pound. Perhaps butter was low just then, for in those days it was a common thing for honey to follow the price of butter.

I left one of the hives with a farmer, and he hived a prime swarm in it, for which I paid him five dollars. In the remaining hive I had a weak swarm hived, paying a dollar for the swarm. I bought a colony of bees besides these, paying $7.00 for hive and bees.

WINTERING UPSIDE DOWN.

The bees were wintered in the cellar, and according to Quinby's instructions the hives were turned upside down. That gave ample ventilation, for when the hives were reversed the entire upper surface was open, all being closed below. I doubt that any better means of ventilation could be devised for wintering bees in the cellar. There is abundant opportunity for the free entrance of air into the hive, without anything to force a current through it. Equally good is the ventilation when all is closed at the top and the whole bottom is open, as when the hives without any bottom-boards are piled up in such a manner that the bottom of a hive rests upon the top of a hive below it at one side, and upon another hive at the other side, and the ventilation is perhaps as good when there is a bottom-board so deep that there is a space of two inches or more under the bottom-bars.

Fig. 4—Heddon Super.

SEASONS 1863—1865.

The four colonies wintered through, and I find charged to the bees' account for 1863 three movable-frame hives at $2.00 each, three box hives at $1.00 for the three, and some surplus boxes at 10 to 20 cents each. These surplus boxes held from 6 to 10 pounds each, some of them having glass on two sides, and some having glass on four sides. Small pieces of comb were fastened in the top of each box as starters. I also bought another colony of bees at $7.00, and I bought Quinby's text-book, "Mysteries of Beekeeping Explained." I think I had previously read this as a borrowed book. I got 82 pounds of honey, worth 15 cents a pound.

I began the year 1864 with seven colonies, which had cost me $23.39; that is, up-to that time I had paid out $23.39 more for the bees than I had taken in from them, reckoning interest at ten per cent, the ruling rate at that time. Besides getting new hives that year, I bought a colony of bees for $5.00, and twenty empty combs at 15 cents each. I took 54 pounds of honey, 39 pounds of it being entered at 30 cents, the balance at 25 cents.

The year 1865 opened up with nine colonies, and the total crop for the season was 10 pounds of honey. Alas! that it was so small, for that year it was worth 35 cents a pound.

FIRST ITALIANS.

In 1866 I got my first Italian queen, paying R. R. Murphy $6.00 for her, and the following year I paid $10.00 for another to Mrs. Ellen S. Tupper, who was at one time editor of a bee journal. The crop for 1866 was 100¾ pounds of honey, which that year was worth 30 cents.

GETTING EVEN.

I took 131 pounds of honey in 1867, worth 25 cents a pound, and this for the first time brought the balance on the right side of the ledger, for I began the season of 1868 with seven colonies and had $10.40 ahead besides. It will be seen, however, that bad wintering had been getting in its work, for there were two colonies less than there were three years before.

There was certainly nothing at all brilliant after seven years of beekeeping to be able to count only two colonies more than the total number I had started with, together with the four I had bought. But there was a fascination in beekeeping for me, and it is very likely I should have kept right on, even if it necessitated buying a fresh start each year. At any rate, my friends could no longer accuse me of squandering money on my bees, for there was that $10.40, and the time I had spent with the bees was just as well spent in that way as in some other form of amusement. Indeed at that time I am not sure that I had much thought that I was ever to get any profit out of the business. Certainly I had no thought that it would ever become a vocation instead of an avocation.

Fig. 5—T Super.

GETS AMERICAN BEE JOURNAL.

In 1869, while away from home, I came across a copy of *The American Bee Journal.* I subscribed for it, and also obtained the first volume of the same journal. That first volume, containing the series of articles by the Baron of Berlepsch on the Dzierzon theory, has been of more service to me than any other volume of any bee journal published, and to this day I probably refer to it oftener than to any other volume that is as much as two or three years old.

Among the most frequent contributors to *The American Bee Journal* when I subscribed for it were H. Alley, D. H. Coggshall, C. Dadant, E. Gallup, A. Grimm, J. L. Hubbard, J. M. Marvin, M. Quinby, A. I. Root, J. H. Thomas, and J. F. Tillinghast, most of which are well-known names a third of a century later. G. M. Doolittle did not appear on the scene till late in 1870.

A. I. Root, under the *nom de plume* of Novice, was then just as full of schemes as he has been since, and was trying a hotbed arrangement for bees, and in my first communication to *The American Bee Journal,* in 1870, I wrote, "I am waiting patiently for Novice to invent a machine for making straight worker-comb; for as yet I have found no way of securing all worker-comb, except to have it built by a weak colony." At that time he probably little thought that he would come so near fulfilling my expectations, sending out tons upon tons of foundation.

ATTEMPT AT COMB FOUNDATION.

I made some attempts myself in that line, simply with plain sheets of wax. I poured a little melted wax into a pail of hot water, and when it cooled I took the sheet of wax and gave it to the bees. It was not an immense success. I dipped a piece of writing paper into melted wax, and gave it to the bees in an upper corner of a frame where no brood was reared, and for years you could hold that frame up to the light and looking through the comb see the writing that was on the paper. Then when foundation came upon the market, what a boon it was!

VISITS A. I. ROOT.

In 1870 I made my first visit to Medina, then several miles from a railroad station. Mr. Root was then a jeweler; his shop had been burned up, and his house (not a large one at that time) was doing duty as both shop and dwelling. Just then he was full of the idea of having maple sap run directly from the trees to the hives. I showed him how to use rotten wood for smoking bees, and he thought it a great improvement over the plan he had been using. I do not now remember what his plan had been, but hardly a tobacco-pipe, for I have heard that he has some objections to the use of tobacco. Pleased with his newly acquired accomplishment, I had hardly left town when he tried its use, and succeeded in setting fire to a hive by means of the sawdust on the ground. Whether it was burned up or merely put into jeopardy I do not now remember. He did not send me the bill for it.

At that time he knew nothing of a bee-smoker, and neither of us then thought that in the next third of a century he would send out into the world three hundred thousand of them.

ADOPTS 18 X 9 FRAME.

In 1870 I made a change in hives. I cannot now tell the size of frames I had been using, but I think the frames were considerably deeper than the regular Langstroth. I say "the *regular* Langstroth," for in reality all movable frames are Langstroths, but the *regular* size is 17⅝ x 9⅛. J. Vandervort, a man well known among the older beekeepers as a manufacturer of foundation mills, had at that time a machine shop in Marengo, and upon his moving away in 1870 I bought out his stock of hives. The frames were 18 x 9, ⅜ of an inch longer than the standard size, and ⅛ of an inch shallower.

CHANGE TO REGULAR LANGSTROTH.

So little a difference in measurement could make no appreciable difference in practical results, yet after going on until I had three or four thousand of such frames, the inconvenience of having such an odd size got to be so great that I felt I must change so as to be in line with the rest of the world, and be able to order hives, frames, etc., such as were on the regular list, without being obliged to have everything made to order. The change to the regular size cost a good deal of money, and a good deal more in labor and trouble, extending over several years.

In that same year, 1870, I got a honey-extractor. With much interest I made my first attempt at extracting, the supreme moment of interest coming when after having given perhaps 200 revolutions to the extractor I looked beneath to see how much honey had run into the pan below. Very vividly, I remember my keen chagrin and disappointment when I found that not a drop of honey had fallen. The machine was one of

Fig. 6—Heddon Slat Honey-board.

the first put on the market, a Peabody extractor (Fig. 2), the entire can revolving, and it had not occurred to me that the same force that threw the honey out of the comb would keep it against the outer wall of the can so long as it kept in motion. When the can stopped revolving, a fair stream of honey ran down into the pan, and I resumed my normal manner of breathing.

TOO RAPID INCREASE.

I began the season of 1870 with eight colonies, increased to 19, and extracted about 400 pounds of honey. This warmed up my zeal considerably. In the winter I lost three colonies, so I commenced the season of 1871 with 16 colonies, took 408 pounds of honey, and, the season being favorable, I increased without much difficulty until I reached thirty or forty, and I thought it would be a nice thing to have an even fifty, so I reached *about* that number, for so many of them were weak, that I am not sure exactly how many it would be fair to call them. I fed them some quite late, too late for them to seal over, and they were put into the cellar with little anxiety as to the result.

DISASTROUS WINTERING.

In the winter they became quite uneasy, and February 11 I took out five colonies, which flew a little, and then I put them back. They continued to become more and more uneasy and to be affected with diarrhoea, and, February 22, I took them all out and found only twenty-three alive. They flew a little, but it was not warm enough for a good cleansing flight; and soon after there came a cold storm with snow a foot deep, and by April I had only three colonies living, two of which I united, making a total of two left from the forty-five or fifty.

It was some comfort to know that nearly every one had lost heavily that winter, but what encouragement was there to continue under such adverse circumstances? I was on the road traveling for Root & Cady all the time, with only an occasional visit to my bees, and no certainty of being there upon any particular date, and evidently with no great knowledge of the business if I had been home all the time. To be sure, I may have got enough money so as to feel that there was no particular money loss, but after eleven years of beekeeping, and after having bought, first and last, quite a number of colonies, here I was with only two colonies to show for all my efforts!

I do not remember, however, that any question as to continuance occurred to me at that time. Perhaps I didn't know enough to be discouraged. Instead of selling off the two colonies and going out of the business, I bought five more colonies early in April. They were in box hives, and one of them died before the season warmed up, so I began the season of 1872 with six colonies. These I increased to nineteen, and I think I took no honey. With the number of empty combs I had on hand, there was nothing to exult over in this increase, especially as the colonies were not in the best condition as to strength.

WINTER IN CINCINNATI.

The thousands who have been charmed by the delightful music rendered under the guidance of the baton of that prince of conductors, Theodore Thomas, of the May Musical Festivals

Fig. 7—Two Carrying with Rope.

held in successive years in Cincinnati, will have no difficulty in understanding that a congenial although somewhat arduous occupation was afforded me when the managers offered me the position of "official agent," charged with doing the thousand and one things needed to be done to carry out their wishes in preparing for the first of these festivals. I began this work in 1872, some six months in advance of the time for the Festival, making my abode in Cincinnati, although I still called Marengo my home. In the winter I went back home, put the bees in the cellar December 7, and then locking up cellar and house for the winter I took my wife and child to Cincinnati, from which place we did not return till late the following May.

The bees were left entirely to their own devices throughout the winter. In the latter part of March the weather at Cincinnati became quite warm, and I wrote to my beekeeping friend, Mr. Lester, to get him to take the bees out of the cellar. He took them out under protest, for Cincinnati weather and Marengo weather are two different things, and when they were taken out, March 31, they were probably ushered into a rather cold world. They were in bad condition when taken out—bees do not always winter in cellar in the best possible manner with their owner several hundred miles away—and when I got home in May I found only three of the nineteen left alive.

THREE YEARS IN CHICAGO.

Immediately upon the close of the Cincinnati Festival I began work for the Mason & Hamlin Organ Co., at their Chicago office, where I stayed three years. My wife and little boy stayed on the farm at Marengo during the summer and spent the winters with me in Chicago. Notwithstanding the fact that I could have only a few days with the bees each summer, I still clung to them. At least I could lie awake nights dreaming and planning as to what might be done with bees and I could do that just as well in Chicago as Marengo.

One thing that resulted from that three years' sojourn in Chicago was an appreciation of country life that I had never had before. The office, 80 and 82 Adams Street, was in the heart of the burnt district left bare by the great fire of 1871, and to one with a love for everything green that grows it was desolate indeed. A few weeds that grew in a vacant lot hard by were a source of pleasure to me; and my chief delight was to stand and admire a bunch of white clover that grew near Clark Street. I think all my years of country life since have been the brighter for the dismal months spent in that burnt district of the great city.

The three colonies that were left in the spring of 1873 were increased to eight in fair condition, and I took perhaps 60 pounds of honey. These eight were put into the cellar Nov. 10, and December 10 Mrs. Miller gave the cellar a good airing by opening the inside cellar door so as to communicate with the upstairs rooms, and then she closed up the house to go into the city to spend the winter with me.

March 30, 1874, I went and took them out of winter quarters and was delighted to find them in superb condition, the whole eight alive and hardly a teacupful of dead bees in all. These eight I increased to 22, taking 390 pounds of honey. Of course they were increased artificially.

I attributed the previous winter's success partly to their having been taken in earlier than ever before, so I decided to take them in still earlier, and went out for that purpose October 29. But the bees decided they would *not* be taken in, and whenever I attempted to take them *in* they boiled *out*. So, just as I had done a good many times before, I had to give up and let them have their own way, leaving Mrs. Miller to get them in when the weather was cool enough for them.

November 19 they had a good flight, and November 20 they were taken in by Mr. Phillips, a farmer with the average knowledge—or perhaps the average ignorance—of bees, aided by "Jeff," Mrs. Miller's factotum, one of the liveliest specimens of the African race that ever jumped, with considerably more than the average fear of bees. December 12 my wife gave the cellar a good airing, and then it was closed up for the winter.

The winter of 1874-5 was one of remarkable severity, and I felt some anxiety about the bees. The last of February my wife went out and warmed up the house and cellar, finding the bees somewhat uneasy, but after being warmed up and aired they became quiet. Then the house was again closed up, and they were left till April 6, when the men took them out.

ITALIANS FROM ADAM GRIMM.

Three of the twenty-two had died, leaving nineteen to begin the season of 1875. May 10 two colonies were received from Adam Grimm, for which I paid thirteen dollars per colony for the purpose of getting Italians to improve my stock, for notwithstanding the several Italian queens I had got, some of my bees were almost black. May 27 I made my first visit, and I did not find the colonies very strong. Two colonies had died of queenlessness, so that with the two Grimm colonies I had still only nineteen.

June 25 I visited Marengo again, and was surprised to find very little gain in the strength of the colonies. The season had been extremely unpropitious. July 7 I made another visit, of three days, and found scarcely any honey in the hives. I made a few new colonies, and by giving empty combs and plenty of room I left them feeling that there was little fear of any swarming for that season.

TROUBLE WITH SWARMING.

But a sudden change must have come over the bees and the season, and the bees must have built up with great rapidity, for letters kept coming to me saying that the bees had swarmed, and Mrs. Miller was kept busy superintending the hiving, "Jeff" doing the work. It was a mixed-up business for them, for I had left the queens clipped, and swarms would issue only to return again, and then in a few days there would be after-swarms, and they didn't know which swarms were likely to have young queens, and which clipped queens. Some swarms probably got away, but in the round-up when I went out again, August 10, I found the whole number of colonies had reached 40, there having been an increase of 12 by natural swarming in addition to the nine colonies I had formed artificially.

BACK TO COUNTRY LIFE.

Clearly, keeping bees at long range was a very unsatisfactory business. City life was also unsatisfactory; a traveling life was worse. So in spite of the reduced chance of making money, I decided for a life in the country, turned my back upon an offer of $2500 and expenses, and engaged to teach school at $1200 and bear my own expenses; all because I wanted to be in the country and have a chance to be with the bees all the time. I have never regretted the choice. If I had kept on at other business, I would have, no doubt, made more money, but I would not have had so good a time, and I doubt if I would be alive now. It's something to be alive, and it's a good deal more to have a happy life.

I did not, however, get away from the city till August 12, 1876, but that was early enough to see that all colonies were well prepared for winter, and to be sure of being with them through the winter.

Six of the 40 colonies were lost in the preceding winter, and the remaining 34 had given 1600 pounds of honey, mostly extracted, and had been increased to 99.

Fig. 8—Carrying with Rope.

IMPROVED WINTERING.

The advantage of being home through the winter was apparent, for in the next four years the average loss was only 2 per cent, while for the preceding four winters it had been nine times as great. A new factor, however, had come in, to which part of the change was to be attributed. There was chance enough to ventilate the cellar, for two chimneys ran

from the ground up through the house, a stovepipe hole opening from the cellar into each. But the only way to warm the
cellar was by keeping fire in the rooms overhead, and by opening the inside cellar-door. One day when I came home from
school—I think it was in December, 1870—I found my wife
had decided to hurry up the manner of warming the cellar,
and had a small stove set up, and throughout the winter there
was a fire there a good part of the time.

FIRST SECTION HONEY.

In 1877 I gave up extracted honey, the introduction of
sections having made such a revolution that it seemed better to
go back to comb honey. The sections of that day were crude
compared with the finished affairs of the present day. One-
piece sections were then unknown, four-piece sections being the
only ones, and there was not a remarkably accurate adjustment
of the dovetailed parts, so that no little force was required to
put the sections together. When a tenon and mortise did not
correspond, pounding with a mallet would make the tenon
smash its way through.

In order to fasten the foundation in the section, the top
piece of the section had a saw-kerf going half way through the
wood on the under side. The top was partly split apart, the
edge of the foundation inserted, then the wood was straightened
back to place. I was not well satisfied with my success in fastening in the foundation, and in 1878 wrote to A. I. Root for a
better plan, describing minutely the plan I had been using, giving a pencil sketch of the board I used on my lap, with the different parts upon it. In June *Gleanings in Bee Culture* my letter appeared in full, pencil sketch and all, and he sent me a
round sum in payment for the letter, but no word of instruction
as to any better way! I hardly knew whether to be glad or mad.

WIDE FRAMES.

The sections were put in wide frames, double-tier, making
a frame hold eight sections (Fig. 3). I had an arrangement by
which the sections, after having been lightly started together,
were all punched into the frame at one stroke, driving them

together at the same time, and another arrangement punched them out after they were filled with honey. The super in which they were put was the same in size as the ten-frame brood-chamber—in fact, there was no difference whatever in the two except that the bottom-board was nailed on to the brood-chamber and an entrance cut into it. The super held seven frames, and that made 56 sections in a super. Lifting these supers when they were filled was no child's play, especially when loading them on the wagon at an out-apiary, and unloading them at home, as I had to do in later years.

BROOD-COMBS AS BAIT.

In order to start the bees promptly to work in the sections, a frame of brood was raised from below, and the sections facing this brood were occupied by the bees at once if honey was coming in. Care had to be taken not to leave the brood too long, for if the bees commenced to seal the sections while it was there they would be capped very dark, the bees carrying some of the old black comb over to the sections to be used in the capping.

BEEKEEPING SOLE BUSINESS.

In 1878, at the close of the school year in June, I decided to give up teaching for a time, and since that time I have had no other business than to work with bees, unless it be to write about them.

In 1880 I began out-apiaries in a tentative sort of way, a few bees in two out-apiaries. In March of that year my wife died. When the bees were got into the cellar for winter I closed up the house, took my boy with me, and went to Johnstown, Pa., to spend the winter with my sister, Mrs. Emma R. Jones. When I returned near the close of the following April, deep snow-banks still surrounded the house, and matters were in anything but a happy condition in the cellar.

DISCOURAGEMENT.

When the bees were ready to begin upon the harvest of 1881, there were 67 colonies left out of the 162 that had been put in the cellar the previous fall. A loss of 59 per cent was additional proof that it is better for the bees and their owner to spend the winter in the same State.

ENCOURAGEMENT.

Beginning 1881 with 67 colonies, I took 7884 pounds of comb honey, and increased to 177 colonies. An average of

Fig. 9—Philo Carrying a Hive.

117⅔ pounds of comb honey per colony, and an increase of 164 per cent, which would be nothing so remarkable in some localities, but I consider it so in a place where there is no basswood, buckwheat, nor anything else to depend upon for a crop except white clover. Certainly it is not the usual thing here, but remember there were only 67 colonies, and if I were again reduced to 67 colonies I think I might do a shade better now.

AVERAGE YIELD DEPENDS MUCH UPON NUMBERS.

In general, I suspect that the number of colonies in a place is not sufficiently taken into account.   I remember at one time A. I. Root's commenting upon the case of a beginner with a very

Fig. 10—Colonies Intended for Out-apiaries.

few colonies making a fine record, and he thought it was because of the great enthusiasm of the beekeeper as a beginner. I think instead of unusual enthusiasm it was unusual opportunities for the bees.   I can easily imagine a place where five colonies might store continuously for five months, and where a hundred colonies on the same ground might not store three weeks.   There might be flowers yielding continuously throughout the entire season, but so small in quantity that, although they might keep a very few colonies storing right along, they would not yield enough for the daily consumption of more than ten to fifty colonies.   Remember that the surplus is the smaller part of the honey gathered by the bees. Adrian Getaz computes that at least 200 pounds of honey is needed for home consumption by an average colony. So far as enthusiasm and interest are concerned, I do not believe my stock of those commodities is any less than it was fifty years ago. A born beekeeper never loses his enthusiasm.

TOTAL CROP RATHER THAN PER COLONY.

Some one may possibly ask, "If you can do so much better with 67 colonies, why not restrict yourself to that number?" But I can't do any better; at least not in any average season. For it is not the yield per colony I care for, unless it should be to boast over it; what I care for is the total amount of net money I can get from my bees. In the year 1897 my average per colony was 71¾ pounds, only about three-fifths as much as in 1881; but as I had in 1897, 239 colonies, my total crop was 17,150 pounds, or more than twice as much as in 1881.

A BAD YEAR.

In the year 1887 my crop of honey was a little more than half a pound per colony, and in the fall I fed 2802 pounds of granulated sugar to keep the bees from starving in winter. But I could not tell then, neither can I now tell whether it was because the season was so bad or because the field was overstocked, for I had 363 colonies in four apiaries. Possibly if I had had only half as many bees, the balance might have been on the other side of the ledger. But I don't know.

Somewhere there surely is a limit beyond which one cannot profitably increase the number of colonies in an apiary, but just where that limit is can perhaps never be learned. If I were obliged to make a guess, I should say about 100 colonies in one apiary is the limit in my locality.

If I were to live my life over again, and knew in advance that I should be a beekeeper, I never would locate in a place with only one source of surplus. When white clover fails here the bottom drops out. Unfortunately the years in which the bottom drops out have been unpleasantly frequent.

In the fall of 1881 I married Miss Sidney Jane Wilson, who was born on the Wilson farm where one of my out-apiaries was for years located. There was some economy in the arrangement, for she could go to the out-apiary for a day's work, and visit her old home at the same time.

A GOOD YEAR.

Of the 177 colonies with which the year 1881 closed, two died in wintering, and I sold one in the spring. That left 174

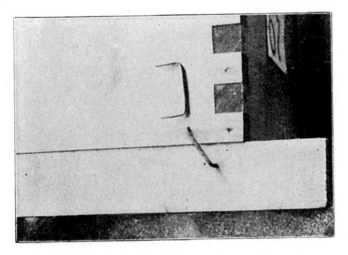

Fig. 11—Hive-staples.

for the season of 1882, and these gave me 16,549 pounds of honey, nearly all in sections. That was 95 pounds per colony, and the increase was only 16 per cent—quite a falling off from the amount per colony of the previous year. But the additional nine thousand pounds in the total crop reconciled me to the "per colony" part of the business. It would be interesting to learn how much the difference in the yield per colony was due to the season, and how much to the increased number, but that is one of the things past finding out.

HEDDON SUPER.

In the year 1883 I tried the Heddon super (Fig.4) to the number of two hundred. The Heddon super is much in form like a T super, but it is divided lengthwise into four compartments. This prevents, of course, the possibility of having separators running the length of the super, so no separators are used. James Heddon and others had reported success in obtaining sections that were straight enough for satisfactory packing in a shipping case, but with me too many sections were bulged, their neighbors being correspondingly hollowed out. I did not continue the use of this super very long.

T SUPER.

In the latter part of the same year I attended the North American convention at Toronto, Canada, and while there D. A. Jones showed me the T super (Fig. 5). I was much impressed with it. The next year I put a number of T supers in use, and the more I tried them the better I liked them. I have tried a number of other kinds since, but nothing that has made me desire to make a change.

THICK TOP-BARS.

When attending that same convention, that very practical Canadian beekeeper, J B. Hall, showed me his thick top-bars, and told me that they prevented the building of so much burr-comb between the top-bars and the sections. Although I made no immediate practical use of this knowledge, it had no little to do with my using thick top-bars afterward. I was at that time using the Heddon slat honey-board (Fig. 6), and the use of it with the frames I had then was a boon. It kept the bottoms of the sections clean, but when it was necessary to open the brood-chamber there was found a solid mass of honey between the honey-board and the top-bars. It was something of a nuisance, too, to have this extra part in the way, and I am very glad that at the present day it can be dispensed with by having top-bars 1⅛ inches wide and ⅞ inch thick, with a space of ¼ inch between top-bar and section. Not that there is an entire absence of burr-combs, but near enough to it so that one can get along much more comfortably than with the slat honey-board. At any rate there is no longer the killing of bees that there was every day the dauby honey-board was replaced.

But it would take up space unnecessarily to follow farther the course of the years, especially as these later years are familiar to more of my readers than are the former years, so I will proceed to fulfill my chief purpose in telling about my

Fig. 12—Bottom-rack.

work throughout the course of the year, reserving, however, the right to refer to the past whenever I like.

SEASONS HAVE CHANGED.

It is only fair to remark, however, that in later years the crops have not always been so good as formerly. At least that is true as to the early crop. The fall crop, however, seems to be on the increase. Just why, I don't know, unless it be that there are two important pickle-factories at Marengo, and the bees have the range of some two hundred acres of cucumbers.

Sweet clover may have a little to do with it, and also heartsease. If the yield of fall honey keeps on the increase, it will
hardly do to say there is only one source of honey—white clover. The season of 1902 emphasized the change in seasons.
During the proper time for white clover, the bees would have
starved if it had not been that they were fed about a thousand
pounds of sugar. Clover grew well, but blossoms were scarce.
The bloom, however, kept increasing, and during the latter part
of August and the first part of September a number of colonies stored fifty pounds and more each. How much of the
honey was from clover I cannot tell. As late as the last half of
October I saw bees busy on both red and white clover.

TAKING BEES OUT OF CELLAR.

The difficulty of wintering bees, at the North, is not entirely without its compensations. I am almost willing to meet
some losses, for the sake of the sharp interest with which I look
forward to the time of taking the bees out of the cellar in the
spring. I live on a place of 37 acres, about a mile from the
railroad station, and on my way down town a number of soft-
maple trees are growing. How eagerly I watch for the first
bursting of the buds! and when the red of the blossom actually
begins to push forth, with what a thrill of pleasure I say, "The
bees can get out on the first good day!"

In former years I did sometimes bring out the bees earlier,
because they seemed so uneasy, but I doubt if I gained anything by it. I have known years when a cold, freezing time
came on at the time of maple bloom and I did not take out the
bees for a good many days, but generally I go by the blooming
of the soft maples. So I watch the thermometer and the clouds,
and usually in a day or two there comes a morning with the
sun shining, and the mercury at 45 or 50 degrees, with the prospect of going a good deal higher through the day.

TAKING OUT WITH A RUSH.

This is one of the times when I want outside help, for
carrying two or three hundred colonies of bees out of the cellar is not very light work if it be done with a rush; and I want

them all out as soon as possible so as to have a good flight before night. If any should be brought out too late to fly, it may turn cold before the next morning, when a lot of bees might fly out to meet their death. To be sure, I could get along without outside help by having one of the women-folks help me, for my hives have cleats on each end, the cleats being clear across the hive, so that a rope can be slipped over them, and one can take hold of the rope at each side, making the work not so very hard. Indeed, the two women have sometimes rendered efficient service by taking a hive between them, as shown in Fig. 7. An endless rope is used, making it the work of a very few seconds to throw the rope over each end of the hive. The same rope may be used to make the work lighter for a single person (Fig. 8). But the work is not so quickly adjusted as when two persons use it.

On the whole, it is better to have a strong man who can pick up each hive without any ceremony, carry it directly to its place, and set it on its stand. In this work the end-cleats of the hive serve an important purpose, for the carrier can let the full weight of the hive come on his forearms by having an arm under each cleat, each hand lightly clasping the hive on the opposite side (Fig. 9).

CELLAR AIRED BEFORE CARRYING.

When it is warm enough to carry out bees, it will be understood that the cellar is likely to become a good deal warmer than 45 degrees, the temperature near which it is desirable to keep the cellar throughout the winter. So if carrying out is undertaken without any previous preparation, when the cellar-door is opened the bees will pour out of the hives and out of the cellar-door, sailing about in confusion, causing some loss and making the work of carrying out exceedingly unpleasant. This must be avoided; so the previous evening, as soon as it becomes dusk, cellar door and window are thrown wide open.

Having the cellar open the previous night makes it much pleasanter to carry out the bees, which do not generally come out of their hives till some time after being set on their stands. If at any time a colony seems inclined to come out of the hive, a little smoke is given at the entrance. At other times it would be bad to have smoke in the cellar, but as the bees are immediately to have a chance to fly, it does no harm to have the cellar filled with smoke. The hive entrances are left open; and as the hives have been taken into the cellar with covers and bottom-boards just as on the summer stands, the work can be done rapidly.

Before each hive leaves the cellar, I make sure there are live bees in it, by placing my ear at the entrance. If I hear

Fig. 13—Entrance-blocks.

nothing I blow into the entrance. That generally brings an immediate response, but sometimes I will blow several times before getting a sleepy reply from a strong colony. That pleases me. If any are dead they are piled to one side in the cellar.

PLACING OF COLONIES.

Colonies intended for the home apiary are set upon their stands. Those for the out-apiaries are set upon the ground not far from the cellar, being placed in pairs, two hives almost touching, then a space of a foot or more between that pair and the next pair, so as to occupy as little room as possible (Fig. 10). Sometimes some attempt is made to have colonies occupy the same stands they occupied the previous year, but oftener no attention is paid to this. Close attention, however, is paid to selecting the colonies that are to be in the home apiary.

BEST BEES FOR HOME APIARY.

The hives with queens having the best records were all marked the previous fall by having a stick tacked on the front. These are all put in the home apiary—not that queens will be reared from all of them. The one or two very best colonies may furnish all the young queens, the rest will furnish choice drones. By doing this from year to year I ought to have better stock than if I allowed the poorest drones to remain in the home apiary.

TAKING BEES ALL OUT AT ONCE.

Some object to taking all the bees out at the same time, for fear of so much excitement that bees will swarm out and return to the wrong hives. I have never had much trouble in that way. Neither have I had any evil results from putting colonies on stands different from the ones they occupied the previous fall.

I am not sure that I can tell for certain just why there should be this difference in different apiaries, but I think I can see some reason for it. As already mentioned, the cellar is left wide open all night the night before the bees are carried out, and it is possible that just in that little thing lies the secret of the difference. When the weather begins to warm up in the spring before it is time to carry out the bees, it often happens that there comes a warm day when the outside temperature runs up to 50 degrees or more, and possibly this may continue more than a day. Such times are hard on the ventilation of the cellar.

TEMPERATURE AND VENTILATION.

Please remember that the ventilation of the cellar depends on the difference of the weight of the air in the cellar and the weight of the outside air. Also remember that the difference in weight depends on the difference in temperature. Warm air is lighter than cold air. So when the air outside the cellar is colder and heavier than that inside, it forces itself in and crowds up the warm air, precisely in the same way—although not with the same degree of force—that water would pour into the cellar if a body of water surrounded the cellar. If the water were lighter than the air, no water would flow into the cellar. So long as the outside air is colder than the inside, ventilation continues.

Suppose, now, that the air in the cellar stands at 45 or 50 degrees, and that the outside air becomes warmed up to the same temperature. There will be an equilibrium in weight, and there will be no ventilation. The air in the cellar is all the time becoming vitiated by the breathing of the bees, and, no matter what the ventilation of the *hives*, it can do little good so long as there is no pure air in the *cellar*. The bees become frantic in their desire for fresh air, and if carried out while in this condition they will rush out of the hive, the excitement becoming so great that soon after being put on their stands whole colonies will swarm. If the cellar has been open all night, they will find little change of air on being carried out, and so will not fly out of the hives for the sake of getting air, but only to take their cleansing flight.

Of course, there is an understanding with the women-folks about the time the bees are taken out, lest they spot the clothes on the line on a wash-day; but the bees have the right of way, and if there is a clash, the wash-day must be postponed.

SIZE OF ENTRANCE.

While the bees were in the cellar they had an entrance $12\frac{1}{8}$ x 2 inches, and during the cool days of spring, after they are taken out of the cellar, it is no longer desirable to have so large an entrance. So, as soon as the bees are on their stands, the entrance is closed down to a very small one by means of an entrance-block. Before describing this I must tell you about the hive and the bottom-board.

CLEATS FOR HIVES.

The hive is the ordinary 8-frame dovetailed, only I insist upon having on each end a plain cleat $13\frac{7}{8}$ x $1\frac{1}{2}$ x $\frac{7}{8}$. There are more reasons than one for having this cleat, rather than the usual hand-holes. It is more convenient to take hold of when one wants to lift a hive. Latterly the manufacturers use a very short cleat, which is a great improvement on the hand-hole, but it does not allow one to carry the hive with the weight resting on the whole forearm, as shown in Fig. 9. This way of carrying a hive is one gotten up by Philo Woodruff, the hired man who helped me for several years, evidently to make the work easier for him. One day he was carrying a hive that had no cleats, only hand-holes, perhaps the only one of that kind he had ever carried. He seemed disgusted with it, and as he set the hive down he grumbled, "I wish the man who made them hand-holes had to carry them."

Another advantage of the cleats is the strength it gives to the rabbeted ends of the hive. Without the cleat the rabbet leaves the hive-end at the top only 7/16 of an inch thick for more than ¾ of an inch of its depth, and the splitting off of this part is unpleasantly frequent. With the added cleat the thickness is three times as much, and it never splits off.

These cleats, not being regularly made by manufacturers, can be had only by having them made to order, so hives are generally made without them, but quite a number of experienced beekeepers are quietly using them because of their distinct advantage, notwithstanding the inconvenience of having them made to order.

BOTTOM-BOARD.

The bottom-board is a plain box, two inches deep, open at one end. It is made of six pieces of ⅞ stuff; two pieces 22½ x 2 , one piece 12⅛ x 2, and three pieces 13⅞ x 7½. When so desired, the bottom-board is fastened to the hive by means of four staples 1½ in. wide, with points ¾ inch long (Fig. 11).

With such a bottom board there is a space two inches deep under the bottom-bars, a very nice thing in winter, and at any other time when there is no danger of bees building down, but quite too deep for harvest time. Formerly I made the bottom-board reversible, reversing it in summer so as to use the shallow side, but latterly I leave the deep side up, summer and winter.

Of course, with a 2-inch space under the bottom-bars the bees would build down, sometimes even as early as dandelion bloom.   Before that time I shove under the bottom-bars a bottom-rack.   As material for a rack there are two pieces 18 x 1 x ¾, and 21 pieces 10½ x ⅜ x 3/16.   The little pieces are nailed upon the ¾-inch sides of the two larger pieces, ladder-fashion, with ½-inch space between each two strips.   The strips are allowed to project over at each side about an inch.

Fig. 14—Wagonload of bees.

I value this bottom-rack highly. It prevents building down, and at the same time gives the bees nearly the full benefit of the deep space, preventing overheating in hot weather, thus serving as no small factor in the prevention of swarming.   It also saves the labor of lifting the hive off the bottom-board to reverse the bottom-board and then lifting the hive back again, spring and fall.   Instead of being made in the way described, a board 10½ inches long may be split up irregularly and used for the cross-pieces.   Such a bottom rack is shown at Fig. 12.

ENTRANCE BLOCK.

Now for that entrance-block.   Formerly I made it heavy (Fig. 13), but now it is thin, ⅛ inch or so thick, 12 inches long and 3 inches wide. It is lightly nailed upon the hive by one or two small nails, and at one lower corner a notch 1 inch square or less is cut out. I think that small entrance helps to prevent "drifting" when the bees take their first flight.

GIVING STORES.

When the bees are being carried out, if any are noted as suspiciously light, they are marked, and the next day frames of honey are given them. If, unfortunately, these are not to be had, sections of honey are put in the hive in wide frames, or shoved under.

HAULING BEES.

As soon as the bees have had a good flight, those not in the home apiary are ready to be hauled away. I like to get them away as soon as possible, so as to have advantage of the spring pasturage at the out-apiaries, but sometimes the condition of the roads causes delay. I first hauled four colonies at a time on a one-horse wagon, which you may imagine was very slow work. That was years ago, and the number has been gradually increased until now 40 or 50 colonies are taken at a load.

WAGON FOR HAULING.

After several changes, I used for a good while a common farm-wagon with heavy springs put under the box. Nine colonies were put in the box; then a rack (Fig. 15) (made in two parts for convenience in handling) was put on the box, and 22 colonies were set on the rack, making 31 colonies in a load. After that I used a flat hayrack or a drayman's platform, taking 40 or 50 colonies at a load.

PREPARATIONS FOR HAULING.

All the hives have fixed-distance frames, so no preparation is needed in the way of fastening frames in place before hauling. The only thing to do is to fasten the cover and close the entrance. The cover is fastened to the hive by two staples (the same as those used to fasten the bottom-board to the hive), one staple at the middle on each side. Hives that were brought from the out-apiaries the previous fall have the covers already fastened, for they have never been opened since coming home, unless they were so light as to need feeding. If things were always done just right, there never would be any opened because suspiciously light; but things are not always done just right.

The entrance is of course closed with wire cloth, and after trying a good many entrance-closers I have settled down upon the simplest of all. It is a piece of wire cloth just large enough to close the 12⅛ entrance and project an inch or so up on the

Fig. 15—Rack for Hauling Bees.

front of the hive. To make the edges at the bottom and at the two ends more firm, and to prevent them from raveling, the wire cloth is cut about 13½ x 4, and then about ¾ of an inch folded over at the bottom and at each end. These edges are folded over the edge of a saw. When finished, the closer is 12⅛ inches long or a trifle less, so it will easily fit in the bottom-board. The closer is put in place, a piece of lath 13½ inches long is pushed up against it, and fastened by a nail in the middle of the lath. Then to make it more secure, a nail at each end is placed perpendicularly against the lath and driven a short distance into the outer rim of the bottom-board. The three nails used to fasten the lath are finishing or wire casing nails $2\frac{1}{2}$ inches long or longer. Being so long and not driven in very deep, one can generally pull them out with the fingers.

At Fig. 16, in the middle of the cut, will be seen an entrance-closer, above it being the lath to fasten the closer in place.

Before the hives are put on the wagon I make sure there is no possible leak in any of them. This is hardly necessary where everything is in good condition, but some of my covers and bottom-boards are pretty old, and I must plug up any hole that would possibly allow a bee to escape.

When the hives are placed on their stands in the out-apiary, the entrance-closers are removed, a little smoke being used if the bees appear belligerent. Then the entrances are closed. with the entrance-blocks.

I speak of taking bees to out-apiaries as if I were still keeping up out-apiaries. As a matter of fact, I have had no bees away from the home apiary since 1909. That year I kept bees in the Wilson apiary for the last time, having given up the Hastings apiary some years before, and the Belden apiary still earlier. But it is more convenient, sometimes, to speak of past things as if present, so the reader will please pardon any discrepancy that may appear in this book at any time on that account.

NUMBERING HIVES.

Numbers for hives are made in this way: Pieces of tin $4 \times 2\frac{1}{2}$ inches have a small hole punched in each one, near the edge, about midway of one of the longer sides. With $\frac{1}{2}$-inch wire nails, nail them on the top of a wooden hive cover or other plane surface. Then give them a couple of coats of white paint, and, when dry, put the numbers on them, from 1 upward, with black paint. There is room to make figures large enough to be seen distinctly at quite a distance. These tin tags are fastened on the fronts of the hives with $\frac{3}{4}$ or inch wire nails driven in not very deep, making it easy to change them at any time from one hive to another.

I have also used manilla tags with figures printed on them, but the figures are not seen at so great a distance as on the white tin tags. The tin tags cost more in the first place, but are cheaper in the long run, for they last twenty years or more, while the manilla scarcely last a fifth of that time in satisfactory shape.

ORDER OF NUMBERS.

When the hives are put on the stands in the spring, the numbers are all mixed up. The first thing to be done is to enter upon the record book these numbers. The first hive in the first row should be No. 1, the next No. 2, and so on; but in the place of No. 1 stands perhaps 231; on the place of No. 2 stands 174, etc. So, on the new record book I write No. 1 (231) on the first page at the top; one-third the way down the page I write No. 2 (174), and so on.

Just as soon as convenient the tags are taken off the hives where they are wrong, and the right ones put on. If on No. 1 the tag says 231, then that tag is taken off and the tag that says 1 is put on.

THE RECORD BOOK.

I can tell more or less of the history of every colony of bees since I began keeping bees in 1861. At first I kept the record of each colony from year to year in the same book, but for a good many years I have had a new book each year. The book I like is 12 x 5½ inches, containing about 160 pages (Fig. 17). Three colonies are kept on each page, so the book is a good deal larger than I need, for I have never had quite 400 colonies. But a good many pages are used for memoranda and other things, and it is better to have too much room than too little. While the size of the book is not so very important, the binding is. If the book were bound the same as the book in which you are now reading, it would come to pieces if it should be left out long enough in a soaking rain. Of course a book should never be left out in a rain, but of course it sometimes is. So I want a book that will suffer no greater harm than to have the cover come off if it should be rain-soaked. It must be

stitched together through the middle, so that the one set
of stitches does the whole business, the first leaf being continuous with the last leaf, the second continuous with the next to
the last, and so on.

HISTORY OF QUEENS.

While the record book is very important to keep track of
the work from day to day, it is perhaps more important for the
purpose of tracing the history of queens from year to year. On
each page is left a margin of about ¾ of an inch. In that
margin is put the last two figures of the year in which the
queen is born, '99 if she was born in 1899, '01 if in 1901, and
so on. In that margin is also found anything important to
have recorded about the queen. "Very cross" may be in the
margin if the workers distinguish themselves in that direction;
"seals white" if the capping of sections was uncommonly
white; "dark" if the workers were unusually dark, etc. Especially am I interested in the memoranda in the margin relat-
ing to swarming and storing. You will find *sw* if the colony of
that queen swarmed last year; *no c* if no queen-cells were found
in the hive during the whole of last season; *2k* if I twice killed
queen-cells that were started. No doubt the printer will feel
like putting some periods after these contractions. Please don't
do it, Mr. Printer, for I never take time to use such embellish-
ments when making entries. The number of sections stored by
the progeny of the queen the preceding year has a place in this
margin; *24 sec* if 24 sections were stored; *160 sec* if so many
sections were stored. If an unusual number of sections was
reached, that record follows the queen as long as she lives. For
instance, in the year 1902 may be found in one case on the margin, *44 sec, 60 sec in 1900, 178 in 1899.* That means that the
progeny of that queen stored 44 sections in the preceding year,
1901, 60 sections in 1900, and 178 sections in 1899. An unusual record, considering the character of the seasons in 1900
and 1901. If, in the year 1902, a 1900 queen is by any means
replaced by a young queen, a line is drawn through the *00* and
02 is written below it.

As soon as I have entered in the record the old numbers

that were on the hives, as previously mentioned, I am ready to enter the respective ages of the queens. If, for instance, I find at the beginning, No. 1 (231), I turn to No. 231 in last year's record and find the year set down for the age of the queen, and put it in the new book at No. 1. This I do throughout all the numbers.

ADVANTAGE OF BOOK FOR RECORD.

I do not need to be in the apiary to do this work; it can be done in the house just as well. Indeed I spend a good deal of time in the house with my record book, studying and planning,

Fig. 16—Entrance-closers.

perhaps lying on the lounge. I had two out-apiaries, one three miles north at Jack Wilson's, on the old farm where my wife was born; the other five miles southeast at cousin Hastings'. Frequently I studied my book most of the way in going to one of these apiaries, making my plans and jotting down memoranda of what was to be done when I got there. That saves time. Another advantage is that my records are safe from interference, for with slates, stones, etc., in the apiary, there is always danger that records may be changed, either through accident or mischievous design. One disadvantage of the book is the danger of forgetting it. One may forget it at an out-apiary, and then have to make a special trip to get it. I've done that.

SPRING OVERHAULING.

After the bees are hauled to the out-apiaries, I am ready for the spring overhauling as soon as the weather is right for it. I do not want to open up the hives except at a time when it is warm enough for bees to fly freely. Too much danger of chilling the brood. Sometimes there may come one good day followed by a week of weather too bad for bees to fly. So I may commence overhauling in April, and perhaps not till in May; and if I do begin in April I may not get all done till well on in May.

HIVE-SEAT.

Having due regard for my own comfort, I want a seat when I work at a hive. Mr. Doolittle once tried to poke fun at me in convention, because I accidentally admitted that I sat down to work at bees. If I were obliged to work all the season without a seat, I am afraid I would have to give up the business from exhaustion. Moreover, if I had the strength of a Samson I don't think I should waste it stooping over hives, so long as I could get a seat. I generally have three or four seats about the apiary, and they may not all be of the same kind. A common glass-box is more used than any other. To make it convenient for carrying, a strap of leather or cloth may be nailed to two diagonally opposite corners on the bottom. Or the cover may be nailed on the box with a hand-hole in the middle. The box being of three different dimensions, one has a choice as to height of seat. It is a little curious to know what a difference there is in this respect as to the preferences of different persons. My assistant never uses the highest seat the box affords, while I never use the lowest.

Fig. 18 shows a hive-seat with a strap-handle, the kind I prefer; Fig. 19 shows one with hand-hole, which my assistant prefers.

A DIGRESSION.

Perhaps I ought to digress a little, and tell you about my help. Years ago, my wife, her sister Emma, and sometimes my boy Charlie (I have no other children), all worked with me at the bees. Those were delightful days. I think Charlie would have made a very bright beekeeper, but somehow he did not take kindly to the business, and has spent his later years in the army and government service. My wife is one of the sort who is never happy unless she is doing something for some one else, so for years she has been confined to the house so as to help make a pleasant home for others, sometimes of my relatives, sometimes of hers. Ever since the year of our Lord eighteen hundred and ninety-eight there has dwelt with us my wife's mother, Mrs. Margaret Wilson, a blessed old Scotch saint, whose presence in the home I feel to be much like the presence of the ark in the house of Obed-edom, when "it was told King David, saying, The Lord hath blessed the house of Obed-edom, and all that pertaineth unto him, because of the ark of God." She is a great consumer of honey, and her temper is correspondingly sweet.

ASSISTANT BEEKEEPER.

So for a number of years Miss Emma M. Wilson has given me the only assistance I have had in the apiary. Hired help does some such work as carrying out and hauling bees, putting together hives, etc., unloading honey brought from the out-apiaries, taking sections out of supers, etc. Sometimes it has been a convenience that I could call on the hired help in the employ of my good brother-in-law, Ghordis Stull. Ghordis has the place pretty well filled with raspberries and strawberries, and he is 'way up in such matters. Previous to his occupancy of the place it was chiefly in grass, for I could give no attention to cultivated crops. The only thing I pretend to oversee of the farm work is the cultivation of the rose-beds. I could hardly live without roses, and my wife is an expert in chrysanthemums. With the fruit crop I have nothing whatever to do except with the finished product, and only so much of that as we can finish in the house—by no means a small quantity.

Miss Wilson was a school-teacher with health run down, and in 1882 she stopped a year for the outdoor life of bee-keeping. She is still stopping. Although never rugged in health, I think she has never missed a day's work in the apiary during all the years since, when there was work to be done. Small of stature and frail of build, she yet has a remarkable capacity for work, perhaps owing to the fact that she is full-blooded Scotch, and she will go through more colonies in a day than I can, do my best. I think, however, that the bees prefer just a little to have me work with them. They have more time to get out of the way, and not so many of them get killed.

T-SUPER SEAT.

Well, I started in for a digression, but I didn't mean to write a history. We were talking about seats. Another kind of seat is made of an old T super. A piece of lath is nailed to opposite diagonal corners, and another piece nailed to the other two corners. That stiffens and strengthens it, so it makes a good seat for one who doesn't like a low seat.

HIVE-TOOLS.

Of all the hive-tools I have tried, I like best the Muench tool (Fig. 20). Its broad, semi-circular end with sharp edge can hardly be excelled for the purpose of raising covers and supers, and when the other end is thrust between two frames, a quarter turn separates the frames with the least possible effort. Miss Wilson has a liking for the Root tool. I have not used it much, but it has the special advantage that it is a fine scraper. Besides the hive-tool for opening the hive and starting the frames, if the hives are to be cleaned out, another tool is needed.

After trying a number of different things for hive-cleaners, I have been best satisfied with a hatchet, the handle sawed short, so that it will not be in the way when working in the bottom of the hive, the edge dull and a perfectly straight line and the outside part of the blade also ground to a straignt line and at right angles with the edge. The right-angled corner is to clean out the corners of the hive. In cleaning, the hatchet is moved rapidly back and forth, or rather from side to side,

the blade being held at right angles to the surface being cleaned.
The weight of the hatchet is quite a help, something like a fly-
wheel in machinery.

It would be a nice thing to clean the propolis out of all
hives every spring, because I am in a region for profitable

Fig. 17—Record books.

propolis production if it ever comes to be a staple article of
commerce; but it takes some time to clean the hives, and it is
not done every spring.

PREPARING TO CLEAN HIVES.

If the hives are to be cleaned, an empty clean hive is ready
in advance. The empty hive is placed at right angles to the
hive to be overhauled, the back end of the empty hive near the

front end of the other hive, thus leaving plenty of room for my seat beside the full hive, and leaving the empty hive within easy reach.

OPENING HIVE.

A single puff at the entrance if the smoker is going well, or two or three puffs if it is yet scarcely under headway, notifies the guards that they needn't bother to come out if they feel a little jar. The cover is cracked open the least bit at one corner by the tool, then the other corner is cracked open and the cover lifted. It could be lifted without using the tool twice, simply prying up one corner enough, but that would jar the bees more, and excite them. The desire is to get along with the smallest amount of jar and smoke possible, for the queen is to be found, and too much smoke or jarring will set the bees to running so the queen cannot be found. As soon as the cover is raised, a little smoke is blown across the tops of the frames, not down into the hive. While it is bad to use too much smoke, it is also bad to use too little, for if the bees are once thoroughly aroused it takes more smoke to subdue them than it does to keep them under in the first place.

CLEANING HIVES.

When the cover is removed the dummy is taken out. If the dummy was on the near side, the frames are all crowded to that side, allowing me to lift out the further frame. Whether that further frame is now to be put into the empty hive depends upon circumstances. It is to be put in if the next frame contains brood; otherwise not. For I want the brood-nest to begin with the frame next to the further outside frame, at least that is generally the way. Then I can tell at any time afterward how many frames of brood are in a hive, merely by finding where the brood begins on the side next me. One after another the frames are changed into the empty hive, making sure that at least those containing brood maintain their original relative positions.

When the old hive is empty, then it is set off the stand and the other takes its place. The order of proceeding may be changed by first setting the full hive off the stand and putting the empty one in its place. Or the change may be made when half the frames have changed their places. The last makes the lifting a little lighter, but takes more time.

The empty hive is now to be cleaned out, the hatchet being used for all but the rabbet, which is a separate contract. Propolis is used in large quantities in my locality, and the trough formed by the tin rabbet will, in the course of years, become completely filled.

Fig. 18—Hive-seat with Strap-handle.

In the matter of propolis, there is a difference in bees as well as in localities. The worst daubers I ever had were the so-called Punics or Tunisians from the north of Africa. One colony put so much propolis at an upper entrance that I rolled up a ball of it somewhere between the size of a hickorynut and a blackwalnut.

To clean out the rabbet the small end of the hive-tool is well adapted. Holding it perpendicularly, with the edge of the tool diagonally in the trough, I play it backward and forward until the trough is emptied of propolis. Still better is a screwdriver, rather sharp, ground to just the right width to fit easily in the trough.

The empty hive is now used to take the place of the next hive to be overhauled, which in its turn is cleaned and then used again, and so on.

While the frames are being changed from one hive to the other, observations and necessary changes are made. If there is no cleaning of hives, then the work is shortened. The dummy is taken out, and one frame is also taken out so as to leave freer working room. This one frame may be put in an empty hive standing convenient; or it may be leaned against the hive being operated on, or against an adjoining hive. If the dummy was on the near side, then the frames are all pushed toward me, two or three being started at a time, and when all are started the tool is pushed down between the further frame and the side of the hive, and all the frames at one push shoved toward me enough to give plenty of room at the further side. If the frames are Hoffman (a few hives contain Hoffman frames) then it is necessary to start each frame separately before it can be lifted out.

WATCHING FOR QUEEN.

As the frames are being handled, the thing that receives closer attention than anything else is to see the queen so as to know whether she is clipped or not. For if a colony should have an unclipped queen there is a fair chance that it might swarm and decamp; and it is possible that almost any colony may have superseded its queen the previous fall, leaving it with an unclipped queen.

IMPLEMENT FOR CLIPPING.

If the queen is unclipped, of course I clip her. Nearly always I use a pair of scissors for clipping, although I have tried a knife. The strongest argument in favor of the knife is that a knife is always on hand. But it is just as easy to have a pair of scissors always on hand. They may be tied to the record book, and the record book is sure to be always on hand. Most of the time I have had a pair of embroidery scissors tied to my record book with a string long enough to allow the scissors to be freely used, but I have been surprised to find that much larger scissors will do very good work. Latterly

I have used a common pair of gentleman's pocket scissors, and I am not sure but I like them as well as the embroidery scissors. It is just as easy to have a pair of these as a knife constantly in the pocket. To make good work clipping, a knife

Fig. 19—Hive-seat with Hand-holes.

should be very sharp, and I find it is harder to have a *sharp* knife constantly on hand than a sharp pair of scissors. Neither is it so necessary that the scissors be sharp.

FINDING QUEEN.

Before a queen is clipped she must be found. I have seen some attempt at rules for finding a queen, but after all is said, you must do more or less hunting for a queen if you would find her. I generally begin looking on the first frame of brood I come to—hardly worth while to look on any frame before the brood is reached—and as I raise the frame out of the hive I

keep watch of the side next me. Then when the frame is lifted
out of the hive, before looking at the opposite side, I glance
at the nearest side of the next frame in the hive; for it requires
scarcely any time to do this, and if she happens to be in sight it
will be a saving of time to lift out immediately the frame she
is on. Not seeing her on the frame in the hive, I look over both
sides of the frame in my hand, and continue thus through all
the frames. Although it was not worth while to look for her
on any comb before the brood-nest was reached, it is worth
while to look for her on the comb or combs remaining after
passing over those that contain brood, for in trying to get away
from the light she will go to the outside combs.

This trying to get away from the light on the part of the
queen, by going from one comb to the other, makes me go over
the combs as rapidly as possible without looking too closely, for
if I do not see her with a slight looking, the chances are that she
is on another comb, and I count it better to run the chance of
going over the combs again, rather than to go too slowly. For
if one goes over the combs *slowly enough*, it is a pretty safe
thing to say that the queen will be driven clear to the other side
of the hive.

My assistant, however, who is an expert at finding queens,
holds a different theory, and as a consequence her practice is
different. She thinks it better to go more slowly and make
sure of finding the queen the first time going over. She takes
more time to go over the combs the first time, but she doesn't
often have to go over the combs a second time; so perhaps
one way is as good as the other.

If the queen is not found the second time going over, she
may be found the third time, but it is quite possible that she is
hid in such a way that it may be impossible to find her with
long searching. So it is economy to close the hive, and try again
another day, or at least to wait half an hour.

AIDS TO FINDING QUEEN.

If, for some special reason, it is very important to find the
queen without any postponement, sometimes the combs are put
in pairs. Two of the combs are put in an empty hive, the two
being close together; then another pair is put an inch or more

distant from the first pair, and the remaining combs in the hive
on the stand are arranged in pairs the same way. Wherever the
queen is, it will not be long before she will be in the middle of
whatever pair of combs she is on. Going on with work at another hive, I return after a little, and look again for the queen.
Lifting out the comb nearest me, I look first on the side of its

Fig. 20—Muench Hive-tool.

mate in the hive, and if I do not see the queen there, I quickly
look on the opposite side of the comb in my hand. I am pretty
sure to find her in the middle of one of the pairs.

If the pairs are sufficiently separated from each other (I
don't mean the two combs of each pair separated, for the two
combs in each pair should be as close together as possible, but
that one pair should be far enough from another pair so that

the bees should not communicate), the bees will, after standing long enough, show signs of uneasiness by running over the combs, all but the one pair that has the queen on, and the quietness of the bees on that one pair is sufficient warrant for seeking the queen there.

If the bees get to running, it is hardly worth while to continue the search for the queen until they have quieted down. Sometimes she will be on the side or the bottom of the hive, and will be found only by lifting out all the combs.

BEE-STRAINER.

A strainer may be used for straining the bees through and leaving the queen. A queen-excluder is fastened to the bottom of an empty hive-body, and that makes the strainer. The strainer is set over a hive-body in which there is a frame of brood but no bees—at least it must be certain that the queen cannot possible be in the hive-body under the strainer. Then all the bees are shaken and brushed from the combs into the strainer. The workers will go down through the excluder, being hurried by a little smoke if necessary, while the queen will be left in the strainer.

On the whole the queen is generally found so easily by the ordinary looking over the combs that it is seldom that any other plan is resorted to.

It happens once in a great while that the queen is on the cover when it is lifted off the hive, so it is well to glance over the under surface of the cover as it is removed from the hive. Once in a great while I have known the queen after no little searching to be on the shoulder or some other part of the operator. How she managed to get there I don't know.

CATCHING THE QUEEN.

When the queen is found, she must be caught before she is clipped. I want to catch her by the thorax or just back of the thorax, and if she is in motion, by the time I reach for the thorax it will have passed along out of reach. So I make a reach more as if attempting to catch her by the head, and the movement she makes is likely to bring my thumb and finger down on each side of her thorax, and in that position she is held firmly on the comb (Fig. 21). There is no danger of hurting the queen by giving a pretty hard squeeze on the thorax, and indeed there is not so very much danger if the hold is further back and the abdomen gets a little squeeze.

Then the thumb and finger are slid up off the thorax, at the same time pressed together, and this gives me a grip on the wings, when she is lifted from the comb, fairly caught (Fig. 22).

All this is done with the right hand, generally, although occasionally she is caught with the left hand. At any rate, she

Fig. 21—Catching the Queen.

is now shifted to the left hand, and held between the thumb and finger, back up, head and thorax between thumb and finger, head pointing to the left, ready to clip (Fig. 23).

CLIPPING THE QUEEN.

Then one blade of the scissors is slipped under the two wings of one side, and they are cut off as short as they can conveniently be clipped (Fig. 24).

The queen will be just as helpless about flying if only the

larger wing on one side is clipped, and clipping the one wing will not mar her looks so much, but when a queen is scurrying across a comb, or when you get just a glimpse of her in the hive, it is much easier to tell at a glance that she is clipped if both wings on one side are cut off.

ADVANTAGE OF CLIPPING.

Although nowadays the practice of clipping has become quite general, there are a few who doubt its advisability. I would not like to dispense with clipping if I had only one apiary and were on hand all the time, and with out-apiaries and no one to watch them it seems a necessity. If a colony swarms with a clipped queen, it cannot go off. True, the queen may possibly be lost, but it is better to lose the queen than to lose both bees and queen.

If there were no other reason for it, I should want my queens clipped for the sake of keeping a proper record of them. A colony, for example, distinguishes itself by storing more than any other colony. I want to breed next spring from the queen of that colony. But she may be superseded in the fall after that big harvest, and if she is not clipped there is no way for me to tell in the following season whether she has been superseded or not. Indeed I can hardly see how it is possible to keep proper track of a queen without having her clipped.

Sometimes when a queen is being found, she will quickly run under and out of the way, giving one a mere glimpse of her, so that it is not easy to say whether it was a queen or a worker that was seen, in which case the missing wings aid in recognizing her. To this, however, it may be replied that there is less need to find queens where they are not kept clipped.

BEE-SMOKERS.

You who have used smokers ever since you began working with bees hardly know how to appreciate them. At least it is doubtful if you appreciate them as much as you would if you had done as I did when I first began beekeeping, going around with a pan of coals and a burning brand on it, or else a lighted

piece of rotten wood (indeed this last was quite an improvement over the first), the only bellows I had being a sound
pair of lungs. Any one of the various makes of smokers I have
tried will do quite satisfactory work. I have used up more
Clark smokers than any others. Although low in price, the
Clark is really more expensive than any other. It works beau-

Fig. 22—Caught!

tifully while new, but the "new" wears off entirely too soon.
The bellows become incapacitated by reason of the smoke
sucked into it, and then there is no good way to clean it out.

CONTINUOUS AND CUT-OFF BLAST.

The Bingham, Corneil, Crane, and others, are all good.
The cut-off blast lengthens the life of a smoker, but shortens its
blast. The continuous blast, as in the Clark, allows one to send

the smoke with more force, but, as already mentioned, shortens the life of the smoker, because the bellows becomes foul with smoke. The Crane has the advantage of the full strength of the blast without the weakening of the cut-off, and works to perfection for a long time. Still, in the course of time, the metal valve becomes dirty, and it must be cleaned. Fortunately the part containing the valve can be taken off, allowing all to be made just as clean as when new. It takes quite a bit of time to do this, but it is time well spent, and one cleaning a year, even with heavy use, is sufficient. Those who do not care for so strong a blast will prefer a Bingham, Corneil, or other smoker with a cut-off never needing to be cleaned, while those who like the strong blast will be willing to spend the time occasionally cleaning the Crane. The latest Root smokers are the favorite of all.

CLEATS ON SMOKERS.

Using a smoker all day long is a hard thing on the muscles that work the bellows, and the stiffer the spring of the bellows the more tiresome the work. But unless the spring be quite stiff, the smoker will drop out of the hand when the grasp is relaxed so as to allow the bellows to open. I think it was W. L. Coggshall who suggested little cleats on the smoker, and these cleats have given great satisfaction. They are merely strips of wood one-fourth inch by one-eighth, extending across the upper end of each bellows-board and about half way down the sides (Fig. 80). The sharp edges of the cleats cling to the fingers, allowing the spring to be—I don't know just how much weaker, but I should guess only half as strong as without cleats. Most of the latest smokers are now made so that no cleats are needed.

SMOKER-FUEL.

It is a matter of much importance to have plenty of the right fuel and lighting material. Time is precious during the busy season, and it is trying on the temper to have to spend much time getting a smoker started, or relighting it when it has gone out. There are a great many different things that can be used for fuel, and it is largely a matter of convenience as to what is best for each one. Pine needles, rotten wood, sound wood, excelsior rammed down hard, planer shavings, greasy cotton-waste thrown away along the railroad, peat, rags, corn-cobs, old bags—in fact almost anything that will burn may be used in a smoker. Whatever is used, however, there should be a good stock of it on hand thoroughly dry, with no chance for the rain to reach it.

Fig. 23—Ready for Clipping.

GREEN FUEL.

And yet there are times when something green is better. When a continuous and strong smoke is wanted, after a hot fire has been started in the smoker, it is a good thing to fill the smoker with green sticks from a growing tree. The hot fire and the continuous blowing make it burn freely, and the smoke from green wood is sharper than that from dry.

But it is only on special occasions that it is desirable to have green wood, and it should at all other times be not only dry but very dry. Nothing is better as a standard fuel than sound hard wood sawed into proper lengths and split up into pieces about a quarter of an inch thick. The only objection is that such wood is rather expensive, for it takes a great deal of time to prepare it. Much the same thing without the cost of preparation may be had at any woodpile where hard wood has been chopped—I mean the chips to be found there—and that has been the favorite smoker-fuel "in this locality" for some time. When the weather is dry, the chips may be picked up in the chip-yard and filled directly into the smoker, but a stock is always kept on hand well covered up, ready to use immediately after the heaviest shower of rain.

SMOKER-KINDLING.

When live coals are at hand in the cook-stove, nothing is handier than to put a few of them in the smoker to start the fire. These are not always at hand. I have used for kindling carpenter's shavings, kerosene, rotten wood of some hard wood, especially apple, that kind of rotten wood that is somewhat spongy and will be sure to burn if the least spark touches it—all these have given more or less satisfaction, but nothing quite so much as saltpeter-rags. Like the right kind of rotten wood, the least spark will light a saltpeter-rag so that it will be sure to go, but it is not so slow in its action as the rotten wood, and makes a much greater heat, so that chips of sound hard wood will be at once started into a secure fire.

SALTPETER-RAGS.

To prepare the saltpeter-rags a crock is kept constantly standing, containing a solution of saltpeter. The strength of the solution is not a matter of great nicety. A quarter or half a pound of saltpeter may be used to a gallon of water, and if it evaporates so that the solution becomes stronger, water may be added. A cotton rag dipped in this solution will be ready for use as soon as dried. As a matter of convenience, quite a lot of rags are prepared at a time. They are wrung out of the solution and spread out to dry in the sun, and when thoroughly dry are put in the tool-basket, which always contains a supply. When taken out of the crock, the rags may be wrung quite dry, thus containing not so much saltpeter, or they may be wrung out just enough so the liquid will not run off on the ground and waste, in which condition they will be strongly dosed with saltpeter.

A plentiful supply of dry smoker-fuel, with a corresponding stock of saltpeter-rags, is a great saving of the "disposition."

POUNDING BEES OFF COMB.

Mention was made of getting bees off combs. Sometimes shaking is used altogether, sometimes brushing, and sometimes both. The weight of the comb has something to do with the manner of shaking. The most of the shaking—in fact all of the shaking, unless the combs be very heavy or the bees be shaken on the ground—is done as shown in Fig. 26. Perhaps it might better be called pounding bees off the comb. The comb is held by the corner with one hand, while the other hand pounds sharply on the hand that holds the comb. By this manner of pounding I can get almost every bee off a comb with a few strokes, unless the comb be too heavy.

DOOLITTLE PLAN OF SHAKING.

With a very heavy comb, G. M. Doolittle's plan is better, and is the one used. Let the ends of the top-bar be supported by the first two fingers of each hand, the thumbs some distance above. Keeping the thumb and fingers well apart, let the frame drop, and as it drops strike it hard with the balls of the thumbs, then catch it with the fingers, raise it and repeat the operation. The bees are jarred both up and down, and don't know which way to brace themselves to hold on, so a very few shakes will get most of them off.

PENDULUM PLAN OF SHAKING.

Often it is desirable to shake the bees back into the hive.

In that case brushing may be better than shaking, but the pounding plan serves very well. A space may be made by shoving the combs apart, and the frames to be pounded held well down in the hive. But many times it is as well to shake the bees on the ground. This may not be so advisable if the queen is likely to be among the shaken bees. Yet I have often shaken the queen off among the bees on the ground, and I am not sure that she ever failed to find her way with the bees back into the hive. When the bees are to be shaken on the ground the pendulum plan is used almost altogether. With the right hand I take hold of one end of the top-bar, letting the frame hang with the bottom-bar pointing forward, and then swinging the frame backward like a pendulum I let it swing again forward, and then as it falls back I let the lower end of the top-bar strike the ground in such position that a diagonal from the point that strikes the ground to the opposite end of the bottom-bar shall be nearly vertical. It is easier than the other plans, and takes less time.

BEE-BRUSHES.

Sometimes it is not desirable to get all the bees off, in which case, or with very light combs, no brushing is needed. But if all the bees are to be cleaned off, and the combs are not very light, then brushing must be resorted to. I know of no brush better than one made of some growing plant, such as asparagus, sweet clover, goldenrod, aster, etc., no little bit of a thing, but a good big bunch, well tied together with a string (Fig. 27).

But like many a thing that costs nothing, these weed brushes are very expensive, for they dry up so that a fresh one must be made every day, and that takes a good deal of time. So I generally use a Coggshall brush (Fig. 28). The essential thing about a Coggshall brush is that it must be made of long broom-corn with a very thin brush, and not trimmed at all at the ends. One of these is always in the tool-basket.

Of course no shaking or pounding of combs is admissible if queen-cells are on the combs that are considered of any value.

TOOL-BASKET.

The tool-basket spoken of is simply a common splint basket (Fig. 29). At different times I have had different arrangements for carrying the things most generally needed, at least two different tool-boxes having been made for that special purpose with separate compartments for the various articles. But the basket is lighter, and although things get a little mixed up in it, it seems to have the preference at present. At one time I tried to keep an outfit at each apiary—smoker, hive-

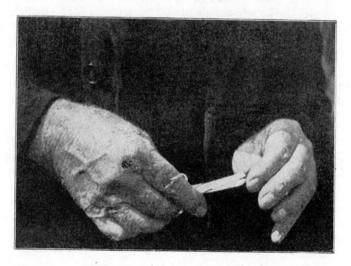

Fig. 24—Clipping the Queen.

tools, etc.—so that there should be no need to carry anything from one apiary to another, but one gets used to tools and prefers to use the same ones day after day, so the basket is used.

CONTENTS OF TOOL-BASKET.

Of course, the number of objects carried in a basket must be somewhat limited. The bulkiest part is the apron, sleeves, and gloves of my assistant. The record book must always be present. Then there will be smokers, hive-tools, hammer, cages, matches (although matches are always kept covered with the fuel in each apiary), saltpeter-rags, nails, and any other light objects that may happen to be needed at any particular time. Of course there will be heavier articles, not convenient to carry from one apiary to another, and each apiary must have its own, as a hive with a closed entrance and a robber-cloth, ready to contain at any time frames of brood or honey safe from robbers. Generally, however, there will be no need to be so careful against robbers, and the one or two frames lifted out of a hive will be leaned up against it, taking pains to stand any frame where the hot rays of the sun may not strike too directly upon it, and to stand it up straight enough so it will not sag with its own weight..

RESTING FRAME DIAGONALLY IN HIVE.

With one frame out of the hive there will be room enough for the rest to be moved about in the hive, and returned to it as soon as examined. Sometimes when it is desired to set a frame back in the hive very quickly, or when a queen has been caught and is held in the fingers, so that the frame must be handled with one hand, it is convenient to set the frame in the hive resting diagonally, as shown in Fig. 36. The frame is lowered until one end of the top-bar rests upon one rabbet, and then the bottom-bar is allowed to rest upon the other rabbet.

Perhaps oftener, however, I use both hands to handle a frame, even while holding a queen with one hand. While searching for the queen the frame is held in both hands, and as soon as she is seen the end of the frame held by the right hand is rested upon the hive, the right hand catches the queen, and she is then allowed to run upon the leg of my trousers, upon the thigh (it is an exceedingly rare thing that a laying queen will offer to fly), and then I catch her in the hollow of my right hand, holding her in the hollow formed by the three fingers, while with the thumb and forefinger I am free to handle the frame at leisure.

BEES BALLING QUEEN.

When a colony is being overhauled, it sometimes happens that the queen is found balled. This balling is likely more because the colony, being frightened, is seeking to protect the queen than because of any hostility to her. Fig. 30 shows a queen thus balled, or rather the balling bees are shown, the queen being hidden by them. The ball is small, whereas a ball of bees bent on the destruction of a strange queen is liable to be as large as a hickorynut, or larger.

Whether the object of the bees be to protect the queen or not, anything that tends to excite them sufficiently may lead them to do violence to the queen. So when I find the queen thus balled, I always close the hive immediately, not generally touching it again till the next day, when everything will be found all right.

MAKING RECORDS.

After the overhauling of a colony is completed, a record thereof must be made. If May 10, 1902, should be the date of the visit, and if I should clip the queen at that visit, I would make the entry, "May 10 cl q (01)," which means that I clipped the queen May 10, and that she was a queen reared in 1901. If, later in the season, I should clip a queen reared that same season, the entry would be "cl q (02)," meaning that the queen was reared in 1902. In either case the year of the birth of the old queen in the left-hand margin has a line drawn through it, and the birth-year of the new queen is written under it. If I find a clipped queen in the hive, then the entry is "q cl," which means the queen was already clipped. It might not seem important to enter that the queen was already clipped, but if I do not find her the first or second time looking over the combs I leave it till another day, leaving the blank after the date, and that keeps me in mind of the fact that I have not yet seen the queen.

After clipping the wing of the queen I put her on the top of a frame directly over the brood-nest. If you hold her on your finger over the brood-nest she displays a great degree of perverseness and persists in crawling up your hand, right away from her proper home. So I let her crawl upon a leaf, little stick or other object, lay this on the frames, and she will directly go down into the cluster.

Not always, however. Too often she will run about over the tops of the frames, and even over the side of the hive, and when thus excited there is some danger she may be balled when she gets down in the hive. So I like better to have a frame of brood covered with bees, lying flat, or held flat, by an assistant, and then I drop the queen right among the bees on the middle of the comb.

Fig. 25—Home from the Out-apiary.

On this first visit I also generally enter in the record book the amount of brood present. If the record is "2 br," or "3 br," it means that two combs or three combs are fairly well filled with brood—at least half filled with brood. If the record is "br in 2," that means that brood is found in two combs, but that at least one of them is less than half full. So you will see that "br in 3" might be a good deal less than "2 br", for "2 br" might mean two very full combs, and at the least will be as much as one very full comb, while "br in 3" may mean there is only a little spot of brood in each of three combs.

Any other item that needs especial mention will be recorded, but generally there is no record made beyond those mentioned.

MENDING COMBS.

In handling the combs, if any are found with drone-comb or with holes in them, and if we are not too crowded for time, the defects are remedied. Very likely I may turn over these combs to my assistant, who mends them before they are returned to the hive. The usual plan is to mend them in this way:

She takes a common tea-knife with a thin, narrow, sharp blade, cuts out the piece of drone-comb if the hole is not already made, lays the frame over a piece of worker-comb (this piece of worker-comb may be the part or whole of some old or objectionable comb), with the point of the knife marks out the exact size and shape of the hole, removes the frame, cuts out the piece and crowds it into the hole.

Or the following plan may be used, especially if the frame is wired: After the hole is made (the mice have probably made the holes in the wired frames), the cells on one side are cut away to the base for a distance of $\frac{1}{8}$ to $\frac{1}{4}$ inch from the hole, and a piece of foundation cut to the right size is placed over the hole and the edge pressed down upon the base that surrounds the hole. The foundation must not be too cold. Before fall these patches cannot be detected, unless by the lighter color where the foundation has been used.

HIVES NOT PAINTED.

Now that the apiary is all in running order, you may want to take a look at it. You "don't think it looks remarkably neat"? Neither do I. If I had only a dozen colonies and were keeping them for the pleasure of it, I should have their hives painted, perhaps ornamented with scroll work, but please remember that I am keeping them for profit, and I cannot afford anything for looks. I suppose they would last longer if painted, but hardly enough longer to pay for the paint. Besides, in the many changes constantly taking place, how do I know that I may not want to throw these aside and adopt a new hive?

CHANGES IN HIVES.

I have already changed five times, having begun in 1861 with a full-sized sugar-barrel, changing the next year to Quinby box hives, then to a movable-frame hive made by J. F. Lester, and afterward when J. Vandervort, the foundation-mill man, came and lived perhaps a year in Marengo, I bought out his stock of hives. I supposed they were the exact Langstroth pattern, but they had frames 18 x 9 inches, not different enough to make any appreciable difference in results, but different enough so that they were not standard, and after I had a few thousand of them on hand and wanted to change to the regular Langstroth size, the trouble I had would be hard to describe. I still have some of them, but not in regular use. These hives were 10-frame, and in course of time I cut them down and made them 8-frame. Then I changed to the 8-frame dove-tailed hive, and I don't know what the next change will be.

Another reason for not painting the hives is that I am afraid bees do not do quite so well in painted as in unpainted hives, especially in winter.

Except the full-sized cleat already mentioned on each end, my hives are the regular dovetailed. But the frames are Miller frames.

LOOSE-HANGING FRAMES.

For a good many years handling frames was much slower work than it is today, because for a good many years I had loose-hanging frames. In moving the frames from one side of the hive toward the other, each frame had to be moved separately. It would not do to shove two or more at a time, because in so doing bees would be mashed between the frames. Then when the frames were returned to place each one had to be carefully adjusted, judging by the eye when it was at the right distance from its neighbor. This was slow work, and when done with the utmost care it was only approximately exact. There was no dummy to lift out to make extra room; and the frames had to be crowded together so as to make room to get a first frame out. That disarranged the spacing of several of the frames, even if there were no other occasion for disarranging them.

SELF-SPACING FRAMES.

Then there came a time of struggling for some self-spacing arrangement, closed-end, partly closed-end, and what not. I tried a good many different kinds. Closed-ends were probably warmer for wintering, and were certainly self-spacing, but it took time to avoid killing bees, and the trouble with propolis was no small matter. Half-closed ends were the same in kind, only different in degree.

Of these last the Hoffman is probably the most popular. and I put in use enough to fill a few hives, and some of them are still in use. When new they work very nicely, but as propolis accumulates the difficulty of handling increases, and the frames become more and more crowded, until it is almost impossible to get out the dummy, the easier thing being to pry out with a good deal of force the first frame, either with or without the dummy. Indeed, the difficulty of getting out the frames is so great that the sight of a set of Hoffman frames when the cover is removed always produces something like a shudder.

Although I could not have anything in the line of closed-ends I wanted the advantage of the self-spacing and not finding anything on the market to suit me I was, in a manner, compelled to adopt something of my own "get-up," and so for several years I have used with much satisfaction the Miller frame (Fig. 95).

MILLER FRAME.

The frame is of course of the regular Langstroth size, $17\frac{5}{8}$ x $9\frac{1}{8}$. Top-bar, bottom-bar, and end-bars are uniform in width, $1\frac{1}{8}$ inches throughout their entire dimensions. The top-bar is $\frac{7}{8}$ inch thick, with the usual saw-kerf to receive the foundation, and close beside this is another kerf to receive the wedge that fastens in the foundation. The length of the top-bar is $18\frac{5}{8}$ inches, and $\frac{7}{8}$ x 9/16 is rabbeted out of each end to receive the end-bar. The end-bar is 8 9/16 x $1\frac{1}{8}$ x $\frac{3}{8}$. The bottom-bar consists of two pieces, each $17\frac{5}{8}$ x $\frac{1}{2}$ x $\frac{1}{4}$. This allows $\frac{1}{8}$ inch between the two parts to receive the foundation, making the bottom-bar $1\frac{1}{8}$ inches wide when nailed.

In Fig. 95 the frame is upside down, one-half of the bottom-bar nailed on, the other half above, while below is seen the long strip that serves as a wedge to fasten in the foundation.

Some of my latest frames, however, have the bottom-bar in one piece, 1⅛ inches wide, and I'm not sure but I prefer them. The only object in having the bottom-bar in two pieces is the convenience of an exact fit of the foundation without the trouble of cutting it carefully to the right size. With the bottom-bar all in one piece, the foundation fitting down close upon it, and melted wax run along the joint, the bees may be less inclined to gnaw a passage under the foundation than with the double bottom-bar without the melted wax.

Fig. 26—Pounding Bees Off Comb.

SPACING-NAILS.

The side-spacing, which holds the frame at the proper distance from its next neighbor, is accomplished by means of common wire nails. These nails are 1¼ inches long, and rather heavy, about 3/32 inch in thickness, with a head less than one-fourth inch across. By means of a wooden gauge which allows them to be driven only to a fixed depth, they are driven in to such a depth that the head remains projecting out a fourth of an inch.

Each frame has four spacing nails. A nail is driven into each end of the top-bar on opposite sides, the nail being about an inch and a half from the extreme end of the top-bar, and a fourth of an inch from its upper surface. About two and a fourth inches from the bottom of the frame a nail is driven into each end-bar, these nails being also on opposite sides. Hold the frame up before you in its natural position, each hand holding one end of the top-bar, and the two nails at the right end will be on the side from you, while the two nails at the left end will be on the side nearest you.

The object of having the nails so heavy is so that they may not be driven further into the wood when the frames are crowded hard together. Once in a great while the wood is split by having so heavy a nail driven, and if such a nail could be obtained it would be better to have a lighter nail with a head a fourth of an inch thick, so that it could be driven automatically to place without the need of a gauge, and without the possibility of being driven further in by any amount of crowding.

I have never tried the metal spacers now used on what are still called Hoffman frames, but it seems to me they must be an immense improvement over the original Hoffman frames, such as I had. I think, however, I should still prefer such a nail as I have mentioned, because there is less opposing surface, and so less chance for propolis. Such nails are in use in Europe.

Objection has been made to metal spacers because they are in the way of the uncapping-knife. But why should I, who do not use an uncapping knife, be denied the frame that is best for my use, because, forsooth, it doesn't suit an uncapper? Yet I must say I am very skeptical as to the objections to metal spacers on even extracting frames. The spacers are only at one end of the frame at each side, and if the knife starts at the spacer-end it does not seem necessary to dull it on the spacers. I have tried it enough to form something of an opinion, and I have been told by those who ought to know that the objection is a thing largely of imagination.

END-SPACING.

The end-spacing is done by means of the usual frame staple, about three-eighths of an inch wide. The staple is driven into the end-bar, immediately under the lug of the top-bar. This lug being only half an inch long, there is room for a bee to pass between the end of the lug and the upper edge of the hive-end, so no propolis is deposited there. I like this feature as much as some dislike it. They complain that with so

Fig. 27—Weed Brushes.

short a top-bar the frames drop down in the hive, a nuisance not to be tolerated. I do not have this trouble, although the hold of the top-bar on the tin support is so slight that if the work were not exact I can easily imagine the frames dropping there. Possibly those who complain do not have very exact work. I am not sure but I would rather put up with a little dropping down of frames, rather than to have the ends of the top-bars glued.

It will be seen that while the frames are automatically spaced very firmly, the points of contact are so small that the frames are always easily movable. These points of contact are the thin metal edges upon which the top-bars rest, the two end-staples, and the four nail-heads. The same spacing is in use in other frames, only staples are used for side-spacing instead of nails. The staples do not seem quite so substantial, and there is more danger, when the frames are crowded hard together, that the staples may be driven in deeper, or that the head of the staple may dig into the adjoining wood.

The top-bar and end-bar being 1⅛ wide, and the spacing of the nails ¼ inch, the frames are spaced just 1⅜ from center to center. It is just possible that a little wider spacing than 1⅜ might be better, but 1⅜ is the general fashion, and so far as possible I like to adopt standard goods. I may be asked, then, why should I use a frame not regularly made by manu-facturers. Possibly prejudice has a little to do in the case, but I think the Miller frame enough better than anything I can find listed, that I prefer to be out of fashion so long as I can find nothing listed that is quite close to what I want.

USING STANDARD GOODS.

In general I think it is best to adopt standard goods. They can be more cheaply made, and it is more convenient to get them. It cost me no small sum to change my frames so little as to make them only ⅜ of an inch less in length and an eighth of an inch more in depth, but I made the change, and made it solely because my frames were not of standard size. Years ago I changed from four-piece to one-piece sections solely because I wanted to be in fashion, although I think I prefer the one-piece now.

WORKING FOR IMPROVEMENT.

At the same time it is one's privilege—perhaps one's duty to make some effort toward improvement, if one can only keep from thinking that a thing is necessarily an improvement because it is different from what has been. The things and plans gotten up by me that were different from others would make a pretty long list. Unfortunately, a full trial has in most cases convinced me that my supposed improvements were no improvements at all, so they were cast aside. A few, however, have stood the test; the Miller feeder and the Miller introducing cage having become standard articles on the price-lists, while bottom-starters, the robber-cloth, bottom-board, and some other things have had from my brother beekeepers a reception of which I have no reason to complain. While the tendency toward something different needs to be kept in bounds

Fig. 28—Coggshall Bee-brush.

it would be a sad thing if no changes had been made, and we were set back just where we were a quarter or half a century ago.

GETTING COMBS BUILT DOWN TO BOTTOM-BARS.

While upon the subject of frames, I may as well tell how I manage to have them entirely filled with straight combs which are built out to the end-bars and clear down to the bottom-bars, a thing I experimented upon for a long time before reaching success. The foundation is cut so as to make a close fit in length, and the width is about half an inch more than the inside depth of the frame. The frame is all complete except that one of the two pieces of the bottom-bar is not yet nailed on. The frame is laid on a board of the usual kind, which fits inside the frame and has stops on the edges so that when the foundation is laid on the board it will lie centrally in the frame. The half of the bottom-bar that is nailed on lies on the under side. The foundation is put in place, and one edge is crowded into the saw-kerf in the top-bar. Then the lacking half of the bottom-bar is put in place, and a light nail at the middle is driven down through both parts. Then the frame is raised and the ends of the two halves of the bottom-bar are squeezed together so as to pinch the foundation, and nailed there. Then the usual wedge is wedged into the fine saw-kerf in the top-bar.

As already said, I am not sure but it is just as well, or better, to have the bottom-bar in one piece, with the foundation cut to fit close upon it.

FOUNDATION-SPLINTS.

Now we are ready for the important part. Little sticks or splints about 1/16 of an inch square, and about ¼ inch shorter than the inside depth of the frame, are thrown into a square shallow tin pan that contains hot beeswax. They will froth up because of the moisture frying out of them. When the frothing ceases, and the splints are saturated with wax, then they are ready for use. The frame of foundation is laid on the board as before; with a pair of plyers a splint is lifted out of the wax (kept just hot enough over a gasoline stove), and placed upon the foundation so that the splint shall be perpendicular when the frame is hung in the hive. As fast as a splint is laid in place, an assistant immediately presses it down into the foundation with the wetted end of a board. About 1½ inches from each end-bar is placed a splint, and between these two splints three others at equal distances(Fig. 31). When these are built out they make beautiful combs, and the splints do not seem to be at all in the way (**Fig.**32).

Five splints in a frame works all right for medium brood foundation, but in 1909 I filled a number of frames with light brood foundation, and used seven splints in a frame.

A little experience will enable one to judge, when putting

in the splints, how hot to keep the wax. If too hot there will be too light a coating of wax.

It must not be understood that the mere use of these splints will under any and all circumstances result in faultless combs built securely down to the bottom-bar. It seems to be the natural thing for bees to leave a free passageway under the comb, no matter whether the thing that comes next below the comb be the floor-board of the hive or the bottom-bar of the frame. So if a frame be given when little storing is going on, the bees will deliberately dig away the foundation at the bottom; and even if it has been built down but the cells not very fully drawn out, they will do more or less at gnawing a passage. To make a success, the frames should be given at a time when work shall go on uninterruptedly until full-depth cells reach the bottom-bar.

In Fig. 32 will be seen two such frames of splinted foundation that have been built out and filled with honey. The upper one is built out solid to the frame all around, while the lower one has a hole at one of the lower corners, through which a queen can play hide-and-seek.

In Fig. 33 are two that have been built out and filled with brood. They are built out solid to the wood, excepting one hole in each at one of the lower corners, but these two holes are covered up by the fingers so that you cannot see them. Look carefully at the frame at the left hand, and you will see at least three places where the capping is slightly elevated, because of the splints beneath.

BROOD TO THE TOP-BAR.

Incidentally your attention may be called to this comb as a fine specimen of one well filled with brood. It is literally *filled*, all the cells, sealed and unsealed, containing brood. It shows that there is no necessity for shallow frames to have brood clear to the top-bar. At the time when it is desired to get bees to start work in sections, the brood will be up so high in the combs that bees will start in the sections just as promptly with standard frames as with those that are shallower. *After* the bees have been at work storing for some time, the brood in the standard frame will not be as near the top-bar as in a shallow frame, but that will be no hindrance to the *continuance* of storing in supers.

For a long time it puzzled me to understand why others should say that in a Langstroth frame a space of one or two inches would be left under the top-bar where no brood would be reared, while in my hives, in the height of brood-rearing, frame after frame would be filled with brood clear to the top-bar. It was urged that the trouble arose because the frame was too deep. Finally it was suggested that horizontal wiring allowed enough sagging so that the upper cells were stretched just enough so they would not be used for brood. In my frames, with foundation-splints, there was no chance for stretching, and so the row of cells next to the top-bar and bottom-bar could alike be used by the queen.

Even if brood were not reared in the upper part of a Langstroth frame, I should still prefer that depth for comb honey, whatever might be true as to extracted honey. At one time I had two hives with shallow frames, and the amount of pollen in sections filled over those shallow frames was greater than in all the other thousands of sections filled over the Langstroth frames.

Please do not misunderstand that all my combs look like the four in Figs. 32 and 33. Many of them do, but more do not, because so many of them were built in seasons of comparative dearth.

There is another way to get combs built down to the bottom-bar. Suppose you have a comb with a passageway under it more or less of its length. Cut it free from the bottom-bar, and then cut straight across an inch or more above the bottom-bar; then turn this piece upside down and let it rest on the bottom-bar. The bees will immediately fasten this piece to the bottom-bar (of course it must be at a time when bees are working freely), and very soon they will fill in the gap above the piece.

HIVE-DUMMY.

A good dummy is a matter of no light importance. It is handy to fill up vacant space, its chief use being to make an easy thing of removing the first comb from a hive. With self-spacing frames there can be no crowding together of the frames so as to give one of them extra room as is the case with loose-hanging frames, and if a hive be filled full of self-spacing frames it would be about impossible to remove the first frame after a fair amount of propolis is present. A dummy at one side is the thing to help out.

An eight-frame dovetailed hive is $12\frac{1}{8}$ inches wide inside. Eight frames spaced $1\frac{3}{8}$ inches from center to center will oc-cupy 11 inches, leaving at one side a space of $1\frac{1}{8}$ inches, abund

Fig. 29—Tool-basket.

ance of room to lift out the first frame easily. A dummy put into that space will prevent the bees from filling it up with comb, and it ought never to be difficult to lift out the dummy. If a dummy a trifle more than a fourth of an inch thick be put in, leaving a fourth of an inch between dummy and frame, there will be left between the dummy and the side of the hive a space little more than half an inch, a space that the bees will never fill with comb in such a place. As propolis accumulates, however, this space will become less.

The dummy should be light and at the same time quite

substantial, and the one I use fulfills these requirements (Fig.
42). The principal board of the dummy is 16⅛ x 8¾ x 5/16,
of pine. The other parts are of some tougher wood. The top-
bar is 18⅞ x 5/16 x 5/16. Each end cleat is 8⅜ x 5/16.

It will be seen that the dummy is neither so long nor deep
as a frame. That makes it easier to handle, and being at the
side of the hive it never makes any trouble. If I were making
new dummies, I think I would make the principal board 15
inches long instead of 16⅛. It would be easier to handle, and
bees are little inclined to fill in comb at the ends of the dummy.
While the cut-off top-bars in the frames work nicely, they do
not work so well in dummies, as I found upon trying a number
of them. The principal objection to this dummy is that the
top-bar, being only 5/16 square, is sometimes broken off, or
pulled off, when the dummy is pried out of a hive where it is
glued in. Some of them are made over in a simple way that
is very satisfactory. The top-bar is entirely torn off, and for a
lug at each end is used a common tenpenny wire nail, which is
3 inches long and ⅛ inch thick. Lay the nail on top of the
dummy, with the point projecting as far as it can and yet admit the dummy into the hive. The head of the nail will not allow it to lie down flat. All the better. Hammer on the head
till the nail does lie flat. Now take a piece of tin 3½ to 4
inches long and wide enough to cover the part of the nail that
lies on the dummy, not including the head. Lay this tin on
top, bend down over each side, and near the lower end drive
through two light wire nails an inch long or longer, and clinch.
There's a feeling of solid comfort every time one opens a hive
containing such a dummy.

HIVE-COVERS.

At the risk of losing caste as a beekeeper, I am obliged to
confess that I never got up "a hive of my own," never even
tried to plan one, but I have tried no little to get up a hive-
cover to suit me. A hive is so seldom moved that I care less for
its weight, but when I, or more particularly, my female assistants, have to lift covers all day long, when hot and tired, a
pound difference in weight is quite an item. The first covers I
had for movable-frame hives were 8 inches deep and weighed

about 18 pounds. Needless to detail the different covers I have devised and tried, with upper surfaces of tin, oilcloth, and wood, painted and unpainted. Although I don't paint hive-bodies, I want covers painted or at least waterproof. Some of my covers have been the common plain board cover, and I don't like them. Some of them are of two boards united at the middle by a V-shaped tin slid into saw-kerfs, and I like these

Fig. 30—Balled Queen.

still less. A new board cover is a nice thing. After a little it warps, and then it is not a nice thing. Put a cleat on each end so it can not warp—cast-iron cleats, if you like—and it will twist so that there will be a grinning opening at one corner to allow bees to walk out and cold to walk in, to say nothing of robber-bees.

TIN COVERS WITH DEAD-AIR SPACE.

I have fifty covers that I like very much. They are double-board covers, the boards being ⅜ thick, the grain of the upper and lower boards running in opposite directions, with a ⅜ dead-air space between them; at least it would be dead-air if it were not for cracks, and I do not consider the cracks a necessary part if the covers were properly made. The whole is covered with tin and painted white. The lower surface is perfectly flat, with no cleat projecting downward, for such cleats do not help rapid and easy handling. Such a cover is light, safe from warping and twisting, is cooler in summer than the plain board cover, and warmer in winter. The greatest objection is the cost; I think they cost 25 cents or more each.

Two of these tin covers will be seen at Fig. 37, the one at the right showing the under surface of the cover.

ZINC COVERS.

Fifty other covers are made on the same plan and covered with zinc. These are not painted. So long as they remain whole there is no need of paint, and whenever there seems to be a possibility of their approaching anything like a leaking condition they can be covered with paint. The same might be said of the tin, only I expect the zinc to stand the weather unpainted much longer than the tin would.

At Fig. 38 may be seen two of these zinc hive-covers. The one at the right shows the upper or zinc surface. The left one shows the under or wood surface; and if you look at the right end of this last cover you will see that the upper layer of thin board projects three-fourths of an inch so as to serve as a handle. One of these covers weighs five pounds.

A cover sent me by The A. I. Root Company covered with paper and painted, has been in use several years, and so far it seems to stand as well as zinc or tin. Possibly this paper may do as well as the metal and save expense. I would rather pay a good price for a good cover, rain-proof, bee-proof, non-warping, non-twisting, with a dead-air space, than to take a poor cover as a gift.

The hundred covers I have mentioned were made specially

to order, but I am glad to see that The A. I. Root Company have now on their list a cover made on the same principle.

My hive-stands are simple and inexpensive (Fig. 39). They are made of common fence-boards 6 inches wide. Two pieces 32 inches long are nailed upon two other pieces or cleats 24 inches long. That's all. Of course the longer pieces are uppermost, leaving the cleats below. Two similar cleats, but loose, lie on the ground under the first-mentioned cleats. This makes it equivalent to cleats of two-inch stuff, with the decided advantage that only the loose cleat will rot away by lying on the ground, without spoiling the whole stand. These stands are leveled with a spirit-level before the hives are placed on them (sometimes not till afterward), being made perfectly level from side to side, with the rear one or two inches higher than the front. Each of these stands is intended for two hives, with a space of 2 to 4 inches between the two hives. It is much easier to level a stand like this than to level one for a single hive. There are other advantages.

For years I was well satisfied with these stands, but longer experience has made me become greatly dissatisfied with them. More than a square foot of the under surface of the bottom-board lies flat upon the boards of the stand. When it rains the water soaks in between these two surfaces, and favors rotting. Worse still, it makes the nicest kind of a place for the large wood-ants to make a nest and honeycomb the wood of the bottom-board. Perhaps the coming stand is of cement with but a small surface in actual contact with the bottom-board.

HIVES IN PAIRS.

This putting in pairs is quite a saving of room; for if room were allowed for working on each side of a hive, only two-thirds the number could be got into the row. But so far as the bees are concerned, it is equivalent to putting in double the number; that is, there is no more danger of a bee going into the wrong hive by mistake, than if only a single hive stood where each pair stands. If hives stood very close together at regular intervals, a bee might by mistake go into the wrong hive; but if a colony of bees is in the habit, as mine sometimes are in the spring, of going into the south end of their entrance, they will never make the mistake of entering at the north end, as you will quickly see if you plug up, alternately, the north and south ends of the entrance. When the north end is closed it does not affect the bees at all, but close the south end and dire consternation follows. To the bees the pair of hives is much the same as a single hive, and they will not make the mistake of entering the wrong end.

Fig. 31—Foundation with splint supports.

A space of 2 feet or so is left between one pair of hives and the next pair, so as to leave plenty of room for a seat.

GROUPS OF FOUR HIVES.

In two of the apiaries there is still further economy of room by placing a second row close to the first, the hives standing back to back. That, you will see, makes the hives in groups of four. I do not know of any arrangement that will allow a larger amount of hives to stand on a given surface. The difference in the amount of travel in the course of a year in such an arrangement as compared with one without any grouping, is a matter not to be despised.

SHADE.

Trees shade most of the hives at least a part of the day, and at one end of the home apiary the trees were so thick that I cut out part of them. I had previously thought that shade was important, and that with sufficient shade there was never any danger of bees suffering from heat, but after having combs melt down in a hive so densely shaded by trees that the sun did not shine on it all day long, I changed my mind. I value the shade these trees give, not so much for the good it does the bees, but for the comfort of the operator working at them. I don't believe bees suffer as much from the hot sun shining directly on the hives as they do from having the air shut off from them by surrounding objects. I have had combs melt down in hives, the honey running in a stream on the ground, one of the hives at least being in a shade of trees so dense the sun never shone on it, and I suspect it was for lack of air. A dense growth of corn was directly back of the hives and a dense growth of young trees and underbrush in front. I didn't know enough to notice this, although when working at the bees my shirt would be as wet as if dipped in the river. I had the young trees thinned out and trimmed up, the corn-ground in grass, so the air could get through, and now I work with more comfort, and no comb has melted down for 30 years.

Sometimes I have found it desirable to shade one or more hives singly. An armful of the longest fresh-cut grass obtainable is laid on the hive-cover, and weighted down with two or three sticks of stove-wood. But I do not think anything of the kind is needed on double covers.

MOVABLE SHADE.

For hives that are not in the shade, especially during certain parts of the day, a movable shade (Fig. 58) is a great comfort to the operator when the sun shines with blistering heat. Four standards are made of 7/16-inch rod iron. Take a piece of the iron 6 feet 2 inches long; bend the upper end into

a ring or eye, and sharpen the lower end. Twelve inches from
the point or lower end bend the rod at right angles. Two inches
higher up bend again at right angles, leaving the rod straight
except that knee of two inches, upon which you can set your
foot and drive it into the ground as when spading.

The cloth used for the shade is about as large as an ordinary bed sheet, and is usually the linen lap-robe, which is always at hand, and on which a string is kept tied on each corner
so as to be always ready to set up in a twinkling. The string
has both ends tied around the cloth at the corner, leaving the
string in the form of a loop. The loop is thrust through the
eye of the standard, looped back over the eye, and there you
are.

When the sun is not far from the horizon, only two standards are used, from which the lap-robe hangs as a wall between
the operator and the sun.

FEEDING MEAL.

I used to read about feeding meal in the spring. I tried
it, put out rye-meal, and not a bee would touch it; baited them
with honey, and if they took the honey they left the meal.
Finally, one day, I saw a bee alight on a dish of flour set in a
sunny place. It went at it in a rollicking manner as if delighted. I was more delighted. At last I had in some way got the
thing right, and my bees would take meal. The bee loaded up,
and lugged off its load, and I waited for it and others to come
for more. They didn't come, and that was the first and last
load taken that year. I cannot tell now exactly when the
change came about, neither do I know that I have done anything different, but I have no trouble now in getting the bees
to take bushels of meal. I suppose the simple explanation is
that there was plenty of natural pollen for the few bees I had
in the first years, but not enough for the larger number of
colonies I had later.

About as soon as the bees are set out in the spring, I begin
feeding them meal, although some years I do not offer them
any substitute for pollen. For this purpose I like shallow boxes,
and generally use old hive-covers 4 inches deep. These are
placed in a sunny spot about a foot apart, one end raised three

or four inches higher than the other. This may be done by
putting a stone under one end, although I generally place them
along the edge of a little ditch where no stone is needed, and
they can be whirled around as if on a central pivot. One feed-
box is used for every 10 to 20 colonies, although I am guided
rather by what the bees seem to need, adding more boxes as fast
as the ones already given are crowded with bees.

SUBSTITUTES FOR POLLEN.

I can hardly tell what I have not used for meal. I have
used meal or flour of pretty much all the grains, bran, shorts,
and all the different feeds used for cows in this noted dairy
region, including even the yellow meal brought from glucose
factories for cow-feed, although, if this last were known, it
might be reported that I filled paraffin combs with glucose and
sealed them over with a hot butcher-knife. I think this glucose
meal is perhaps the poorest feed I have used. As to the rest I
hardly know which is best, and I have of late used principally
corn and oats ground together, partly because I was using that
for horse and cow feed, and partly because I think it may be
as good as any.

When the feed-boxes are put in place, in the morning (and
I commence this feeding just as soon as the bees are out of the
cellar), I put in each box at the raised end about four to six
quarts (the quantity is not very material) of the feed. The
more compact, and the less scattered the feed the better. The
bees will gradually dig it down until it is all settled in the lower
end of the box, just the same as so much water would settle
there. This may take an hour, or it may take six, according to
circumstances. As often as they dig it down, I reverse the
position of the box, just whirling it around if it stands on the
edge of the ditch. This brings the meal again at the raised end
of the box. When the bees have dug it down level there is little
to be seen on the top except the hulls of the oats, and what fun
it is to see the bees burrow in this, sometimes clear out of sight!

It is always a source of amusement to see the bees working
on this meal, and the young folks watch them by the half-hour.
By night the oatmeal and finer parts of the corn are nearly all
worked out, and after the bees have stopped working, the boxes

are emptied, piled up, one on top of another, and at the top, one placed upside down so that no dew or rain may affect them. If I think it is not worked out pretty clean, I may let them work it over the next day, putting three or four times as much in a box. When the bees are done with it, there will be empty oat-hulls on top, and the coarse part of the corn on the bottom. It does not matter if it is not worked out clean, for it is fed to the horses or cows afterward.

After the first day's feeding, the boxes must be filled in good season in the morning, or the bees annoy very much by

Fig. 32—Combs of Honey.

being in the way, and throughout the day, while the bees are at work, if I go around the feed-boxes to turn them, or for any other purpose, I must look sharp where I set my feet, or bees will be killed, as they are quite thick over the ground, brushing the meal off their bodies and packing their loads. Before many days the meal-boxes are deserted for the now plenty natural pollen, although if you watch the bees, as they go laden into the hives, even when working thickest in the boxes, you will see a good many carrying in heavy loads of natural pollen.

It seems to be a beneficent natural law, that bees do not like to crowd one another in their search for pollen or nectar, or else the meal-boxes would be untouched and all the bees would work upon the insufficient supply of pollen. In consequence of this law it is necessary to furnish a sufficient number of boxes, for although the bees will work quite thick if only 5 boxes are left for 150 colonies, they will work scarcely thicker if only one box is left.

OUTDOOR FEEDING.

I have fed barrels of sugar syrup in the open air, and it is possible that circumstances may arise to induce me to do it again, but I doubt.

There are serious objections to this outdoor feeding. You are not sure what portion of it your own bees will get, if other bees are in flying distance. Considerable experience has proved to me that by this method of feeding, the strong colonies get the lion's share, and the weak colonies very little. Moreover, I have seen indications that part of the colonies get none, both of the weak and strong. You are also dependent on the weather, as wet and chilly days may come, when bees cannot fly.

As already mentioned, when bees are brought out of the cellar, colonies are marked that are suspiciously light, and their immediate wants supplied as soon as possible. But with eight-frame hives there will be a good many colonies that will run short of stores before there is any chance for them to supply themselves from outside.

STIMULATIVE FEEDING.

Some would say that I ought to practice stimulative feeding for the sake of hastening the work of building up the colony. But it takes a good deal of wisdom to know at all times just how to manage stimulative feeding so as not to do harm instead of good; and I am not certain that I have the wisdom.

Whatever else may be true about spring, I am pretty fully settled in the belief that it is of first importance that the bees should have an abundant supply of stores, whether such supply be furnished from day to day by the beekeeper,

or stored up by the bees themselves six months or a year previously. Moreover, I believe they build up more rapidly if they
have not only enough to use from day to day, but a reserve or
visible supply for future use. If a colony comes out of the
cellar strong, and with combs full of stores, I have some doubts
if I can hasten its building up by any tinkering I can do. So
my feeding in spring is to make sure they have abundant stores,
rather than for the stimulation of frequent giving.

RAPID CONSUMPTION OF STORES.

After so many years of experience in that line, I am nevertheless still surprised sometimes to find how rapidly the stores
have diminished under the constantly increasing demands made
by brood-rearing. So there is little danger of getting too much
honey in the hive. It is not enough to have sufficient to last
till the white-clover harvest begins. To be sure, that might be
all right so far as the building-up of the colony is concerned.
But no honey will be put in the supers so long as there are
empty cells in the brood-chamber, and it is better to have
enough honey left in the brood-chamber so that the first white
honey shall go straight into the supers.

SURPLUS COMBS OF HONEY.

Nothing is better than to have plenty of full combs of
sealed honey saved over from the previous year, with which to
supply any colony that may need them. If I were as good a
beekeeper as I ought to be, there would always be enough of
these so that nothing else would be needed to take their place.
But I am not as good a beekeeper as I ought to be, and while
some years I may have all the extra combs of honey that can
be used, at other times they may run short, even to not having
enough to supply the pinching wants of colonies just taken
from the cellar. There may, however, be some combs at least
partly filled that have been taken from colonies that died in
winter, or from the uniting of colonies in spring, and these
may supplement the number of combs saved up from the previous year.

FEEDING SECTIONS OF COMB HONEY.

When the combs of honey are all gone, the next best thing is to give sections in wide frames. This seems like an extravagant thing to do; but if the sections contain dark or objectionable honey, and if they can be cleaned out and used for baits, there is no very great extravagance about it. I have given sections by sliding them under the bottom-bars, a thing very easily done with bottom-boards two inches deep, but such sections are ruined for use as baits, and all you can do with the empty comb in them is to melt it into wax.

FEEDING TO FILL COMBS.

If neither combs of sealed honey nor suitable sections are to be had, then feeding with Miller feeders is in order. But colonies that need feeding in spring are not always very strong, and a weak colony makes rather poor work on a feeder at that time. Instead of distributing feeders to all colonies that need feeding, they are limited to a small number of the very strongest, whether these need feeding or not. Then filled combs are taken from these strong colonies and given to the needy colonies whether at home or in the out-apiaries, for the feeders are generally used only at home.

It may be that these strong colonies are already well supplied with honey. Whatever honey they have is taken from them, unless it be in combs containing brood, and empty combs given in place. The feeder is put directly on the brood-chamber. After the bees get a fair start on the feeder an upper story with empty combs may be given, but just at first they will make a better start without this second story. When the feeder is put on 5 or 10 pounds of sugar is poured in, and an equal quantity of water poured on the sugar. It is much better to have the water hot. It would be well to fill the feeder full, but in that case a good portion of it would be left to get cold, and faster work will be done if no more is given each day than will be taken that day. Very often when I go around to the feeders next morning I find most of them with sugar still in the feeder, but the liquid all taken. That doesn't matter; more water can be added. Indeed, 12 or 15 pounds of sugar may be put in the feeder, and then each day only so much water as the bees will use out that day; for they are not likely to do much at night unless the weather be quite warm.

There come times, however, when the feeding must be rushed, and there can be no puttering with getting one colony to store for another. One of those times came in the year 1902. The second week in June, at the time when in a good season

Fig. 33—Combs of Brood.

there ought to be lively work piling on supers, I found nearly every colony on the point of starvation. If there was any difference the strongest colonies were the worst. The combs were filled with brood, requiring large daily consumption, stores in the hive were exhausted, and not enough for daily supplies coming in. It would hardly be proper economy to have combs filled with honey saved up for such emergencies, seeing that they are not expected to come often, so the whole force of feeders, some fifty, were put into action.

Part were put in the home apiary and part taken to the

out-apiaries. When going to an out-apiary a bag of sugar was taken along. Water was put in the wash-boiler on the cook-stove and a good fire built under it. A good-sized tin pail was filled half full or more with the heated water, then sugar was poured in till the pail was nearly full, and it was stirred with a stick till fairly well dissolved, which did not take very long. The syrup was then poured into the feeder on one of the hives, a pail half full of water was taken in and poured into the boil-er, and then another colony was fed, and this was continued till all the feeders were supplied. The next day or so the feeders were shifted to another set of hives, until all were fed.

FEEDING IN JUNE.

You will notice this is considerably different from the early spring feeding. The colonies were stronger in June, the weather warmer, and the bees made rapid work carrying down the feed. It was better to dissolve the sugar before putting it in the feeders (perhaps it is better at any time), for then there was no danger of having dry sugar left in the feeder. Perhaps there was no real gain in using hot water when the colonies were strong and the weather warm. I tried cold water in some cases, and it worked all right, only it took more stirring.

ORIGINAL MILLER FEEDER.

Most of my feeders are of the original pattern (Fig. 40). At Fig. 41 is seen one of them dissected. The lower part is an ordinary section-super. On this rests the feeder proper, with the little board at one end removed, also the little board at one side, so as to show the inside wall under which the syrup may flow, and the outside wall, which lacks enough of coming to the top so that the bees can come up over it and go down into the feed.

IMPROVED MILLER FEEDER.

The improved Miller feeder of the catalogs, instead of being all in one has two parts, and the bees go up through the middle. I thought it was an important improvement to allow the bees to go up the middle instead of up the two sides, because the heat ought to be greater at the middle. After a thorough trial of the two, side by side, I am obliged to admit that the improvement is one in theory only, and that the bees go up the sides whenever they will go up the middle, and it seems a little better to have the feed all in one dish.

If it were not for the expense of keeping two sets of feeders, I should like to keep a set of Doolittle division-board feeders, for there may come a time when it is cool and bees will not take feed readily from a Miller feeder, yet would take it from a division-board feeder, because closer to the brood-nest. But most of the time I should prefer the Miller, so that has the preference.

CROCK-AND-PLATE FEEDER.

I have used the crock-and-plate feeder (Fig 43), and it answers a very good purpose. It has the advantage that any one can make a feeder at a minute's notice with materials always ready to hand. Take a gallon crock, fill it half full of granulated sugar; then fill nearly full of water, all the better if stirred till dissolved; cover over the crock a thickness of flannel or other woolen cloth, or else four or five thicknesses of cheesecloth; over this lay a dinner-plate upside down; then with one hand under the crock and the other over the plate, quickly turn the whole thing upside down. Of course a smaller quantity of feed may be used if desired.

The feeder is then set over the frames of a colony, an empty hive-body placed over, and all covered up so no bee can get to it except through the regular hive-entrance.

WATERING-CROCK.

This crock-and-plate feeder is a good one for those who like outdoor feeding, if only a small quantity is to be fed. It also makes a good watering place for bees, if one does not mind the trouble. Better than this is a six-gallon crock standing upright with a few sticks of firewood in it for a watering-crock (Fig. 44). A little salt thrown into the water helps to keep it sweet, and prevents it from being a breeding place for mosquitoes.

CORK CHIPS FOR WATERING.

But I hit upon something that is so effective, so cheap, and so little trouble, that I can hardly imagine anything better. Go to your grocer and ask him to save you some cork chips, such as he gets in kegs of grapes, and probably throws away. Take a pail or other vessel (I use a half-barrel), put in as much

Fig. 34—Part of Home Apiary (from Northwest).

water as you like, and on this put so much of the cork chips that the water will barely come up enough for the bees to reach. A bee can not drown in this. When the water gets low, a fresh supply can be poured in, and it does no great harm to pour it directly on the bees. They climb easily to the top of the cork after their bath. The cork remains effective throughout a whole season.

It is important to start the watering-place early in the season, before the bees make a start at some pump or other place where they will be troublesome.

LACK OF SYSTEM.

I would like to say that I am very methodical about over-hauling and seeing to the building-up of colonies, from the time they are placed on the summer stands till the honey harvest begins, but it would hardly be in accordance with facts. Conditions of bees or weather may make a difference in the course of action. Possibly some other duties aside from the direct care of the bees may make a difference. So when I attempt to tell things just as they are, my want of system confronts me, and makes the task somewhat difficult.

At this point I fancy I can hear some of my good friends saying, "Why don't you keep a smaller number of colonies, so that you can have system enough to be able to tell a straight story, and derive more pleasure and profit?" I know it would be more pleasure; but as to the profit, I doubt. If I had so few that I could at all times do every thing by a perfect system, I am afraid I should have part of the time a good deal of idle time on my hands. Neither is it fair for me to charge my lack of system entirely to the number of colonies. Some of it comes from ignorance in not knowing how to do any better, some of it from changing plans constantly, and perhaps some of it from lack of energy in doing every thing just at the right time.

DIVISION-BOARDS.

In former years I made some attempt to keep the bees warmer by the use of a division-board, closing down to the number of combs actually needed at the time by the bees. I was disappointed to find no clear proof that any great good came from it. Since then the experiments of Gaston Bonnier have shown that combs serve as good a purpose as a division-board, so the trouble of moving a division-board from time to time to accommodate the size of the colony is avoided.

VERY WEAK COLONIES IN SPRING.

I have had, one time and another, a good many very weak colonies in the spring, and I am puzzled to know what to do with them. It seems of no use to unite them, for I have united five into one, and the united colony seemed to do no better than one left separate. About all I try to do is to keep the queen alive till I find some queenless colony with which to unite them.

One year I took the queens of five or six very weak colonies, put them in small cages, and laid the cages on top of the frames, under the quilt, over a strong colony. When I next overhauled this colony, its queen was gone, probably killed by the bees on account of the presence of other queens, but the queens in the cages were in good condition, and became afterward the mothers of fine colonies. I had put two of the queens in one cage, as I was short of cages, and did not attach much value to the queens, and these two did as well as the others. Of course this was an exception to the general rule.

In my locality I do not think the colonies can ever become strong and populous too early in the season. Theoretically, at least, then, I see that every colony as soon as it comes out of the cellar has plenty of stores to last it for some time. I know this is a very indefinite amount. Perhaps I might make it more definite by saying, for an ordinary colony, the equivalent of two full combs of stores. If they do not have so much I supply them. I formerly thought it desirable to have any feed given them as far as possible from the brood-nest, so that they might have the feeling that they were accumulating from abroad. Further observation makes me place less confidence in this.

STRONG VERSUS WEAK COLONIES.

I think that with increasing years I have an increasing aversion to weak colonies. At the time of the honey harvest 40,000 bees in two colonies will not begin to store as much as the same bees would do if they were all in one colony. Of course you have thought of that, but possibly you have not noticed so clearly that something like the same rule holds good about building up in spring. Take a colony that comes out of the cellar with only enough bees to cover two combs. It will remain at a standstill for a long time. Indeed, it may not stand still, but may become weaker, so that it will not have as much brood June 1 as May 1, with a possibility of pegging out altogether before the harvest opens. On the other hand a col-

ony with bees enough to cover well three frames is likely to
hold its own, beginning to increase slowly as soon as weather
permits; and if it has bees enough to cover four frames it will
walk right along increasing its brood-nest.

GIVING BROOD TO STRONGER.

Shall I take frames of brood from strong colonies to give
to the weaklings? Not I. For the damage to the strong colonies will more than overbalance the benefit to the weaklings. If
any taking from one colony to give another is done in the spring,
it will be to take from the weak to give to those not so weak.
If one colony has four frames of brood and another two, taking from the stronger frames for the weaker would leave
both so weak they would not build up very rapidly, whereas
taking one from the two-frame colony and giving it to the
four-frame colony would make the latter build up so much faster that it could pay back with interest the borrowed frame.

GIVING BROOD TO WEAKER.

Not till a colony has six or eight frames of brood is it
desirable to draw from it brood for weaker colonies, and there's
no hurry about it then. When a colony has its hive so crowded
with brood that the queen seems to need more room, then a
frame of brood can be taken from it to help others. The first
to be helped are not the weakest, but the strongest of those
with less than four frames of brood. When the three-framers
are all brought up to four frames, it is time enough to help
the weaker ones. Toward the last the little fellows can be
helped up quite rapidly. Perhaps a colony with two or three
brood (if you will allow me to use brood for short when I mean
frames of brood) has had brood taken from it, leaving it with
only one brood. It has stood for several weeks, and now it can
have three or four brood given to it, setting it well on its feet.

When brood is thus taken, generally the adhering bees are
taken with the brood, of course making sure that no queen is
taken. Where a single brood is given with adhering bees to a
colony, I have never known any harm to come to the queen of
the reinforced colony. In rare cases I have had the queen

killed when several frames of brood have been given at a time to a very weak colony. A precautionary rule is that when more than one brood is given at a time, each one is taken from a different colony.

GIVING SECOND STORY.

When a colony is beginning to be crowded and there are no colonies needing help, and sometimes even when others do need help, a second story is given. This second story is given below.

Fig. 35—Part of Home Apiary (from Southwest).

Putting an empty story below does not cool off the bees like putting one above does. The bees can move down as fast as they need the room. Indeed, this second story is often given long before it is needed, and sometimes two empty stories are given, for it is a nice thing to have the combs in the care of the bees. They will be kept free from moths, and if any are mouldy they will be nicely cleaned out ready for use when wanted.

Sometimes when a colony is very strong and a story of empty combs is given below, a frame of brood is taken from the upper hive and put below, an empty comb being put in its place above. But unless the colony is very strong, this hinders rather than helps the building up.

So good a beekeeper as G. M. Doolittle practiced giving the extra story on top. I protested, at least mentally, against dissipating the heat of the colony in that way. Yet in the spring of 1914 I did exactly that thing myself! By the middle of May colonies were unusually strong, and there were no longer any weak colonies to which brood could be given after being taken from the stronger colonies. The only thing to do was to give extra stories to colonies which needed more room, or else to limit the queen to one story, a very unwise thing up to the time of giving supers. So I began giving to the strongest colonies an upper story, putting in it two brood from below. I put the extra story above instead of below, not because it was better for the bees, nor to gratify Doolittle, but because that was the easier thing for the beekeeper, and the bees would just have to stand it. A day or two later it began to be evident that any colony in the apiary might need more room, and so I made a wholesale business of giving an extra story to each colony, with the exception of one or two. To make the work still easier for the beekeeper, instead of putting two frames of brood in the upper story, I merely put in it five empty combs. That took less than half the time, and would take much less time when it came to putting on supers, especially in the case of a colony which had started no brood above. That gave plenty of room above for the queen to use if she needed it. If she didn't need it no harm was done beyond cooling off the heads of the bees more than they might like.

I may say here that after a good deal of experience with colonies having two stories I find that there is no trouble from having the queen stay exclusively in one or other of the stories. She passes up and down freely, keeping filled with brood in both stories as many combs as the bees will care for.

SUBSEQUENT OVERHAULING.

Any overhauling subsequent to the first is an easy matter. As a broodless frame was left at the further side at the first overhauling, and the brood-nest commenced with the next frame, I can count that the bees will continue this arrangement, only in some cases there will be brood found in the outside frame. So in any examination after the first, I commence at the near side; and when I come to the first frame of brood, I need go no further, for I know that the brood-nest will occupy all the rest of the combs except the outside one. If they have not plenty of feed, of course it can be given, although it may not often be necessary to give stores the second time, for in this locality they can get good supplies from fruit bloom. I

Fig. 36—Comb Resting Diagonally in Hive.

suppose they can forage upon 10,000 fruit trees without going a mile.

If, however, the first frame of brood I come to contains only sealed brood, I must look further to see whether they have eggs or very young brood, for it is possible they may have become queenless. If eggs are plentiful, but no unsealed brood, I know that they have a young queen which has commenced laying, and I must find her and clip her wings.

If there is nothing but sealed brood, and no eggs, I am not sure whether they have a queen or not, and it is not safe to give them one till I do know, so I give them, from another col-

ony, a comb containing eggs and young brood. I make a record
of giving them this young brood thus: "May 20, no eg gybr,'
(no eggs; gave young brood), and in perhaps a week I look to
see in what condition they are. If I find queen-cells started I
am pretty sure they have no queen.

QUEENLESS COLONIES.

What shall be done in that case depends. If the colony is
weak, it is at once broken up, brood and bees being given
wherever they may be needed, and I heave a sigh of relief to
think I am rid of the weakling. If it is strong—an accident
may have happened to the queen of a strong colony at the last
overhauling—it may be broken up and the brood and bees distributed where they will do the most good, but more likely a
weaker colony with a good queen will be united with it. Just
possibly, the queen-cells started may be allowed to go on to
completion.

BROOD AS A STIMULANT.

If it happened that they had a virgin queen when the
young brood was given them, the presence of this brood is supposed to stimulate the queen to lay the sooner, and I may find
eggs on this later inspection. It may be, however, that I shall
find neither eggs nor queen-cell, in which case I consider it
probable that they have a queen which has not yet commenced
to lay, and they are left for examination later.

LAYING WORKERS.

Although laying workers are not so likely to be found
early in the year, it is still possible. In some cases the scattered condition of the brood awakens immediate suspicion. This
scattered condition is shown in Fig. 59, but the picture does not
clearly show how the sealed brood projects above the surface
like so many little marbles, being thus projected because drone-
brood is in worker cells.

Often the presence of laying workers can be detected before there is any sealed brood, by the fact that drone-cells are

chosen in preference to worker-cells, that is, drone-cells will be filled with eggs or brood—perhaps two or more eggs in a cell—while plenty of unused worker-cells seem handy. Eggs in queen-cells are also likely to be found, and if you find a queen-cell with more than one egg in it you may be pretty sure laying workers have set up business. Sometimes a dozen of eggs may be found in one queen-cell. An egg in a queen-cell with no other brood or eggs present is a pretty sure sign of laying workers.

Fig. 37—Painted Tin Hive-covers.

TREATMENT OF LAYING-WORKER COLONIES.

When a colony of laying workers is found early in the season, about the only thing to do is to break it up, and it matters little what is done with the bees. They are old, and of little value. Indeed, there are never any very young bees with laying workers, when the bees are Italians or blacks, and it may be the best thing in all cases to break them up, distributing the bees and combs to other colonies.

Yet if a strong colony is found at any time with laying workers, and if, for any reason, it may seem desirable to con-

tinue the colony, a queen-cell, or a virgin queen just hatched
may be given, for it is not easy to get them to accept a laying
queen.

DRONE-LAYING QUEENS.

Drone-brood in worker-cells may be present with no laying workers—the work of a drone-laying or failing queen. The
brood in that case, however, will not be so scattering as in Fig.
59. Such a colony is more amenable to treatment, and can be
well utilized by uniting with a weak colony having a laying
queen.

BREAKING UP FAULTY COLONIES.

When fruit blossoms are about ready to burst forth, and
bees are carrying pollen whenever it is warm enough, I do not
expect to lose any more colonies except those that are queenless
or have faulty queens. But I do expect to have the satisfaction
of breaking up every colony that does not have a good queen,
for when I find a colony that is queenless or one whose queen
is more or less a drone-layer, it is no longer any satisfaction to
me to nurse it and coax it along for the sake of saying I have
not lost that colony. The real satisfaction is in having it out of
the way. Time was when it seemed a nice thing in case of
finding a strong colony without a queen to give it young brood
and let it rear a queen; but much observation has shown that a
queen reared thus early is only an aggravation nine times out
of ten. So when a colony is found that is not queen-right, it is
remorselessly broken up, and distributed amongst other colonies, or united with a weak colony having a good queen. The
breaking-up of such colonies does not make the number less
in the long run, for by fall the number can be made greater
than if no breaking-up had taken place.

RECORD ENTRIES.

While care is taken to omit no entry in the book that will
be of future importance, there is really not such a great deal
of writing done, as will be readily understood when it is remembered that only one page is allotted to three colonies, allowing

only 22 square inches for each. It is seldom that a colony requires more than its allotted space in the season, hardly half the space being used on the average. There is a great deal of monotony about the entries, and there are a few words which are so frequently used that abbreviations aid much in saving room and time for making entries. Some abbreviations that are constantly used are as follows: b for bees, br for brood, c or qc for queen-cell, g for gave, k for killed or destroyed (kc means

Fig. 38—Zinc Hive-covers.

I destroyed the queen-cells), q for queen, s for saw, but sc means sealed queen-cell, t for took, v for virgin queen, ☐ for super.

PLACE FOR PENCIL.

To make sure of always having a pencil handy to make entries, it is tied to the book, as is also a pair of scissors for clipping queens unless the latter is replaced by a pair of pocket scissors. A strong string is put in the middle of the book, passed around the back and tied, and to this is tied a long string that holds the pencil and another for the scissors. To prevent

the scissors hanging open with its two sharp points, a common
rubber band is so fastened on the handles as to hold them together. While the band holds the scissors together when not
in use, its elasticity allows their free use when needed.

KILLING GRASS.

This is a good time to salt the ground at and about the
entrances of the hives, to kill the grass, although too often I
leave it till it has to be cut with a sickle. Grass growing in
front of the hive annoys the bees, and that growing at the side
annoys the operator, especially if the operator is of the female
persuasion, and the grass is wet with dew or rain.

HARBINGERS OF HARVEST.

There are certain things always noticed by a beekeeper,
with much interest, as heralding the beginning of spring or of
the honey harvest. Among these are the singing of frogs, the
advent of bluebirds, and the opening of various blossoms. With
me the highest interest centers in white clover. As I go back
and forth to the out-apiaries, I am always watching the patches
of white clover along the roadside. If your attention has never
been called to it, you will be surprised to find how long it is
from the time the first blossom may be seen, till clover opens
out so bees will work upon it. I usually see a stray blossom
days before it seems to have any company. In my location I do
not count upon anything usually besides white clover for surplus, so no wonder I am interested in it.

VARIOUS HONEY PLANTS.

Yet there are a good many other plants whose help, all
taken together, is not to be despised. If I kept only a few
colonies, it is quite possible that I might secure some surplus
from more than one of them.

Dandelions help no little in brood-rearing.

Raspberries are eagerly visited by the bees, but there are
not enough of them to give a noticeable amount of raspberry
honey. It is a very pleasant sight to see the bees thickly covering a field of raspberries in full bloom (Fig. 45).

Red clover may yet be of importance. Whether it be the
change in the bees or the change in the season I do not know,
but formerly I never saw a bee on red clover except at rare
intervals, and now it is quite common. I think it may be that
the bees are different.

Alsike clover is becoming common.

SWEET CLOVER.

It is hard to tell just how much, but I think the bees gather
quite a little from sweet clover (Fig. 46). The earlier part of
the sweet-clover bloom is probably of no great value, because
it comes at the same time as white clover, but it continues after
white clover is gone, thus making it of greater value. It has a
habit of throwing out fresh shoots of blossoms on the lower
part of the stalk after the whole stalk has gone to seed and appears dead, and thus it continues the blooming season till
freezing weather comes on. A branch of this kind will be seen
at the right in Fig. 46. I value sweet clover for hay.

Yellow sweet clover blooms from two to four weeks earlier
than white sweet clover, and on that account is of less value in
a year when common white clover yields well. But in the years
when common white clover is a failure yellow sweet clover may
be of very great value, for so far as I know there are no years
of failure with either kind of sweet clover. There may be no
small advantage in having the annual variety of yellow sweet
clover.

Alfalfa (Fig. 47) has become quite common here, a boom
for it having started about 1912. But it is a rare thing to see a
bee at work upon it, and I think it is generally understood that
it does not yield nectar east of the Mississippi.

GIANT WHITE CLOVER.

A new honey plant was mentioned a good deal in foreign
bee journals, a giant white clover, called Colossal Ladino (Fig.
48). I succeeded in getting some seed from Switzerland, sowed
a few of them in the window in the winter, and had the plants
blooming in the summer of 1902. For the purpose of compari-
son you will see in Fig. 48, at the right, a branch of red clover,

and at the left a plant of common white or Dutch clover, both grown on the same ground. As you will see by looking at the picture, the new plant has leaves as large as those of red clover and in appearance I think they are identical. The blossom, however, which you will see toward the left, looks precisely like a large white-clover blossom. The habit of growth, too, is that of the common white clover, running along the ground and taking root as it goes. A look at the picture will show this, the roots being seen coming from the stalk at the left.

Just how much value there is in this new clover I do not know. As will be seen, it grows much larger than the common white, but only as its leaves and leaf stems are larger, for it does not grow up and throw out branches like red clover. It died out the second winter.

LINDEN, CATNIP, GOLDENROD, ASTERS, HEARTSEASE.

Linden or basswood (Fig. 49) is a scarce article, the flavor of linden honey being seldom perceptible in any honey stored by my bees. I take great pleasure, however, in the sight of a row of lindens running from the public road up to the house (Fig. 50).

Catnip (Fig. 51) is scattered about in some places quite plentifully where it has the protection of hedges, for which it seems to have a great liking. It has a long season.

Goldenrod (Fig. 52) grows in abundance in several varieties, and while other insects may be seen upon it in great numbers, a bee is seldom seen upon it. Much the same may be said of the asters (Figs. 53 and 54). In some places both these plants are said to be well visited by the bees.

The summer of 1902 was very wet, and for the first time in my observation heartsease (Fig. 55) was busily worked upon by the bees. Probably it was not plentiful enough before. At any rate it has now become a honey plant of importance. In some localities heartease is, I believe, the chief honey plant producing amber honey. But I *think* it yields very light honey here.

CUCUMBERS.

I think the white-clover crop, for some reason, is more

unreliable than it was years ago. Some years there is a profusion of clover bloom, but there seems to be no nectar in it. As some compensation, I think there is more fall pasturage than formerly. One reason for this is that two pickle-factories are located at Marengo, and my bees have the run of one or two hundred acres of cucumbers. And yet I must confess that I am not at all sure what cucumber honey is. Sometimes the honey stored at the time of cucumber bloom is objectionable in flavor, and sometimes the flavor is fine. Two or three years the bees

Fig. 39—Hive-stand.

at the Hastings apiary stored in the fall some fine honey, remarkable for whiteness, and I've no idea what it was gathered from unless it was heartsease. On the whole I am in a poor honey region, and would have sought a better one long ago but for ties other than the bees.

ARTIFICIAL PASTURAGE.

I have made some effort to increase the pasturage for my bees. Of spider-plant I raised only a few plants. It seemed too difficult to raise to make me care to experiment with it on a larger scale. Possibly if I knew better how to manage it, the difficulty might disappear. Or, on other soil it might be less difficult to manage. The same might be said of the other things I have tried. My soil is clay loam, and hilly, although I live in a prairie State. I am at least a mile distant from prairie soil. I had an acre of as fine figwort as one would care to see. It died root and branch the second winter; even the young plants that had come from seed the previous summer. It was on the lowest ground I had, very rich, and much like prairie.

When the boom for Chapman's honey plant (*Echinops spherocephalus*) was on, I was among the first to get it, and I succeeded in having a large patch. Bees were on it in large numbers, but close observation showed that a great proportion of them were loafing as if something about the plant had made them drunk. I concluded I did not get nectar enough from it to pay for the use of the land, to say nothing of cultivation.

One year I raised half an acre of sunflowers, and I have tried other things. but given them up.

APPLE BLOOM.

Quite likely if a second crop of apple bloom came a month or two later than the usual time, I might get some surplus from that; but coming so early I think there are hardly bees enough to store it. Still, the bees are at this time using large quantities of honey for brood, and so the apple bloom is of very great value. Another advantage is that the great quantity of bloom has somewhat the effect of prolonging its time, for the latest blossoms, that with a few trees would amount to little or nothing, are enough to keep the bees busy. So it happens that often I can scarcely recognize any interim between fruit bloom and clover. A few items from a memorandum for 1882 may be interesting.

MEMORANDA OF 1882.

April 4.—Last bees taken out of cellar.

May 8.—Plum bloom out. Bees still work on meal and sugar syrup.

May 10.—Wild plum, dandelion, cherry, pear, Siberian, Duchess of Oldenberg.

May 31.—Saw first clover blossom.
June 5.—Apple about done.
June 12.—Commenced giving supers.
June 13.—Clover full bloom—plentiful.
June 20.—Locust out.
August 1.—Clover failing.
August 5.—Robber bees trouble.

You will notice that the earliest apple bloom (Duchess of Oldenberg) commenced May 10, while the Janets and other late bloomers were still in blossom on June 5, several days after the first clover was seen, making about four weeks of apple bloom. Possibly this was unusual—certainly the clover lasted unusually long, about 7½ weeks from the time the bees commenced working on it, for they do not seem to commence work till after the blossoms have been out some time..

TIME FOR GIVING SUPERS.

You see that I did not commence putting supers on till 12 days after I saw the first clover blossom, and if I had had only a dozen colonies, I might have waited later, but with a large number I must commence in time so that all shall be on as soon as needed. Usually I put on supers as nearly as convenient to ten days after seeing the very first white-clover blossom. A little time before bees commence work in supers, little bits of pure white wax will be seen stuck on the old comb about the upper part, yet I hardly wait for this, but go rather by the clover.

Another year (1884), I saw the first clover blossom on May 21, apple being still in full bloom; and I commenced putting on supers June 2. One year, I remember, clover failed on July 4, the earliest I ever remember.

MEMORANDA OF 1901.

Turning to another year, the year 1901, I give a few entries:
March 17.—Bluebirds, prairie chickens, robins, larks.
March 25.—Frogs.
April 5.—Soft maple.

April 28.—Dandelion.
May 1.—Hard maple, plum.
May 2.—Cherry.
May 5.—Apple.
May 6.—Strawberry.
May 23.—White clover.
June 20.—Sweet clover.
June 29.—Linden.

WHITE CLOVER UNCERTAIN.

That year, 1901, had perhaps the finest show of white-clover bloom ever known, but it was a dead failure, perhaps on account of the terrible drouth, although sometimes white clover blossoms bountifully and fails to yield honey when nothing that can be seen in the way of weather is at all at fault. About the middle of August the bees began storing, perhaps from cucumbers and sweet clover, and gave a surplus of 16 pounds a colony. It would have been better to have had it all stored in brood-frames, I think.

The following year, 1902, was still more exceptional. As already told, the bees would have starved in June but for feeding, yet later on they did some good work, some colonies yielding as much as 72 sections. The bulk of this was stored toward the last of August or later.

Fig. 70 is from a photo taken Oct. 1. In the picture the bee appears to be perfectly still, but these are not moving pictures, and I assure you that that bee was in very lively motion when taken.

OVERSTOCKING.

To a beekeeper who has more bees than he thinks advisable to keep in the home apiary, pasturage and overstocking are subjects of intense interest. The two subjects are intimately connected. They are subjects so elusive, so difficult to learn anything about very positively, that if I could well help myself I think I should dismiss them altogether from contemplation. But, like Banquo's ghost, they will not down. I must decide, whether I will or not, how many colonies will overstock the home field, unless I make the idiotic determination to keep all at home with the almost certain result of obtaining no surplus. I do not expect ever to have any positive knowledge upon the subject, because if I could find out with certainty just what number of colonies a given area would support in one year, I have no kind of assurance that the same kind of year will ever occur again. So I act upon the *guess* that in my locality it is never wise to have more than 100 colonies in one apiary, and possibly 75 would be better.

SURPLUS ARRANGEMENTS.

The first surplus honey I obtained worth mentioning was secured in boxes holding somewhere from 6 to 10 pounds. The boxes had glass on one or more sides, and were placed on the top of box hives. Then for a year or more my surplus was extracted honey obtained with the old Peabody extractor (Fig. 2), in which the whole affair, can and all, revolves.

SECTIONS.

Then I started on sections of the four-piece kind, and later used one-piece. I have used the $4\frac{1}{4}$ x $4\frac{1}{4}$ x $1\frac{7}{8}$ size much more than any other. I have used a few hundreds of the tall sections, but my market does not seem to like them any better than the square sections, if as well. I have tried $4\frac{1}{4}$ square sections of several widths, 1 15/16 inches wide, 7 to the foot, also 8, 9, and 10 to the foot. I have made some trial of plain sections, but for my market I am not sure that there is advantage enough in them to make me change from the two-beeway sections.

T SUPERS.

The T supers I use are $12\frac{1}{8}$ wide inside, just right for eight- frame hives. Just why I adopted this size I do not know, for at that time I was using 10-frame hives, and it was a little awkward to use a super so much narrower than the hive. But at least part of the time I used only eight frames in the 10-frame hives.

HOW TO MAKE A T SUPER.

So many have asked me how to make a T super that it may be well to give directions here. It is a plain box without top or bottom, the inside width being the same as that of the hive and the depth ¼ inch more than the depth of the sections to be used. Mine being for the 8-frame dovetailed hive, and for 4¼ x 4¼ sections, are 17⅜ inches long, inside measure, 12⅛ inches wide, and 4½ inches deep. If they were all to be made over again, I think I might prefer to have them ⅛ inch

Fig. 40—Original Miller Feeder.

shorter. Unless the lumber is very thoroughly seasoned, the depth should be a little more than ¼ inch more than the depth of the sections. To support the sections, three T tins are need-ed, and there must be something to support these T tins, 3 sup-ports on each side. With your super lying before you upside down, make a mark on the edge of each side at the middle. Now, half way between this mark and each inside end of the super, make another mark. These three marks on each side will tell you where the middle of each support is to be. Most of the supers have for these 6 supports pieces of sheet iron 1⅛ x 1 inch. Lay the piece flat on the edge of the side of the super, and fasten it by 2 nails about $\frac{1}{4}$ inch from the inside edge of the side of the super. As the wall of the super is $\frac{7}{8}$ thick, that will allow the support to project inside about $\frac{1}{4}$ inch, and the support is of course 1 inch wide. Some of the latest of my supers, instead of these squares of sheet iron, have staples as supports. A staple is driven in about $\frac{1}{4}$ inch from the inside edge, then bent over and hammered down flat. The staples are an inch wide. To support the sections at each end of the super a strip of tin is nailed on. It is $13\frac{1}{4}$ x $\frac{5}{8}$, and is nailed on so as to project inward $\frac{1}{4}$ inch. The 12-inch T tins are bought ready made. The super is hardly long enough to close the top of the hive. I like this. When the harvest is booming I let the super be shoved forward enough so there will be at the back end a space of $\frac{1}{4}$ inch for ventilation, which is an important factor to prevent swarming. But the sections near this ventilation will not be finished so rapidly, and at the beginning and toward the close of the season a cleat is nailed on the super to close fully the opening. Yet I remember at least one year when it worked the other way, and the sections were sealed sooner at the open end than at the closed end. Perhaps it was because the weather was very hot.

The separators used are plain wood, and are generally bought new every year, for it is about as cheap to buy new as to clean the old, and more satisfactory. The usual follower fills out the super, wedged in with a super-spring.

TOP VENTILATION OF SUPERS.

In working for extracted honey it is an easy thing to give a good deal of ventilation to each story, and it works well as a great hindrance to swarming. It makes no great difference if the bees should not seal the combs so well at the openings for ventilation. For years I dreamed of trying to have some way of having the same advantage for comb honey. To be sure, it had worked well enough, at least part of the time, to have a space for ventilation between hive and super at the back end. But to have ventilation between each two supers could hardly fail to make bad work about sealing where the openings came.

If we could only have ventilation at the center, where sealing is first done, instead of at the ends where the last sealing is done! Well, why not at the center? In 1912 I tried it, making a ventilation-cover. Here is the bill of material for it: 2 pieces 20 x 4⅝ x ¼; 2 pieces 4 x 4⅝ x ¼; 2 pieces 13⅞ x ½ x ½; 2 pieces 7 x ½ x ½.

At each side will be one of the 20-inch pieces, and between them, one at each end, the 4-inch pieces. These will be nailed upon the 13⅞ pieces, one at each end, and the 7-inch pieces will come at the inside ends of the 4-inch pieces. We now have a cover with a central opening 12 x 4⅝ inches. This is laid upon the super with the ½-inch square pieces uppermost, and on this is placed the usual cover. If desired, this ventilation-cover can be lightly nailed to the hive-cover, to be removed at the close of the super-season. These ventilation-covers have not been thoroughly tested, but give promise of being an acquisition.

<h3 style="text-align:center">SUPER SPRINGS.</h3>

Until the introduction of super springs, my supers of sections were wedged together by crowding in behind the follower a straight stick about as long as the inside length of the super, and ½ x ¼ inch. I find the super springs a very great improvement. When the sections are filled into the super, the corners, which have been wet, are not yet entirely dry, and no matter how tightly wedged, as they dry out there will be shrinkage of the contents of the super, so that in some cases the wedge-stick will drop down. The metal springs will adjust themselves to this, and continue to press the sections together, although with less force, after all have entirely dried out. It is easier to put the springs in, and very much easier to take them out. In a word, the sticks are not always a fit, and the springs are.

Another thing of perhaps still more importance is that the stick, being crowded in diagonally, forms a pocket in which the bees are apt to congregate when one is trying to get them out of the super, and it is very hard to dislodge them from this pocket. The spring forms no such pocket.

I am not sure whether it is better to use one spring or two to a super.

The T tins are not fastened to the super, but loose (Fig. 5).

SECTIONS READY IN ADVANCE.

The work of getting sections and supers ready for use has been all done long before the time for putting on, and something will be said about how that work is done.

At the time the supers are needed for putting on the hives, they are all nicely piled up in the storeroom of the shop, ready to carry out.

Years ago I thought I was doing pretty well if I had ready in advance as much as 4 supers filled with sections for each colony. Certainly, if I could average, one year with another, 96 finished sections per colony, it would not be such a bad thing. But if preparation is to be made in advance, it must be not for an average crop, but for the largest crop possible. Allowance must be made, too, for unfinished sections that will be taken off at the close of the season, and also for a good many that the bees have not begun on at all. Being caught short of sections and having to get them ready right in the rush of harvest made me change my mind as to the number that should be ready in advance. Several times I had to change my mind, each time setting the mark a little higher, for as the years went by the big yields of big years became bigger. One reason for this was no doubt the improvement in pasturage. Another was the improvement in bees by continuous breeding from the best storers.

AN EMPHATIC SEASON.

The year 1903 was one of the years that emphasized the need of having a big stock of sections ready in advance. It emphasized also the variableness of the seasons. Another item of no small importance was the harvests of the present and future as compared with the past. Some have said that, with the advance of civilization, the plow and the ax have cut off our resources for nectar, and we are no more to expect such crops as we have had in the past. We shall see where the year 1903 put the emphasis in that matter.

A furnace put in the cellar somewhat late the previous winter had made bad work with the wintering, so that by the 12th of May, 1903, I could muster only 124 colonies all told, and some of them were very weak indeed. The dense carpet of white clover promised well, provided the weather was good (as it turned out there was too much cold and wet for best expectations), but enough supers were piled ready-filled to satisfy any reasonable demands. The cool wet weather hindered storing no little, but was no doubt an advantage in the long run, for it kept the clover growing and blowing, and I don't know really when it did cease to yield.

The season was remarkably early, so that second stories were given some colonies by May 13, and May 25 we began giving supers. Three days later there were evidences of abundant storing. July 1 we began taking off supers, and from that on had a busy time both taking off and putting on—no trouble with robber-bees; supers could be set on hives and left till the bees all ran out of their own accord, standing all day if necessary. This up to July 18, after which time the bees would have spells of letting up, only to go at it afresh after the pause.

Finally it began to dawn on us that our stock of filled supers was running dangerously low. More sections were ordered. Getting them ready as needed was added to our already heavy task. We were kept on the jump till near the middle of August. Then came the National convention at Los Angeles. Some 12,000 finished sections were piled up in the house, but a lot more were on the hives, and I hesitated about going. But my assistant insisted I should go; the bees had let up on storing, and I thought it would do no great harm to leave all sections on till I got back, so I left August 12, getting back the 28th.

Scarcely had I got out of sight when the bees made a fresh start as fierce as ever, and gave Miss Wilson the busy time of her life. Up at 4 o'clock in the morning to get sections ready, then to one of the apiaries to take off and put on supers, with no let-up in the work of going through colonies to keep down swarming. Yes, indeed, there was swarming galore, and had been all through the season. It is generally understood that when bees are busily engaged at storing they give up all thoughts of swarming. Not in 1903. I'm not sure I ever knew so bad a season for swarming. We fought our best to prevent it, but every now and then the bees would get the start of us.

Some 6000 finished sections were taken off during my 16 days' absence, and on my return I found everything about the work kept up in as good shape as if I had been at home. And Miss Wilson was still alive.

Fig. 41—Miller Feeder Dissected.

We didn't get the last sections off the hives till well along in September, and the final footing up was not conducive to despondency. From 124 colonies, spring count, we had 18,150 pounds of comb honey (about 20,000 finished sections), increasing to 284 colonies; or an average of more than 146 pounds per colony, with 129 per cent increase. As the storing was mainly by one set of colonies and the increase by another, it would perhaps be fairer to say that 100 colonies averaged 181½ pounds per colony with no increase, and that each of the remaining colonies was increased to 7⅔ colonies with no surplus.

The best colony gave 300 sections, and several colonies were close on its heels.

Clearly, in such a season as 1903 it would not do to have ready only 4 supers per colony, and I did some figuring to determine what would be the right number. That average of 146 pounds per colony was equivalent to about 160 sections per colony. With 24 sections to the super, these 160 sections would lack 8 sections of filling 7 supers. There were probably more than 8 unfinished and empty sections per colony, so it will be readily seen that for another year like 1903 it will be a conservative estimate to count on having 7 supers of sections ready in advance for each colony. Such a year may never come again, but then again it may. So remembering the old saw, "It is better to be ready and not go than to go and not be ready," it will be the wise thing to have 7 supers filled in advance each year. If they are not needed they will keep over all right, even if kept so long as 4 or 5 years.

Perhaps it will be well, as a general rule, to have ready as many as will be needed in your best year, and then an extra super besides for each colony. That, of course, might make it more, or it might make it less, than 7 supers to the colony.

A PHENOMENAL SEASON.

Just ten years later came the season of 1913, again upsetting all figures. The season opened with 83 colonies; 11 of these were devoted to extracting-combs, and 72 to sections, and these 72 had no help from the other 11. There was abundance of fruit bloom and dandelion, and colonies became strong. May 27 appeared the first bloom on alsike and white clover, just as fruit bloom closed. Two days later we began putting on supers, and the bees were not long about occupying them. There was a steady flow from clover for at least 11 weeks, and I don't know how much longer, for about August 18 sweet clover and heartsease began to mix in, continuing till Sept. 20, supers being taken off Sept. 22. Thus there was a continuous flow, with scarcely a break, for about 16 weeks. Timely rains occurred to keep the bloom at its best, but they generally occurred in the night, allowing the bees to be on their job the next morning.

After the flow was well under way, with every prospect of continuance, Miss Wilson began to urge that more sections should be ordered. I laughed at her. I said, "There is no need of more than 7 supers per colony, spring count. We had at the beginning of the season 660 supers ready to put on the hives. That's a little more than 9 supers per colony. We never have needed anything like that number of supers, and never will. No matter how hard the bees are working now, there are always setbacks, as you will see, and at the close of the season we will have empty supers to burn." But with Scotch persistence she kept insisting, and finally I ordered more sections, with no expectation they would be needed. It would, however, satisfy Miss Wilson, and the sections would keep for another season. But the expected setbacks did not come, and the big flow kept right on flowing until the 660 supers had been put on the hives, and we began to put on some of the fresh lot. Then Miss Wilson had the laugh on me. I bore it calmly.

The increase from these 72 colonies was only one colony, the other 11 colonies furnishing all needed increase.

There was no stinting of surplus room. As fast as needed an empty super was added below, and as a sort of safety valve an empty super was kept on top. Throughout the whole of July there was on the hives an average of 5 supers each. A few colonies had as many as 7 or 8 supers each at one time.

June 24 we began taking off supers. Each colony had careful credit for all honey taken from it. Not only were full sections counted, but sections partly filled were estimated and credited. Footed up at the close of the season, there were 19,186 sections, or an average of 266.47 sections per colony, for the 72 colonies, spring count. If reduced to pounds it would probably be about 244 pounds per colony.

The number of finished, marketable sections was 17,684, or 245.6 sections per colony, spring count. Reduced to pounds, that would be something like 225 pounds per colony.

Returning to the total credits, the poorest colony was credited with 68 sections, the best with 402. Only 10 colonies

gave less than 200 sections each. The best six colonies gave
respectively 383,384,384, 390, 395, 402.

Whether you count the total 266.47 sections per colony, or
only the 245.6 finished sections, I think that 1913 crop stands as
the world's record for the best yield of comb honey for as many
as 72 colonies. It could hardly be expected that I should not
feel a little proud of holding such a record; but I am not proud
that in such a season there should be as many as 10 colonies
giving less than 200 sections each. I can take no pride in the
season; that's one of God's good gifts; I can only take pride in
good management and careful breeding; and for those am I not
equally indebted to the same God?

SHOP FOR BEE WORK.

The shop (Fig. 71) in which the filled supers are stored is
a plain wooden building 18 x 24, two-story, with a bee-cellar
under it. The bee-cellar, however, has not been used for some
years. The upper story is used for storing empty supers, hives,
and other articles not very heavy, or such as are not often
needed. The outside door opens into the middle of the east
side of the house into a storeroom; immediately in front of you
as you enter are the stairs leading to the upper story, and at
your right a door opens into the workroom. In this workroom is a coal stove, and the room, being ceiled up, is comfort-
able in the severest weather.

ROOM FOR QUEEN.

Up to the time of putting on supers the queen has had
unlimited room with the design of encouraging the rearing of
as much brood as possible. When the harvest begins, she may
have as much as 6, 9, 11, even up to 14 frames well occupied
with brood and eggs. A good deal depends on the season, as
well as the queen. At one time I thought I ought to be able to
make a success of continuing the two stories of brood-frames
throughout the harvest. It seems that when a colony is so
strong as to have 12 or 14 frames of brood, there ought to be
no difficulty in having good super-work done by putting the
supers above the two stories; and one season of failure the only

super I had filled was on a two-story colony. But I was never able to have that thing repeated, and whatever the reason may be, I have not been able to make a success of putting comb-honey supers on two-story colonies. Even if the two-story plan would work all right it involves much extra lifting.

REDUCING TO ONE STORY.

So before putting on supers the colonies are reduced to one story each. If a colony has 9, 10, or more frames of brood, all but 8 are taken away. The surplus frames of brood are given

Fig. 42—Hive-dummy.

to those which have less than 8 frames of brood each, the effort being to have in each hive 8 frames well filled with brood when a super is given. The season may be such that it will not be possible to have as many as 8 brood in each hive. A colony strong enough to have 6 frames well filled with brood is likely to be in condition for good super-work, but the work will be better if it has 7 or 8. On the other hand the season and the early condition of the bees may be such that when each colony is brought up or down to its 8 frames of brood, a considerable surplus of brood may be left.

DISPOSAL OF EXTRA BROOD.

Circumstances will decide what shall be done with this extra brood. It may be needed for building up nuclei, or for new colonies. It may be piled up temporarily in piles of three, four, or five stories each, to be used later in any manner desired. It does not take three times as many bees to care for the brood in three stories as it does to care for the brood in one story. If two or three stories of brood with adhering bees are piled up, in two or three weeks there will be enough bees there so that when reduced to one story it will be all right for super-work. Or it may be left just as it is, and allowed to store in combs for the next spring's use, or for extracting.

BURR-COMBS.

At the time of putting on supers, it is desirable that there shall be as little inducement as possible toward the building of burr-combs between top-bars and supers. A very strong inducement of that kind consists in the presence of any beginnings of such combs already there. Formerly I had a space of ⅜ of an inch over top-bars, and if a super of sections were placed directly on the hive, burr-combs in abundance would be built.

HEDDON HONEY-BOARD.

In such conditions the Heddon slat honey-board (Fig. 6) was a boon. Between the top-bars and the honey-board was a mass of burr-combs filled with honey, making a disagreeably dauby, sticky, dripping mess when the honey-board was removed; but the space between the honey-board and the bottoms of the sections was left beautifully free from burr-combs, so the section bottoms were left clean. This while everything was new; for if honey-boards were put on a second year without cleaning there would be the beginnings of burr-combs between honey-board and sections, or more than the beginnings if the honey-boards had gone more than one year without cleaning. So at some time before putting on the honey-boards they were carefully cleaned. But cleaning the honey-boards was not enough. The tops of the frames had to be cleaned as well, and this cleaning was done with a common garden-hoe, an assistant smoking the bees out of the way while the top-bars were hoed.

CORRECT BEE-SPACE.

It was a great step in advance when we learned that instead of a space $\frac{3}{8}$ of an inch there should be only $\frac{1}{4}$ inch, or perhaps a shade less. In other words we learned that a bee-space, or that space in which bees were least inclined to put either comb or propolis, was a scant quarter of an inch. With a correct bee-space between top-bars and sections, we can dispense entirely with anything in the shape of a honey-board. There will be a little trouble with the building of bits of comb under the sections, but not enough to make it worth while to use a honey-board. But that trouble will be greatly aggravated if there be any beginnings of burr-combs on the tops of the frames when supers are given. So the tops must be cleaned off wherever there is anything to clean off before the supers are put on the hives.

THICK TOP-BARS.

Another thing that may help to keep down burr-combs is the thickness and width of top bars. My top-bars are $\frac{7}{8}$ thick and $1\frac{1}{8}$ wide, leaving a space of $\frac{1}{4}$ inch between them. There are more burr-combs than I like built between them, and I have wondered whether any other space would be better. If the sides as well as the tops of the top-bars were cleaned off at the time of giving supers, it would help to keep the bottoms of sections clean, but I doubt its paying.

THICK TOP-BARS FOR WHITE SECTIONS.

Even if the $\frac{7}{8}$ thickness of top-bar were of no other advantage, I should want it for the sake of keeping the cappings of the sections white. At one time I had wide frames of sections facing brood-frames (the brood-frames were used to bait the bees up into the supers), and if the brood-frames were left there till the sections were sealed, the sealing would be almost if not quite as dark as the sealing of brood-combs. The bees seem to carry bits of the old, black brood-combs to use in capping the sections. So the thick top-bar increasing the distance of the sections from the brood-combs helps to keep the former whiter.

NO EXCLUDER UNDER SECTIONS.

"Before putting on the super, would you advise me to put a queen-excluder (Fig. 56) over the brood-chamber?" It would increase the space between the brood-combs and the sections, and in that way would be a further help toward prevention of dark cappings on the sections, and it would make a sure thing as to preventing burr-combs on the bottoms of the sections. But I don't believe there would be enough advantage in both ways to pay for the excluders.

I think I heard you say, "But wouldn't it pay to use excluders for the sake of keeping the queen out of the supers?" I may reply that the queen so seldom goes up into a super that not one section in a hundred, sometimes not more than one in a thousand, will be found troubled with brood. So on the whole I hardly think that all the advantages to be gained from using excluders would pay for the time and trouble of using them. I need not consider so very much the cost of them, for I have a lot on hand lying idle. At one time I thought I had a plan for prevention of swarming by the use of excluders, and was so sanguine about it that I got 150 of them. I think a great deal of queen-excluders, and wouldn't like to do without them, but I did not need 150 of them, for my excluder-swarm-prevention plan did not turn out to be a howling success.

EXPERIMENTING ON TOO LARGE A SCALE.

Allow me to digress long enough to confess that one of my weaknesses is being a little too sanguine about new plans while they are yet in the raw, and so experimenting on too large a scale. More than one crop of honey has been lessened by means

of some foolish project that I thought might increase the crop.
But I haven't done as badly as I might have done, for my good
wife has acted somewhat as a balance wheel, advising me to
"go slow" and not experiment on too great a scale, and she has
always been abetted by her sister, who is perhaps over-con-
servative. I could have tested my plan with 15 excluders just
as well as ten times that number, but I knew the plan would
work, and I couldn't wait! I think I didn't consult my wife
about ordering the 150 excluders. As I grow older I may
learn caution, and experiment on a smaller scale, but too much
should not be expected of me.

Fig. 43—Crock-and-plate Feeder.

PLEASURE OF EXPERIMENTING.

As an offset to the mischief done by experimenting on too
large a scale, I may say that one of my keenest enjoyments is
the working out of problems connected with beekeeping. There
is never a time, summer or winter, when I am not cooking one
or more schemes, plans or projects connected with the business.
No doubt more money could be made at beekeeping if everything in the business were fully settled and we knew before-

hand just exactly the right step to take in any given case, but there wouldn't be nearly the fun in it.

BROOD AND POLLEN IN SECTIONS.

It may be asked why it is that I have so little trouble with queens laying in sections, while some others are much troubled in that way. Possibly the thickness of top-bars may have something to do with it, but very likely it may be that the amount of foundation in sections has a bearing on the case. Some use small starters in sections, while my sections are filled as full as possible with foundation. When drone-comb is absent from the brood-nest, there seems to be such a desperate desire for drone-brood that I have known the queen to leave the brood-nest and fill with eggs a patch of drone-comb two or three frames distant from the brood-nest. On the same principle she would go up into the sections if drone-comb were there, and nearly always when I find brood in the sections it is drone-brood. With small starters in sections there is plenty of chance for building drone-comb, but when the sections are full of worker foundation there is no chance for it, hence no special temptation for the queen to go above unless very much crowded for room.

Of course, when brood enters the sections, pollen is likely to follow. Perhaps a more common cause of pollen in sections is the shallowness of brood-frames. Against this, an excluder is powerless to help. I had a little experience with frames shallower than the Langstroth, and had more pollen over one hive with the shallower frames than over fifty of the others.

PREPARING SUPERS OF SECTIONS.

This work is done in the winter, or at least so early in spring that it will not interfere with other work, but as an understanding of it may help just a little toward understanding some of the summer work, I will talk about it here.

CLEANING SUPERS AND T TINS.

The propolis is scraped from the supers by means of the hatchet already mentioned. Cleaning T tins is another matter,

The plan used is the invention of my assistant, and I think I cannot do better than to let her tell about it by copying the following article which she wrote for Gleanings in Bee Culture:

"When we commenced work in the shop, the first super I filled with the nice clean sections, I looked at the T tins all covered with propolis and thought to myself: 'If we are to have sections unstained by propolis it will never do to put them on these dirty T tins. But, oh dear! it will be an endless task to scrape them all. I can never do it. Just then a happy thought

Fig. 44—Watering-crock.

struck me. Why not boil the propolis off? Sure enough, why not?

"I repaired to the kitchen, placed the wash-boiler on the stove (one we use for such work), filled it with water and T tins, then went back to the shop to work, and left them to boil at their own sweet will, delighted to think I had such an inspiration. In about an hour I went back to the kitchen to see how my T tins were progressing. I fully expected to see them all nice and clean, and was most bitterly disappointed to find that they looked even worse than they did when I put them in, as the propolis was more evenly distributed all over them,

"I next tried scrubbing them with a broom in the boiling water, but it would not work. I meditated awhile, then concluded I would try concentrated lye, provided Dr. Miller did not object. I did not know what effect the lye would have on the tins. He said I might try it. I put the boiler back on the stove to try once more. I did not feel quite so sanguine as I poured in part of a can of concentrated lye.

"I did not leave it this time, but anxiously watched to see what effect it would have. It brought it off pretty well, but was not quite strong enough. I put in the rest of the can of lye, and eureka! the propolis disappeared as if by magic. I stirred the tins with the poker to insure the lye reaching all parts of them; then with the tongs I lifted them into a tub and rinsed them off with cold water and set them up in the sun to drain, as bright and as clean as when they came from the tinner's.

"I filled up the boiler with T tins again, and so on, until the strength of the lye was all used up, when I turned it out, filled up the boiler afresh, and began all over again, continuing until they were all done. I used a can of lye to a boiler of water.

"Every time I fill up a super with the nice clean T tins I feel more than paid for the work it took to make them so. I am pretty sure that washing fluid would clean them almost if not quite as well as the concentrated lye, provided it were used strong enough, although I have never tried it. However, I think I should prefer the lye, as it does the work most thoroughly and does not hurt the T tins in the least that I can see.

"If you have a lot of dirty T tins I advise you to clean them in this way, and see if you are not as delighted as I was to see them come out so bright and clean. Be sure to use plenty of water in rinsing them off."

WETTING SECTIONS.

The well-known Hubbard section-press is used for putting the sections together. If the sections are fresh from the manufacturer and as good as they ought to be, they can be put together at once without any preparation. If they have been held over from the previous year they may be so dry that too many of them will break in folding. The joints of these are wet in a somewhat wholesale manner. If they are crated in such a way as to be favorable for it, the whole crate of 500 are wet before being taken from the original package, one side of the crate being removed so as to expose the edges of the sections. If the crate is not of the right kind for this, then the sections are taken from the crate and put in the proper position in an empty crate lying on one side with the top and one end removed. Of course the sections do not lie flat, but on their edges, the grooves of each tier corresponding with the grooves of the other tiers, so that a small stream of water poured into the grooves at the top will readily find its way clear through to the bottom. If necessary the sections must be wedged together, so there will be no room for water to get between them only at the grooves.

A pint funnel is specially prepared for the work. A wooden plug is pushed in from above, projecting below two inches or less. The lower end of the plug is whittled to a point, and either by means of a bad fit or by means of a little channel cut in one side of the plug, there is just leak enough so that when the funnel is filled there will be a continuous fine stream of water running from the point of the plug. Holding the funnel in one hand I pour into it *boiling* water from a tea-kettle held in the other, at the same time holding the funnel so that the stream from the point of the plug shall be directed into the grooves, moving the funnel along just fast enough so that the water shall be sure to go clear through to the bottom. Cold water will not work well.

A plan I like better is to have a vessel of hot water somewhat elevated, with a small rubber tube running from it, so that the stream from it can easily be directed into the grooves. A fountain syringe works nicely.

Before wetting, the box of sections should be stood so that the sections are on end, and then jolted heavily, so as to make the grooves correspond the whole depth of the box. After the sections are wet they swell immediately, making them fit too tightly in the box to be gotten out without much difficulty. The boards are torn off one end of the box, and after the sections are taken out the boards are nailed on again, if it be desired to preserve the box.

FOLDING SECTIONS.

Sometimes I put sections together myself, but generally some boy or girl does the work unless my wife be pressed into service. The operator seated at the machine (Fig. 57) has a pile of sections laid at a convenient height at her left hand, the sections piled so that ends correspond. As fast as the sections are taken from the press they are neatly piled in order on a board at the right of the operator. (I know that some throw the sections indiscriminately into a basket as they leave the press, and it seems this ought to take less time, but I think in the long run my way saves time.) It is desirable that the board upon which the sections are piled should be light, as no great strength is required, and sometimes several thousand folded sections will be piled up ahead, and it is pleasanter to handle the light board. A dummy or almost any board will answer, but oftener hive-covers are used. One of these is of such size that there may be placed upon it side by side three rows of sections with eleven sections in each row. Upon these are placed three other rows, break-joint fashion, with ten sections in each row, and this piling up may continue till the upper rows contain four or less each. Generally the piling goes no higher than to have six sections in the upper rows, making 153 sections a boardful. As fast as one board is filled another takes its place, and the filled board is piled up, unless Miss Wilson is putting in foundation at the time and is ready for a fresh boardful of sections.

SIZE OF STARTERS IN SECTIONS.

Foundation for sections comes from the factory in sheets large enough to fill several sections. At different times the sheets have been of different sizes, but for some time past they have measured $3\frac{7}{8}$ x $15\frac{1}{2}$. This size is just right to make four top starters $3\frac{1}{4}$ inches deep, and four bottom starters $\frac{5}{8}$ inch deep. Occasionally a bottom-starter of this depth makes trouble by lopping over, but not often, and a shallower starter is more likely to be gnawed down by the bees. Moreover, I think the deeper the bottom-starter the more promptly the two starters are fastened together,

With two starters of this size in a 4¼ section, there should be a space of ⅛ inch between the two if it were not that the space is made larger by the melting away of the edges of the starters when they are put in the section (Fig. 60).

CUTTING FOUNDATION.

I have one time and another used different plans for cutting. A simple way, and one that is quite satisfactory, is the following: Take a board 18 x 12 inches or larger; on one

Fig. 45—Field of Raspberries in Bloom.

end nail a block as a stop for the ends of the sheets of foundation to rest against, and on one side nail four blocks about 2¼ inches long as stops for the one edge of the foundation to rest against. It is well also to nail one of these 2¼-inch blocks on the other side near the stop at the end, so as to make a space of 7⅞ inches in which the ends of the foundation shall be confined, otherwise the foundation has a disagreeable habit of sluing off to one side when the first cut is made at the other end. Of course these stops are to be nailed on the upper surface of the board and not on the edges. The two blocks that are nailed nearest the end-stop are to be tight against it, the

others at such intervals as to allow for cutting the 3¼ starters.
The size of these blocks is not important, ⅝ square being a
good size. With a rule of any convenient length ½ x ¼, this
rule being used to guide the knife in cutting, the machine would
now be ready for the foundation if one had an eye accurate
enough to put the rule in the right place. In order to do this
quickly and accurately, nails against which to place the rule
at the right places are partly driven in on both sides; 2½-inch
wire finishing-nails are good for this purpose. The board is
to lie before you, having the side with the four stop-blocks
nearest you. Drive a nail into each side of the board so that
there shall be a space of just 3¼ inches between the end-stop
and the nail. I don't mean you shall mark a point 3¼ inches
from the end-stop and drive your nail there, for that would
make 3¼ inches from the end-stop to the *middle* of the nail,
whereas it should be 3¼ from the stop to the nearest *side* of
the nail. The distances of the other nails from the end-stops
will be as follows: 6½, 9¾, 13, 13⅝, 14¼, 14⅞. Now your
cutting board is all ready for work.

Two knives are needed, one to be heating while the other
is cutting. For heating I use a common kerosene lamp put in
a box deep enough so that when a board is laid over the top of
it and a knife is laid on that board the end of the knife-blade
shall be directly over the lamp, nearly or quite touching the top
of the chimney. I don't know what kind of knife is best. A
Barlow knife makes good work, but I think I like better a
common tea-knife with a thin steel blade broken off, so it is 2½
or 3 inches long, and somewhat square at the point.

Preparatory to cutting, the foundation must be carefully
and evenly placed on the board. Take several sheets and even
them up true and nice, and lay the pile with one end tight
against the end-stop and one side against the side-stops. Now
lay a similar pile close beside it. Beginning at the right-hand
end, place your rule against the left-hand side of the nails, and
with a quick stroke make a cut with the knife held flat against
the rule. If you don't look out you'll hold the rule so that you'll
cut a piece off the tip of the thumb or fingers of the left hand,
but you'll not be likely to do it many times. If you are not
careful to hold the knife flat against the rule you will be likely

to cut into it. To avoid this I have tried covering the rule with
tin, but do not like it so well. The rapidity of the stroke is
important. If your knife is hot enough you can cut clear
down through at one stroke, but that's bad. The edges of the
foundation will be melted together, and you will have trouble
getting them apart. Turn down your lamp, and get it so three
or four strokes will be needed.

Fig. 46—Sweet Clover.

Latterly I have given up heating the knife, and like it
better. The small blade of a pocket-knife is used, and it is kept
very sharp, especially at the point. Three rapid strokes do the
business. The rapidity of the strokes is important, but some
. practice is needed, for with the very quick strokes there is some
danger that the knife will cut into the stock. If the wax is
warm enough two strokes will do.

Although this plan takes more strokes, it still saves time
for there is no heating or changing of knives. It also saves

the time of pulling the pieces apart, for with the hot knife there will always be at least a little melting together at the edges. Of course the cutting must not be done when the foundation is too cold, or it will be more or less broken.

Cutting foundation in a miter-box with a corrugated bread-knife was highly commended. I tried it, and was quite pleased to think it made faster work, although hardly such exact work. Then I timed it by the watch, and was surprised to find that it took more time than the old way.

When the boardful is cut I take a super with a bottom in it, gather up and put into it 48 bottom-starters, also the 48 top-starters, making these last in a neat pile.

Instead of using a single rule, I have for some time preferred to have a rule for every cut, making a saving of time. Take seven rules and lay them on the board on the proper places for cutting. On the ends of the rules, at each side, lay a thin strip of wood 15 inches long or longer—a one-piece section without the grooves does nicely—with one end of each strip tight up against the end-stop. Now nail together in this position, clinching the nails. You will use this with the other side up, the rules above, the side strips below (Fig. 61). Of course the guide nails are not needed with this arrangement. In the picture three of the rules appear all right, but the other four, which are very close together, look as if they were all one. The cutting board rests on a little worktable (Fig. 62), which is quite convenient for this and other purposes.

The sections being folded and the foundation cut, we are now ready for putting starters in the sections. This is the work of Miss Wilson, and she is an expert at it. After trying a number of foundation-fasteners, I have found nothing with which I can do better work than with the Daisy fastener.

DIVISION OF LABOR.

I may remark in passing that when I speak of doing things it does not always mean that I do such things personally, for it may be that some one else does the work entirely. But when any new implement is to be used or new plan tried, I first carefully study it up and try to learn just how it ought to be used, and then I instruct the one who is to make a specialty of that part of the work, and in a short time the specialist far exceeds the instructor. Miss Wilson can put in, I think, five starters to my one; my son Charlie, when a little chap, could distance me in putting together sections; and I think Philo can beat me at taking sections out of supers.

PUTTING STARTERS IN SECTIONS.

The Daisy foundation-fastener is so well known that I need say nothing about the use of the machine itself. As the operator sits at the machine with a small pile of starters in the lap, a boardful of sections is at the left hand at a convenient height, the side of the board toward the operator (Fig. 87). The bottom-starter is put in first, then the top-starter. When the section has its two starters, it is put directly into the super. With a starter as deep as $3\frac{1}{4}$ inches it would hardly do to throw the sections in a basket. Formerly the sections when filled were placed in order on a board the same as the board from which they were taken, and it was a separate job afterward to fill them in the super.

PUTTING SECTIONS IN SUPERS.

By means of an implement of my own devising, which for want of a better name may be called a "super-filler (Fig. 63), the separate job of filling sections in supers is now entirely dispensed with, and the sections go directly from the Daisy fastener into the super, taking no more time to be put into the super than it would take to put them on a board. Indeed, I think it takes a little less time, for there is not the same need of care in placing the sections so that other sections will not be knocked off the board, but the sections are shoved into place in the super in a sort of automatic way. Then, too, it is a comfort to get them directly into the super, for while on a board, even for a short time, there is always danger of some mishap by which a boardful may tumble over and come to grief.

SUPER-FILLER.

I'll tell you how to make a super-filler. Take a board as large as the outside dimensions of your super or larger. (The one in the picture is a board hive-cover.) Nail a cleat on one end of the board, and another cleat on one side as in the picture. These cleats may be ½ by ¼ inch, but the dimensions are not important. Now put a super on the board, shoving one corner snug up in the corner made by the cleats. With a lead pencil, mark on the board, on the inside of the super, where

Fig. 47—Alfalfa.

the sides of the super come. Put eight sections in the super, four on each side, with three T tins in their proper places. With a pencil rule across the board each side of each T tin, so as to show where the T tins come. Now take off the super and its contents, and get six strips, each 11½ inches long and ¼ inch square. Nail these on as shown in the picture, so as to keep at equal distances from the pencil mark of the super at each side, and about a fourth of an inch distant from the marks made for the T tins. The super-filler is now complete.

It stands at a convenient height at the right-hand side of the one who operates the Daisy fastener, with the side-cleat at the further side (Fig. 87). A super is placed on it with one corner of the super tight against the angle made by the cleats; but no T tin is yet put in the super. As the sections come from the fastener they are placed in the super at the end toward the back of the operator. When the first row of six is completed, the T tin is slipped under these sections into its proper place. In a like manner a second row of sections and a T tin; then a third row and a T tin, and lastly the fourth row. Then, without rising, the operator lifts this filled super to one side and gets an empty one.

PUTTING IN SEPARATORS.

Generally these filled supers are not separatored till the day's work of fastening foundation is done. Then a small table is used at which the operator sits. This table is made of three hive bottom-boards, or boards 21 x 14. Stand two of the boards on end; nail the other board on top; nail light boards on one side for a back, or brace with two pieces of lath diagonally, and there's your table (Fig. 62). Being convenient for other purposes, several of these little tables are on hand. The table is placed near a pile of supers to be separatored, and the separators are filled in.

TOP SEPARATORS.

As the sections now stand, there is some space between them endwise, allowing them to be out of square, and making a convenient place for the bees to deposit a disagreeable quantity of propolis. To remedy this, there is crowded in at the top between each two rows of sections a little stick $11\frac{1}{2}$ by $\frac{1}{4}$ by scant $\frac{1}{8}$. Then the follower is wedged in with a super-spring, and when all are done the supers are carried into the south room or storeroom, and piled up to await the harvest time.

BAIT-SECTIONS.

Bait-sections are put in enough supers so that the first super put on each hive shall be baited. Generally only one bait-section is in a super, the bait being in the center, and these baited supers are piled in the storeroom where it will be convenient to reach them first.

Fig. 48—Colossal Ladino Clover.

SATISFACTION IN HAVING SUPERS READY.

There is a feeling of real satisfaction in seeing the larger part of the storeroom filled with piles of supers ready to go on the hives. How many times I have counted them and admired the nice even piles reaching to the ceiling! Perhaps I should not appreciate them so much if I had not, years ago, felt the annoyance of running out of sections or foundation right in the middle of the honey season, waiting days for it, and the honey wasting.

Having spent this much time telling what was done the previous winter, let us get back to warmer weather.

GIVING ADDITIONAL SUPERS.

Understanding now that each colony has had a super given to it about ten days after the very first white-clover blossom has been seen, or sooner, the further history of this super and its possible successors is a matter that varies so much in different seasons that it is difficult to tell it straight. By the way, you may think that I'm always thrilled with the sight of the first clover blossom. I'm not. Scarcely ever a thrill. The colonies are rarely all of them as strong as I would like for the beginning of the harvest, and that first clover blossom is merely a warning that the time for building up for the harvest is becoming very short.

UNCERTAINTY OF SEASONS.

As to giving additional super room, it may or may not be necessary. That first clover bloom may have so few successors that there will be no harvest; or bloom may be abundant with no nectar. So sometimes it happens that after it becomes a clear case that the harvest is a failure, the supers are taken off as innocent of honey as when they were put on. Oftener it happens that the bait-section in each super is filled and sealed and not a cell drawn out in the other sections. From that up, the seasons will vary so that the average number of sections to each colony will be 10, 24, 48, and up to 150 or more, although these latter seasons do not come with any alarming degree of frequency.

If one could know in advance just what the season was going to be, he could tell a good deal better what to do in the way of giving additional super room. One may give so much room that there will be an undue proportion of unfinished sections at the final taking off, or one may leave the bees so crowded for room as to lose part of the crop. I am not likely to make the latter mistake, which I consider a good deal worse than to have too many unfinished sections.

GUESSING ABOUT MORE SUPER ROOM.

On the whole, there is a mixture of judgment and guess-work as to putting on any super after the first. Perhaps the nearest to a general rule in the matter is to give a second super when the first is half filled. If, however, honey seems to be coming in slowly, or if the colony is not strong, and the bees seem to have plenty of room in the super, no second super is given, although the one already there may be nearly filled with honey. On the other hand, if honey seems to be coming with a rush, and the bees seem crowded for room, a second super may be given although there is very little honey in the first. These same conditions continued, a third super may be given when the second is only fairly started and the first not half full, and before the first super is ready to take off there may be four or five supers on the hive.

RISKING IN GOOD SEASON.

In the year 1897—a remarkably prosperous year—there was on the hives in the Wilson apiary, an average of four supers to each colony, some colonies with less than four and some with more before a single super was filled. As I would lie at night thinking it over, I would say to myself, "What if there should come one of those sudden stops to the flow that sometimes occur, and you should be caught with those tons of honey with scarcely any sections finished in the lot? Wouldn't you wish you had gone a little slower, and had the bees finish up what they had, rather than coax them to spread out over more territory?" And then the cold chills would run up and down my back. But the sudden stop didn't come, and the crop was finished in good style. The supers were all well filled with bees, and although I took some chances as to unfinished work, I feel pretty sure that if I had allowed less room it would have been at a loss. But that was a very exceptional case.

Usually, in a fair season, when the harvest is in full blast and fairly along, there will be three, four, or more supers upon each hive, at one time, and in an extra season there may be a few hives having seven, or even eight, supers each. That does

not mean, by any means, that all of them will be finished, for
very likely the last super given will have very little honey in
it when the harvest is over.   But it will not do to let the bees
be crowded for room, and if all the sections on the hive are
about full, if the harvest has not entirely closed an empty
super must be given, in case they *might* need it.

Fig. 49—Linden or Basswood Blossoms.

SUPERS FOR OUT-APIARIES.

If there is guessing about the number of supers to put on
in the home apiary, there is still more guessing as to the number to be taken when starting to an out-apiary.   If I take a
smaller number than needed, I may have to make a special trip
for more.   If I take more than are needed, I will hardly want

to take them back home with me, and they are put in piles and covered up in the hope that they may be used the next time. But there is some danger of their being affected by rain when piled up at the out-apiary, so there is trouble either way. On the whole it is better to take too many than too few, and so there are generally some extra ones at the out-apiaries.

To take supers to the out-apiaries, they are piled up on the wagon in five piles, a lath is nailed from top to bottom on each pile, and they are braced on top with lath (Fig. 64). Fifty empty supers can be taken at a load, but it is not often that as many as forty filled supers are taken at a load.

ADDING SUPERS UNDER OR OVER.

As the harvest advances I am more chary about giving room, and it is given only when the sections already on are pretty well filled. Suppose toward the last of the season I come to a colony that has its sections nearly all filled. There is a possibility that the bees may be able to finish up what they have and a few more in an additional super, but the great probability is that they will do no more than to finish what they have. Although that probability may amount to almost a certainty, I do not act upon it, but go for the possibility and give the extra super. But I put it on top of the others, so that the bees will not commence work in it unless actually crowded into it.

During the early part of the harvest, so long as there is a reasonable expectation that each additional super will be needed, the empty super is put under the others, next to the brood-chamber. Work will commence in it more promptly than when an empty super is placed on top, and that greater promptness in occupying the new super may be the straw to turn the scale on the side of keeping down the desire for swarming. But when a super is put on toward the close of the season, not because it seems really needed, but as a sort of safety valve in case it might be needed, I do not wish to do anything to coax the bees into it, so it is put on top, and the bees can do as they please about entering it. It is true that if an empty super is put under the others at a time when the harvest is nearing its close, the bees may not do a thing in it, but merely go up and down through it and keep to work in the super above. But it is not so well to have them working so far from the brood-nest with empty space beneath.

No bait-section is needed in any super after the first.

EMPTY SUPERS ON TOP.

Latterly I have fallen into the practice of giving an empty super on top, even when an empty super is put under. This for more than one reason. It sometimes happens that the up-

Fig. 50—Row of Lindens in Bloom.

per starter of foundation is not securely fastened the entire length. If fastened half way across the top-bar of the section, it will look all right, but if put under the other supers, next to the brood-chamber, a heavy weight of bees coming upon it suddenly will drag down the foundation at one side. If put on top, the bees will enter the super only gradually, and the foundation will be fastened in place before any great weight of bees comes upon it. This empty super on top gives a less crowded feeling, and may help a little toward preventing swarming. No matter how full or empty the lower super may be, this top super serves as a sort of safety valve, in case any need for more room should arise. The next time there is need to give a super below, this top super is moved down and another empty super put in its place. When the top super is put down, I think the bees start work on it just a bit sooner than if it had not been above.

SWARMING NOT DESIRABLE.

If I were to meet a man perfect in the entire science and art of beekeeping, and were allowed from him an answer to just one question, I would ask for the best and easiest way to prevent swarming, for one who is anxious to secure the largest crop of comb honey. There are localities where a large crop of honey is secured in the fall, and in such places, or in any other place where the honey flow is long enough, a larger crop may be secured by increase, but I am not so sure about that. If a man in such a place start in the spring with 75 colonies, he may get a larger crop by increasing early enough to 150, supposing 150 colonies to be the largest number his field will bear; but would he not have a still larger crop if he had 150 all through the season and made no increase? However that may be, in my locality, which beekeepers generally would consider a poor one, where white clover is the chief if not the only source from which a crop may be expected, and where the harvest is all too short, if, indeed, it comes at all—in such a place I am satisfied that more honey can be harvested by commencing in the spring with the largest number the field will bear and holding at that number, always provided that the means taken to keep down increase shall in no wise interfere with the best work on the part of the bees.

If I were working for extracted honey, I suppose the matter might be managed, to a great extent, if not to the fullest extent, by simply giving abundance of room in every direction; but with comb honey, I do not believe that an abundance of room in the brood-nest is compatible with the largest yield of surplus.

Or, if I were working for extracted honey, I might at the beginning of the harvest put all the brood over an excluder in an upper story, leaving the queen on empty frames below, but that would hardly work for comb-honey production.

MANAGEMENT OF SWARMING COLONIES.

From my first using movable frames, I think I have kept my queens' wings clipped, so my experience in having natural swarms with flying queens has been very limited. But my experience in having swarms issue where and when I did not want them, has been very large. Only extreme modesty and humility prevent my being very proud of so large an experience. If I should ever reach that point where I shall be equally successful in preventing swarms, I make no promise to be either modest or humble.

So long as success in prevention of swarms has not been reached, it remains an important matter to know the best thing to do when swarms do issue. Under ordinary circumstances some one must be on hand to watch for swarms. For several years I have had no watching for swarms and have had no swarms except those which swarmed in spite of my efforts to prevent them. Yet if I had only the one apiary, it is just possible that I might allow swarming, at least so far as to allow the bees to swarm and then return to their old hives. At any rate there are a great many so situated as to allow their bees to go thus far in swarming, and I feel pretty sure that for them there may be some interest in knowing what I did when swarms did issue, so I will give an account of my management when I formerly allowed the bees to swarm.

WATCHING FOR SWARMS.

With as many as 100 colonies in an apiary, the one who is on watch can hardly be allowed to do anything else. The regular noise is so great among so many that the added noise of a swarm is hardly noticed; so sight, not hearing, must be depended on. I have gone on with my regular work and taken a look once in five or ten minutes along the rows to see if any swarms were out, but it is not a very satisfactory way of doing. A bright boy or girl can watch very well, if faithful. It is not necessary, of course, to watch all day; and the weather has much to do with the hours at which swarms may be expected. On a hot morning a swarm may issue as early as six o'clock; but this is exceptional, and if the weather has been cloudy through the day, clearing off bright and warm in the after part, a swarm may issue after 4 o'clock. Ordinarily, however, it is not necessary to be on the lookout before 8 A. M., or much after 2 P. M. I had a swarm issue once in a shower, but that is so unlikely to occur that I would not think it worth while to keep any watch at such a time.

Fig. 51—Catnip.

The watcher will soon learn the points of advantage from which he can easily command a view of the whole apiary, not needing to stir from his seat unless a swarm issues. Sometimes, however, there is so much playing going on among the bees, that there is no alternative but to travel about and take a close look at each colony that shows unusual excitement. It is an advantage at this time to have the hives in long rows. I

have 30 or 40 hives in a row. At the middle is a shady place
to sit. A clock or watch lies in open sight so that a look at
every hive may be taken once in five minutes. If there is no
timepiece to go by, the watcher may become interested in something else, and think the five minutes not up when double that
time has passed; but having the time measured out, he is free
to read or do any thing else between times. At each five minutes, the watcher, who is sitting at the middle of the middle
row, rises, glances along the back row to the north end;
then along the middle row to the north end; then, stepping forward, glances along the front row to the north end; then along
the same row to the south end; then to the south end of the
middle row, and lastly to the south end of the back row. All
this has taken less time than it takes to write it, and the watcher is ready to sit down till another five minutes is up.

     If, however, unusual commotion is seen—and, sighting
along the rows in this way, it can easily be seen—the watcher
goes to the hive for a closer look. Up to the middle of the day
or later, there is not often much excitement, unless there be a
swarm; but after this time so many colonies take their play-
spells that the watcher needs to spend most of his time on his
feet.

ONE-CENT CAGES.

     The watcher is provided with a number of queen-cages.
These are easily made and the material costs less than a cent
apiece. I take a pine block, 5 x 1 x ½ inch, and wrap around it
a piece of wire cloth 4 inches square. The wire cloth is allowed
to project at one end of the block a half-inch. The four sides
of this projecting end are bent down upon the end of the stick
and hammered down tight into place. A piece of fine wire
about 10 inches long is wrapped around the wire cloth, about
an inch from the open end, which will be about the middle of
the stick, and the ends of the wire twisted together. I then
pull out the block, trim off the corners of the end a little so that
it will easily enter the cage, slide the stick in and out of the
cage a number of times so that it will work easily, and the
thing is complete (Fig. 65). When not in use, the block is
pushed clear in, so as to preserve the shape of the cage. Such

cages can be carried in the pocket without danger of being injured.

FINDING QUEEN OF SWARM.

When the watcher finds a swarm issuing, he is pretty dull if he does not become interested in looking for the queen. I do

Fig. 52—Vase of Goldenrod.

not know of any sure way to find the queen, but she is not often missed. I think I can find her most easily by watching on the ground in front of the entrance. Very frequently she comes out at the back end of the hive or at the side, when the hive is raised on blocks. Rarely she may be found at some distance from the hive, on the ground, with a group of bees about her. If not found, she is most likely in the hive, and the

swarm may re-issue in a day or two. She may be lost, but at
this particular time her loss is not so very great. There is no
danger of the swarm being lost; it will return to the hive in a
few minutes; although I have known them to cluster for half
an hour or more before returning. It may happen, sometimes,
that a swarm may go into a hive whose colony has swarmed
a little while before, and where it is always peacefully received.
I do not like this doubling up, but I do not know that I lose
any thing by it, for the bees can store up just as much in one
hive as in another.

When the watcher finds the queen, she is caged. Either
the cage is held down for her to run into, or she is caught and
then caged. After the queen is in the cage, the block is pushed
in an inch or so, and the cage put where the bees can take care
of it. Usually it is thrust into the entrance, close up against
the bottom-bars, so that if a cool night should come there will
be no danger that the bees will desert it.

The watcher keeps a little memorandum book, and puts
down in it the number of the colony that swarmed; for it might
make bad work if it should be forgotten and neglected until the
emergence of a young queen to lead.out an absconding swarm.

DOOLITTLE'S PLAN.

Some years ago Mr. G. M. Doolittle gave a plan for management of swarming colonies when no increase was desired.
I do not think that he uses it now. I do not know that I shall
ever use it again, and yet it was valuable to me, and for some
circumstances nothing may be better. The plan, in brief, was
this: The queen being caged and left in the hive, all queen-
cells are cut out in five days from the time the swarm issued,
and five days later all queen-cells are again cut out and the
queen set at liberty.

I used this one season with great satisfaction, and I do not
remember that any colony thus treated swarmed again.

VARYING DOOLITTLE'S PLAN.

The next season I varied the plan. Instead of leaving the
queen with the colony to remain idle for ten days, I took her

away and gave her to a nucleus, a new colony, or wherever a queen was needed. At the end of the ten days I returned her to the colony, placing her directly upon a comb taken from the middle of the brood-nest. Often, however, I gave them a different queen, for after an absence of ten days I doubt if they could tell their own queen from any other. Besides, they were in a condition to take any queen without grumbling.

After the first year, however, I had some colonies swarm again after the queen was given them. Whether it was the season, the change in the plan, or some other cause, I am unable to say.

PUT-UP PLAN.

I then adopted a plan which relieved me of the necessity of hunting for and cutting out queen-cells. No matter how careful I might be, there was always a possibility that I might overlook a queen-cell, although this very rarely happened, if ever. But it took a great deal of valuable time. I give herewith the plan, which I think is an improvement.

When a swarm issues and returns, it is ready for treatment immediately; although usually it is put down in my memorandum of work to be done, and the time set for it may be the next day or any time within five days, just as suits my convenience. The queen is caged at the time of swarming, and left in the care of the bees, as already mentioned.

Within the five days, I take off the super, and put most of the brood-combs into an empty hive. Indeed, I may take all the brood-combs, for I want in this hive all the combs the colony should have. In the hive left on the stand, I leave or put from one to three frames, generally two. These combs must be sure to have no queen-cells, and may be most safely taken from a young or weak colony having no inclination to swarm. The two combs are put in one side of the hive, two or three dummies placed beside them, and the rest of the hive left vacant.

The question may be asked, "Will not the bees build comb in this vacant part of the hive?" No; at least they do not for me. Queenless colonies are little given to comb-building, and not at all inclined to make a fresh start in a new place.

If I did not do so at the time of taking out the frames, I now shake the bees off from about half the frames, not being particular to shake them off clean. These bees are of course shaken off into the hive on the stand. The supers are now put on this hive with its two or three frames of brood, the cover is put over the supers, and the "put-up" hive filled with brood is placed over all.

Please understand that there is no communication whatever between the lower and the upper hive, each hive having its own cover and bottom-board.

GETTING THE BEES TO DESTROY THE QUEEN-CELLS.

A plenty of bees will be left to care for the brood, the queen will commence laying, all thought of swarming is given up, and every queen-cell torn down by the bees. In perhaps two days I take a peep to see if the queen is laying, for it sometimes happens that at the time when I "put up the queen" (as I call the operation I have just described), there is already a young queen just hatched, and then the old queen is pretty sure to be destroyed. In this latter case I may remove the young queen and give them a laying one, or I may let the young queen remain.

PUTTING DOWN THE QUEEN.

In ten days from the time the swarm issued—sometimes ten days from the time I "put up the queen"—I put down the queen. If by any chance a young queen is in the upper hive, I do not like to put her down until she commences laying and her wing is clipped, for fear of her taking out a swarm. It seems a foolish operation for them to swarm when there is nothing in the hive from which a queen can be reared, but I have had it happen. The operation of putting down is very simple. I lift the hive off the top, place it on the ground, remove the supers, take the hive off the stand, place it on one side, put the hive containing the queen on the stand, and replace the supers.

You will see that this leaves the queen full chance to lay from the minute she is uncaged, and at the time of putting down there will be as much brood as if the queen had remained in her usual place. Most of the bees, of course, adhered to the lower hive when the queen was put up, but by the time she is put down quite a force has hatched out, and these have marked the upper hive as their location. Upon this being taken away, the bees as they return from the field will settle upon the cover, where their hive was, and form a cluster there;

Fig. 53—Two Asters.

finally an explorer will crawl down to the entrance of the hive below, and a line of march in that direction will be established immediately. In a day or two they will go straight to the proper entrance.

GOOD CHANCE FOR NUCLEI.

We left, standing on the ground, the hive with its two combs, which had been taken from the stand. These two combs, when the queen was put up, probably had a good quantity of eggs, and brood in all stages. They now contained none but sealed brood, some queen-cells, and a pretty heavy supply of pollen. Or, it may be that eggs from a choice queen were given, and the queen-cells are to be saved. A goodly number of bees adhere to the two combs and I know of no nicer way to start a new colony than simply to place the hive in a new location. Or, the bees may be shaken off at the old stand and the combs given to a nucleus which needs them.

I may remark in passing, that these queenless colonies will produce queen-cells not excelled by those of a swarming colony, and not surpassed in excellence by those produced by any of the best plans used by queen-breeders. In short, I do not believe it is possible to have better. It must be remembered, however, that all of them are not of equal excellence. For the bees will continue to start cells for several days, and the last ones started will be from larvæ too old to make good queens. You may be able to distinguish these cells by their poorer look, or, if you give the bees several cells, among them at least one or two of the finest looking, they will make no mistake in making the proper selection.

WORKING OF QUEENLESS BEES.

It may be objected that this keeping bees queenless for ten days makes them work with less vigor. I am not sure but it ought, but I must confess I have had no strong proof of it come directly under my own observation. So far as I could tell, these bees seemed to work just as hard when their queen was taken away as before. In the spring of 1885 one colony was, by some means, left entirely away from the proper rows —some three rods from any other colony. I took it away, put it in proper line, and left to catch the returning stragglers a hive containing one comb, this comb having no brood and very little if any honey. This colony having been a very weak one, very few bees returned to the old spot, but these few surprised me by filling a good stock of honey in the empty comb, before they were put with the rest of the colony.

Swarms treated on this "putting up" plan often swarmed again, but if they did they were put up again. An objection to the plan was that these "putups" were in the way and had to be lifted down when any thing was done with supers. Still, for any one who allows the bees to swarm, and who does not object to the lifting, the plan is a good one.

VARYING THE PLAN.

To avoid the heavy lifting, there has been a tendency toward a variation, by way of putting up only two or three frames of brood with the queen. (Indeed the number of frames

Fig. 54—Three Asters.

put up may be anywhere from two to the whole number.) If only two frames are put up, the lifting is light, but there is more work in killing the cells in the lower hive, both at the time of putting up the queen, and at the time of putting down. Putting up the larger number of frames has the advantage that the queen has the chance to lay without hindrance, keeping up the full strength of the colony. On the other hand, when only two frames are put up I *think* the colony is more likely to continue the rest of the season without swarming.

GIVING NUCLEUS TO SWARM.

A plan that has seemed to be as satisfactory as any other, although it is not always convenient to use it, is upon the issuing of a swarm to pick up the queen so as to have her out of the way, remove the old hive from the stand and place on the stand a nucleus in a regular hive. The supers are put upon this hive, and the swarm is left to return at its leisure. This takes little time and trouble, and there is no danger of further swarming. I have seen it stated that when the swarm returns the queen of the nucleus may be killed, but that does not occur "in this locality."

PREVENTION OF SWARMING.

I don't quite like that heading. It may be understood to mean that I am entirely successful in profitably preventing swarming, and I am not certain that I have yet attained to that. I say *profitably* preventing it, for there might be such a thing as preventing it in a way that would hardly pay. If a colony disposed to swarm should be blown up with dynamite, it would probably not swarm again, but its usefulness as a honey-gathering institution would be somewhat impaired. Swarming might also be prevented by means of such character as to involve an amount of trouble that would make it unprofitable; or it might be prevented in such a way as to have a very unprofitable effect upon the honey crop. The thing I am after is *profitable* prevention.

NO DELIGHT IN SWARMS.

I have read of the great delight felt by the beekeeper at the sight of an issuing swarm, the bees whirling and swirling in delirious joy, but such things do not appeal to me. I do not like swarming. I never did. I don't think I ever shall. In my many years of beekeeping experience, I think I never looked upon the issuing of a swarm with feelings other than those akin to pain, unless it might be the first swarm I ever had.

BAD MANNERS OF SWARMS.

I am not an expert at hiving swarms. They don't act nicely for me. After I have climbed a tree with laborious pains and shaken down a swarm with a hive under it at just the right place, the swarm instead of entering in a well-mannered sort of style will just as likely as not keep flying back every time it is shaken down, unless it should take it into its head to give me more exercise by taking another tree. I got a Manum swarm-catcher, but I do not remember that I ever used it with success. One day when I was trying to use it, J. T. Calvert, the energetic business man of The A. I. Root Co., was here. He helped me. He made a catcher of his hands and put the bees in the catcher by main strength. But they wouldn't stay "catched," and they didn't. So I don't like swarming, even if I didn't think it interfered with the honey crop.

WHY DO BEES SWARM?

Upon no other subject connected with beekeeping have I studied so much, tried so many plans, or made so many failures, as with regard to prevention of swarming. If I knew all about just what makes a colony swarm, I would be in better shape to use preventive measures; but I don't know all about it. Of course I know that want of room and want of ventilation may hasten swarming, and possibly some other things of that kind; but after all there is a good deal of mystery about the whole affair.

VENTILATION AND ROOM.

I think it is of some use to take pains to see that the bees are never cramped for room. I believe that raising the hive on blocks ¾ of an inch or more is a good thing. It is also a good thing to rear queens from stock that has shown little inclination to swarming. Indeed, with room enough and ventilation enough it is possible that bees would never swarm. Some one will say to me that bees may swarm with a hogshead of room.

Yes, but the combs may be in such condition that the queen will be cramped for room, even in a hogshead.

NON-SWARMING PILES.

For a good many years I have been in the habit of having in each apiary one or more colonies whose hives were kept as

Fig. 55—Heartsease.

a sort of storehouse where extra frames of brood or honey could be put, to be drawn from as occasion required, but often there has been no drawing, and these "piles" have grown to be four or five stories high with an immense force of bees. I never knew one of them to swarm. But the ventilation was as immense as the force of bees, for each story had an entrance of good size, and perhaps the superabundance of ventilation was the secret of their not swarming.

YOUNG QUEENS AND SWARMING.

It was said that colonies with queens of the current year's rearing would not swarm, and one year I supplied all the colonies of one apiary with young queens about the beginning of the honey harvest. It didn't work.

Once when a colony swarmed, and returned to its hive, I removed its queen and gave it a queen that I think had not been laying more than two or three days. Within three days that queen came out with the swarm. It seems the condition of the colony has more to do with the case than the condition of the queen. C. J. H. Gravenhorst, late editor of *Deutsche Illustrierte Bienenzeitung,* gives what I think is the truth about young queens and swarming: A given colony will not swarm with a queen of this year if the queen was reared *in this colony;* if reared elsewhere it may swarm. Why that difference he did not know. But some have claimed exceptions to this rule.

TAKING TWO FRAMES OF BROOD WEEKLY.

One season I kept eight brood-combs, in the hive, and every week or ten days took out two of the central combs, replacing them with foundation or empty combs. This was to give the queen so much room that there should be no desire to swarm. It was successful in most cases, but there were too many exceptions to make the plan reliable.

TAKING AWAY ALL BROOD.

Afterward I carried the same thing to its extreme limit in a good many cases, taking away all the brood. One frame of brood, however, was left for two or three days, perhaps a week, for fear the bees would be discouraged and desert an entirely empty hive. This one frame of brood was then taken away because it was the common thing for the bees to start queen-cells on it. Yet it is just possible that no swarming would have taken place, in spite of the queen-cells.

FORCED SWARMING.

This plan has come into great prominence lately under the name of *forced, shaken,* or *brushed* swarms. Gravenhorst, the great German authority, practiced and advocated it in the seventies of the last century. L. Stachelhausen was earnest in his advocacy of the plan in this country, and E. R. Root, editor of *Gleanings in Bee Culture,* took it up with great enthusiasm. Probably a good many had done more or less at it independently, for it would naturally suggest itself that taking away all the brood would leave a colony in much the same condition as if they had swarmed; and in actual practice most of those who had tried the plan have found bees no more inclined to swarm after it than after natural swarming.

FORCED VERSUS NATURAL SWARMING.

Many have found the plan a material advance over natural swarming. One very great advantage is sufficient to commend it; the beekeeper is master of the situation, and is not dependent upon the whims of the bees as to when they shall swarm—an inestimable boon to those who have out-apiaries, and indeed to any one who does not wish the trouble of watching for swarms.

It also gives the beekeeper control over the number of bees that shall remain with the swarm. In natural swarming there may be too few bees go with the swarm for best results in storing, while there may still be not enough for any hope of good work in the parent colony, with a possibility of this latter force being still further divided by after-swarms. In the case of a forced swarm, all the bees may be allowed to remain on the old stand except merely enough to care for the brood which is taken away. This brood may then be put on a new stand, and with the addition of a queen or a queen-cell allowed to start out on its career as an independent colony.

SHAKING OFF ALL BEES.

Or the forced swarm may be made still stronger by giving it *all* the bees, and distributing the brood to nuclei, weak col-

onies, or wherever it will do the most good. In no case, however, would it be a prudent thing in this locality to follow the
recommendation of some, by putting the brood on a new stand
without any bees, trusting to the warmth of the weather to
hatch out young bees fast enough to care for the brood. If
such a colony—if you can call it a colony—should not fall a
prey to the robbers, there would in most cases be a serious loss
of brood from starvation and chilling.

Fig. 56—Queen-excluder.

NO FORCED SWARMING TILL QUEEN-CELLS STARTED.

In no case did I practice this forced swarming till I found
by the presence of queen-cells that the bees were thinking of
swarming. There would be less labor in the long run (supposing that all were to be swarmed sooner or later), to do up the
whole business at a suitable time, without waiting for the bees
to take the initiative. Indeed, conditions may be such in some
localities that there might be a loss to wait for queen-cells.

But the harvests here are such that it is usually better to
have swarming delayed. Moreover, a good many of my colonies, if let alone, will go through the entire season without at-

tempting to swarm, and such colonies are the very ones that give the best yields, and forced swarming would be practiced upon them only at a loss.

DISADVÁNTAGE OF.FORCED SWARMING.

With all the advantage forced swarming has over natural swarming, it still leaves something to be desired. As already said, those colonies which hold their force intact throughout the entire season are the ones that give the best results. It is true that in forced swarming the entire force of bees may be left on the old stand, but there are thousands of prospective bees in the brood taken away. If you take away that brood today, you are taking away the bees of tomorrow, and of twenty more days to come.

"But the bees that emerge tomorrow do not emerge as field-bees, and will not be field-bees until they are sixteen days old. If the harvest closes in sixteen days the additional force will only be a lot of useless consumers." While the first part of your statement may be true enough, I cannot say as much for the second.

BEES DO THE WORK MOST NEEDED.

While the bees that emerge tomorrow may do no field-work for sixteen days, they begin housework at a very tender age—housework that would have to be continued by older bees if this brood were taken away. As fast as one of these young bees is ready to begin housework, it takes the place of an older bee, which can now go afield. I know that, as a general rule, the different departments of work are done by bees of certain ages, but I also know that bees accommodate themselves to circumstances. I have seen bees at five days old carrying in pollen because there were no older bees in the hive to perform that duty, and we all know that in early spring nursing and housework are done by bees several months old.

So it is reasonable to believe that at least to a certain extent the necessities of the case rather than the matter of absolute age decide what duties a bee shall perform; and the logical conclusion from that is that the larger force of bees we have in a hive the more storing we shall have even if a good many of the bees be quite young.

Without, perhaps, giving any satisfactory reason for it, I am also quite of the opinion that better work is generally done when bees are allowed to go right along rearing brood at their own sweet will; for toward the close of the harvest they, of their own accord, curtail work in that direction.

Fig. 57—Folding Sections.

NON-SWARMING PREFERRED TO FORCED.

While I yield to no one in my appreciation of the advantages of forced swarming over natural swarming, I believe that the advantages of no swarming whatever over forced swarming are as great as the advantages of forced over natural swarming.

So you will hardly blame me if instead of resting content with forced swarming I continue to pursue that will-o'-the-wisp—in the opinion of many—non-swarming.

KEEPING COLONIES QUEENLESS.

The next season after practicing the removal of two frames of brood, I settled upon a plan which I felt pretty sure would prevent the possibility of swarming. It was a no less radical measure than to keep the colony queenless. I reasoned that as I had never had a queen hatched inside of eleven days from the time the queen was taken away, or from the time the bees started queen-cells, the colony was safe from swarming if once in ten days I took away their brood and gave them fresh; also, that it was only bees over two weeks old that worked in the field; add to this the three weeks that it took from the egg to the full-fledged worker, and it was five weeks or more from the time the egg was laid till the bee became a gatherer. Clearly, then, only such bees as came from eggs laid five weeks or more before the close of the honey harvest were available as gatherers. Why not have the colony queenless during this five weeks? So I took away the queen, leaving in the hive three combs, one of which contained eggs and brood in all stages, the other two containing nothing from which queen-cells could be started.

Once in ten days the comb of young brood with its queen-cells was taken away and a fresh one given them, and at the close of the five weeks, which was about the close of the harvest, the queen was returned.

NOT A SUCCESS.

As a preventive of swarming, it was a complete success. Not one colony thus treated swarmed; how could it? As a means of securing a large crop, I think it was an egregious failure; although I can hardly tell with great definiteness, the season itself being a failure. Possibly the absence of the queen itself had something to do with lessening their stores, but I doubt it. But when all combs of brood but one were taken away, a large force of prospective bees were taken away that would have hatched out in the next twenty-one days.

If I had allowed four or five frames of brood, changing every ten days, the result might have been quite different. Moreover, the one frame they did have was, for the most part, filled with brood so young, that little or none of it hatched while in the hive. If I should try any thing in the same line again, I should keep four or five frames in the hive, and this should be mainly brood well advanced so that much of it would hatch out to replenish the wasting numbers.

KEEPING QUEENS CAGED.

Success was reported by others with the plan of keeping queens caged in the hive during part or the whole of the harvest, and although I tried it on a large scale there was no case of success with me.

FASTENING YOUNG QUEENS IN.

The good old-fashioned way of managing after-swarms was to return them as fast as they came out. This gave the

Fig. 58—Movable Shade.

young queens a chance to fight it out till only one was left, and when only one was left there would be no more swarming. So I planned to let the young queens fight it out without the trouble of returning swarms. I put a queen-excluder between the bottom-board and hive, so that no queen could get out. As no queen could get out, no swarm could leave. When the young queens emerged they could settle their little differences to suit themselves till only one queen was left. I would keep track of what was going on in the hives sufficiently to take away the excluder after all but one queen had been put out

of the way, so the young queen could go out on her wedding
trip. The thing was so certain to work that I spent $37.50
for queen-excluders to put the plan in practice.

SWARMING GALORE.

In due time when queen-cells were sealed the swarms began to issue. Then they returned. Then they came out next
day. Then they returned again. After doing more or less of
this, the time came when the young queens began to emerge.
Business became lively. Swarming once a day did not always
satisfy them. The number of issues in a day became such that
several swarms would be out at a time, and they were not at
all particular to keep separate. Neither were they as methodical as prime swarms about returning to their own hives. Almost any hive seemed to suit them provided there was a good
deal of noise at the entrance, and when swarming got well
under way for the day there were plenty of hives with noise
at the entrance. Whether the excluders leaked queens, or
whatever may have been the reason, there were some cases
of young queens being out, and when there was a young queen
in a swarm there was no telling how many swarms would unite
with it.

ABNORMAL BEHAVIOR.

After a swarm had been balked in its efforts a number of
times there seemed to be a reckless disregard in a good many
cases as to the propriety of returning when they had had
plenty of time to discover that no young queen had come out
with them, and sometimes they would settle and remain clustered for half a day, perhaps several swarms in the cluster.
Nothing so very bad about that, if I had only been entirely
sure that some time they would return; but when I stood gaz-
ing on a bunch of bees as big as my body when I'm in best
condition, and meditated upon the chance of there being a
young queen in the bunch to incite them to sail off into the
ethereal blue—well, it was not the sort of meditation most conducive to composure of mind.

Inside of the hive the program as laid down was pretty
generally carried out; at the proper time the excluder was re-

moved, and in due time the young queen was laying. The plan
is a good one if one could only induce the bees to refrain from
swarming out until only one young queen is left in the hive.
I could not induce them to do that.

REARING QUEENS IN "PUT-UP."

It is not necessary to tell of all the plans that were tried.
One was finally hit upon that proved to be quite satisfactory,
so far as tried.   When the presence of well-advanced queen-

Fig. 59—Brood of Laying Workers.

cells showed that a colony was bent on swarming, all but one
or two frames of brood were taken from the hive and put in
another hive that was "put-up" on top, of course having no
communication with the bees below.   In the old hive below the
old queen was sometimes left, and sometimes the bees were left
without any queen; but in either case care was taken that no
queen-cell was left below, and ten days later search was made
for queen-cells below, or else the brood was exchanged for
brood from a colony where there was no danger of queen-cells,
and the old queen was removed.   To the "put-up" was given,
at the time of putting up, a virgin queen or a ripe queen-cell,

and as soon as the young queen was laying the old hive was taken away and the "put-up" hive was put down in its place. Thus the whole force of the colony was kept together, there was a young queen of the current year's rearing, practically reared in the hive, and that colony was past the anxiety for the season. Some, however, say that such a queen will swarm with them.

GETTING BEES TO DESTROY CELLS.

I said the brood was put up, but said nothing about the bees or the queen-cells. No attention was paid to the queen-cells, and about half the bees were shaken off the combs—perhaps more than half. Just how many bees to leave in the "put-up" hive was not an easy matter to gauge. If too few there would be chilled brood. If too many the young queen would leave with a swarm. Of course the latter danger could be avoided by destroying all queen-cells in the "put-up," but that would make more work, and if there are few enough bees all superfluous cells will be destroyed by the bees themselves, and there will be no danger of swarming.

NUCLEUS TO PREVENT SWARMING.

A modification of the plan sometimes used was to take a nucleus from somewhere else and put in the place of the colony. But in this case the colony was made queenless two or three days in advance. Either plan left the colony without any diminution of its forces, and with no very great check to its work, and these plans might have been continued if it had not been that I struck upon a plan that seemed equally effective but quite a little easier. This was at first called the foundation plan, and afterward the excluder plan. Before speaking of this, however, it will be well to describe the preliminary work, which is the same for all colonies, whether the after treatment will be on the "put-up" plan or some other plan.

PRELIMINARY WORK.

As soon as colonies become strong and are working busily, we begin to be on the lookout for queen-cells. This generally will not be till the bees are at work on clover bloom, although it may happen in some seasons that preparation for swarming begins during the last of fruit bloom. Of late years dandelion has become so important that there is a possibility it may start swarming. Whether it be in apple or clover bloom, we begin to examine some of the strongest colonies to see if any preparations for swarming are made. If we find none in the strongest colonies it is hardly worth while to look through the rest. When, however, we find one or more queen-cells with an egg

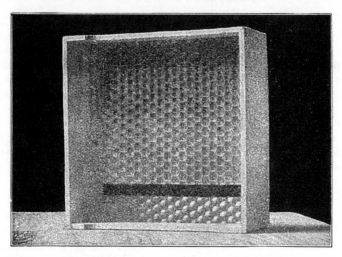

Fig. 60—Top and Bottom Starters in Section.

in each, then it is time to begin a systematic canvass of *all* colonies, and to keep it up in all so long as we continue to find queen-cells in any, except in a case where a colony has already been treated or has treated itself in such a way that it need not be expected to swarm.

COLONIES THAT DO NOT NEED WATCHING.

In struggling with the swarming problem, there are a few things that may be relied upon with some degree of certainty. A swarm that has been hived in an empty hive this season will not send forth a swarm this year, with rare exceptions. Equally safe from swarming is a colony whose queen has been removed

and the colony allowed to rear a new queen, provided only
one queen is allowed to mature. Also a colony kept queenless
about 10 days and then given a laying queen of the current
year's rearing. Colonies that do not come under either of these
heads will need watching until the time comes when bees have
given up starting cells in all colonies.

LOOKING FOR QUEEN-CELLS.

We plan to go through each colony about once in ten days
to look for queen-cells. I say *about* once in ten days, for it is
not always possible to be exact. It may happen that one or
two days in succession will be rainy, and then the ten days
become eleven or twelve. Or, it may be that on account of
some interference with our work that we can see in advance,
we may think it best to shorten the ten days to nine or less.

Suppose we go through a certain colony and find no queen-
cell with as much as an egg in it. The next time around it may
be in the same condition, and so it may continue throughout
the season. In that case there is nothing to be done with that
colony beyond the examination every ten days but to let it
alone and be thankful. Such cases are not so plentiful as I
should like, but I think they are on the increase.

DESTROYING EGGS.

Suppose, however, that upon one of our visits we find one
or more cells containing eggs. We destroy the incipient cells
by mashing them, and in the record-book write after the date,
"keg," a contraction for the expressive, if not very elegant
entry, "killed eggs." It is possible that upon the next visit we
may find no more queen-cells started, and that may be the last
of them for the season. So long as we find only eggs, we do
nothing more than to destroy them.

Generally, however, when eggs are found in cells, the next
visit will find cells with grubs well advanced. When large
grubs are found in cells, then the colony must be treated.

As already mentioned, an easier plan than the "put-up"
plan was struck upon, and for a time that had a run. It may
be called the excluder plan, and I will now give it as we first
practiced it.

EXCLUDER PLAN OF TREATMENT.

We find and cage the queen, destroy all queen-cells, remove the hive from its stand, and put in its place a hive containing three or four frames of foundation. The foundation is on one side of the hive with a dummy next to it. The rest of the hive is left vacant. Upon this hive is put a queen-excluder, and over the excluder the old hive with its brood and bees, and over this the supers as before (Fig. 66). Then the queen is

Fig. 61—Cutting Foundation.

run in at the entrance of the lower hive, and the colony is left for a week or ten days. Ten days is safer.

At the end of the week, or as soon after that time as we can conveniently reach it we take away the lower story with its excluder, and put back the queen in the old hive, which is left on the stand. When we remove the lower story with its three or four frames that a week ago contained foundation, there will be less advance made in those frames than you would be likely to suppose. The vacant part will still be vacant, the amount of honey will be very small, generally only one or two frames will have been occupied by the queen, and possibly nothing beyond eggs will be found. If larvae are found, they will be still small, and not in large quantity. It appears from this that there is some sulking for a time on the part of the queen, or else that the bees are rather slow to prepare the foundation for her. It is possible that this interim without any laying may be an important part of the treatment. I don't know.

SOME FAILURES.

At any rate, in the first two seasons of using the plan, there was no case of any colony making any further preparation for swarming after being thus treated. The third season (1902) every thing did not work so smoothly, but possibly the treatment was not fairly administered in all cases. Some of the colonies did not take kindly to the foundation, and in a few cases it looked as if they might have swarmed out rather than to use the foundation. In one case they built comb and started a brood-nest in the vacant part, leaving the foundation untouched. But there was some excuse for this as the foundation was weather-beaten and hard.

WORKING TOWARD NON-SWARMING.

Of course it is no little work to go through the colonies every ten days up to the time of treatment, and I think it likely that it would work all right to treat every colony on the excluder plan, or some other plan, early in the honey flow, whether they had grubs in queen-cells or not. But there are some colonies that will go through the whole season with never a grub in a queen-cell. Possibly one or more eggs may be found in queen-cells at each of several successive visits; possibly eggs may be found at one visit, and none at succeeding visits. And exactly these colonies that never start cells, or are willing to be thwarted in it, are the ones most likely to give record yields. To interfere with their work, even for a week in a slight degree, is not desirable. There is also another important reason for allowing every colony willing to do so to go through the whole season without any preparation for swarming and without any interference. I am trying all the time to work at least a little toward a non-swarming strain of bees, and if all colonies were treated in advance how would I know which were the non-swarmers from which to choose my breeding stock? Their careful record must be kept.

EMPTY FRAMES USED.

Some time later a little change was made so as to make the queen better satisfied with her new quarters. Instead of putting foundation under the excluder, a brood-frame is put there, at one side. It is preferably one with very little brood in it, the object being merely to hold the queen in the hive, but not to encourage her to do much in the way of laying. As a

Fig. 62—Little Work-table.

further discouragement to laying and comb-building no other comb is put in the hive, nor ever the least starter of foundation. Two or three other frames *entirely empty* are placed beside the brood-comb. No dummy is needed. You might expect that the bees very promptly fill with comb one or more of these empty frames. They don't. At the end of a week or ten days you may find one frame half filled, with a very little comb in the second; perhaps only a little comb in the one frame.

As to the rest, of course the proceeding is just the same as when foundation was used.

DESTROYING QUEEN-CELLS TO PREVENT SWARMING.

Among the first things a beginner thinks he has learned is that destroying queen-cells will prevent swarming, and then he is sorely disappointed to find that he is mistaken about it. But I must confess that I have a good deal more faith in it than I formerly had. Not that I would for a minute trust to it as a sole means to prevent swarming. But I do know that in a good many cases it is efficient. Perhaps one cause of my change of view is the change in my bees. Breeding constantly for improvement in storing, and at the same time giving preference to those least inclined to swarm, it is possible that destroying cells has more effect than it formerly had.

It may be well to give some examples, taking just as they come in order some colonies that needed no other treatment to prevent swarming. I take them from the year 1908, one of the best honey years. The first one I come to had a two-year-old queen, and June 23 I destroyed a grub in just one queen-cell. No other queen-cell was started. If that had not been destroyed, I suppose the colony would have swarmed, and that would have lessened the number of sections produced, which was 181, besides finishing up some "go-backs." The next had a three-year-old queen, and gave 244 sections. June 23 one egg in a cell was destroyed, and that was all for the season. The queen was superseded after August 8. The next had a two-year-old queen, and gave 276 sections. I destroyed, June 15, one egg in a queen-cell, and June 24 one grub. The next had a queen of the previous year and gave 100 sections. It never had even an egg in a queen-cell the whole season. The next had a yearling queen, and gave 145 sections, besides having taken from it, in May, three brood with adhering bees. Not an egg in a queen-cell. The next had a yearling queen, and gave 211 sections. It had one egg in a queen-cell June 6, also July 27 and August 6. That may be enough to show that at least in some cases destroying cells was worth while. Perhaps one colony in three will behave thus well.

THOROUGH WORK AT KILLING CELLS.

Some have said that if a frame or two were lifted from the center of the hive and no cells found in them, there was no need to look further. No such slipshod work will answer here. Every comb in the hive must be carefully examined. It may be that not a cell is found in the hive except upon the very last comb lifted out. Neither will it do to examine a comb with all its bees upon it. The bees must be shaken off, so that the cells can be plainly seen. If at the previous overhauling eggs or cells were killed, or if for any reason it is suspected that the colony is in danger of swarming, then the queen is found, and the comb upon which she is found is put into an empty hive standing near before the bees are shaken off the combs. If any combs were shaken first, it would make it difficult to find the queen.

DEQUEENING TREATMENT.

Latterly no one plan of treatment is followed exclusively. It may be the "put-up" or the excluder plan, or it may be dequeening for about 10 days. The dequeening treatment is the one most generally used. The queen is removed, the queen-cells are killed, and in 10 days the queen-cells are again destroyed and their own queen returned, or another queen given. Sometimes a queenlessness of a week seems to do as well. At any rate, a queen in a provisioned cage may be given in a week, for it will be a little time before she is out ready to lay. Possibly, instead of waiting ten days and giving a laying queen, a ripe queen-cell or a newly born virgin is given at the time of removing the old queen. This has the advantage that if there is any thing like European foul brood in the case, it may be considered somewhat in the light of a cure. It has the disadvantage that my assistant is quite strongly opposed to the idea of having a virgin in a honey-hive, lest she should take it into her head to get the colony to swarm out, a thing that may happen once in a great while in reality, and in the imagination of my assistant quite frequently.

REPLACING WITH BETTER QUEEN.

On the whole, perhaps the most common thing is to replace the removed queen with a young laying queen taken from a nucleus. This will generally result in replacing the old queen with one of better stock, for the young queen will be reared from best stock. If, however, the old queen be an extra-good one, she will be put in a nucleus when removed, and then returned at the proper time. Whether the old queen be returned or a new one given, she is likely to be given with a frame of brood and adhering bees from the nucleus, so there is no interruption in laying. If for any reason she is given in an introducing cage, the cage is thrust into the entrance of the hive, in such way that the bees will be sure to take care of it,

Fig. 63—Super-Filler.

and where it can be looked at at any time without opening the hive. I am not sure but that a queen at the entrance is a little better received than elsewhere. Of course there might be a little danger of chilling in a very cold time.

If the old queen is returned there is a possibility of further attempts at swarming. But if a young queen be given, *after ten days of queenlessness,* that colony is considered settled for the season, and no further watch is kept against swarming.

Somewhat curiously, it is the common thing, upon opening a hive a week after giving the queen, to find one or more queen-cells started. I don't know why. Perhaps the bees have been frightened because of their spell of queenlessness, and want to provide against its happening again. At any rate, when these cells are killed they are not replaced. Possibly the bees would destroy them themselves after finding that the queen was settled to work.

Some think it best, when a queen arrives at a certain age, to replace her with a young queen. It is held by some that a queen does her best work in her first year, and that no queen should be allowed to do a second year's work, because there will always be a gain by replacing her with a younger queen. Some of the men that hold such views, and practice according-ly, are such successful beekeepers that I dare not say they are wrong. Whether it be a difference in bees, in locality, manage-ment, or what not, I do not believe that such practice would be best for me.

I am pretty sure that many of my queens do as good work in the second as in the first year, possibly better. But it is not altogether a question as to whether a queen does as well or better in her second year, comparing it with the first. The question is rather as to what she will do in her second or third year as compared with what would be done by the average young queen that would replace her. However it may be else-where, the rule with my bees is that a queen which distinguishes herself by a good crop of honey in her first year, will keep above the average as long as she lives. And I can count on the bees superseding her at the close of harvest whenever she reaches an age when it would seem profitable for me to re-place her with a younger queen.

Another thing may be worth considering. It is claimed, and with some show of reason, that longevity in bees is an im-portant factor. One colony will be stronger in bees and brood than another beside it, while the latter will store more honey. The explanation given is that the bees in the second colony are longer-lived. It may not be unreasonable to suppose that if one has a strain of bees with queens which live to an unusual age, that the workers will also live to unusual age. So it may be the part of wisdom to encourage those queens which show a disposition to live beyond the usual span.

On these accounts it is my practice to leave the matter of superseding entirely to the bees in all cases, except where for some reason other than age it will seem an improvement to replace with a younger queen. That reason may be that the workers of a queen are unusually vicious, that they do not seal their honey white enough, or there may be some other fault, but generally it will be because they did not store honey enough the previous year. When, then, the colony of such a queen shows persistence in the matter of preparation for swarming, she will be replaced by another as part of the treatment of that colony. But old age alone will not endanger her life.

An item of some interest is the fact that when I look through the colonies in the spring to clip any queen that may have whole wings, I find very little use for the scissors if the previous season was very poor, whereas after a big honey-yield I generally find a good deal of clipping to do. In other words, there seems to be more superseding at the close of a good than of a poor year. Has it only happened to come so, or does a good harvest wear out the queen faster?

THE "JUMBO" HIVE.

At one time I had strong hopes that by the use of a large hive with a large frame I might greatly diminish, if not entirely suppress, swarming. Others reported success with what was called the Jumbo hive. At Fig. 67 will be seen one of these hives. The frame is $2\frac{1}{8}$ inches deeper than the regular Langstroth frame, and if you will look at the front of the hive in the picture you will see that it is $2\frac{1}{8}$ inches higher than the eight-frame dovetailed hive by its side. The Jumbo has ten frames, and the extra depth makes it equivalent to a twelve-frame Langstroth.

I put bees in two of these hives in the home apiary, and waited to see what would result the next summer with much interest. The very first colony to send out a swarm was in one of these Jumbo hives! I was sorry, but it didn't make me sick abed. I had become hardened to failures and disappointments in following after the will-o'-the-wisp—non-swarming.

PILES OF STORIES.

The problem of prevention of swarming would be very much easier if I were running for extracted honey instead of comb. I am very much of the opinion that I could pile up stories as in Fig. 68, and not have one colony in a hundred swarm, the fact that no such pile ever swarmed for me confirming that opinion; and I have had a few such piles every year for a number of years.

VENTILATION TO PREVENT SWARMING.

It is not, I think, so much the abundance of room as the abundance of ventilation that prevents swarming, although the room is important. Notice the opportunity for ventilation in that pile in Fig. 68. The entrance, which you cannot see, is 12 inches wide and 2 inches deep. The second story is shoved forward on the first story so as to make a ventilating space of half an inch at the back between the two stories. The third story is shoved back to make a space in front; and the ventilating space between the third and fourth stories is at the back. Lastly the cover is shoved forward to make a space of half an inch or more. Thus you see there is a fine chance for a free circulation of air right through the whole pile. Alas that such a thing cannot be used for comb honey!

DEMAREE PLAN.

If I were running for extracted honey, I could get along with little or no swarming by following the plan of G. W. Demaree. When the time comes that there is danger of swarming, put into a second story all the frames from below except one containing the least brood, fill up the vacancies with empty combs or frames of foundation, put a queen-excluder between the two stories, and leave the queen in the lower story. Then as the brood hatches out in the second story the combs will be filled with honey and become extracting combs.

SHAKEN SWARM WITHOUT INCREASE.

Another plan that I would enjoy trying if I were running for extracted honey is one variation of forced or shaken swarms. It is the simple plan of making a shaken swarm, say from A, and then piling all the brood from A on another strong colony, B. European beekeepers tell us that with this accession of brood B will not swarm. S. Simmins, of England, and some others, give A half the bees from B. A would be all right for comb honey, but B would not—at least not right away—but it would be all right for extracted honey.

ACCIDENTAL SWARMS.

The best I can do there will sometimes be what might be called accidental swarms. Perhaps a strong colony has in some way lost its queen in the busy season, and when the first-reared young queen emerges—if one is allowed to emerge—there will surely be a swarm issue. Generally such a thing will be headed off before the young queen has a chance to emerge, but once in a great while she gets ahead of me.

Although there is to me nothing entrancing in the sight of such a swarm whirling through the air, there is one thing I do very much enjoy in it—it is the sight of the seething mass hurrying into the hive when dumped in front of it, as in Fig. 69. You will see that a deep bottom-board has been placed in front of No. 32, on which the swarm was dumped (it had previously settled on a low plum tree), and the bees have flowed all over the sides of the bottom-board, and also over the front of the hive. But I don't want the distress of seeing them pouring out of the hive in a swarm for the sake of the pleasure of seeing them hustle back into the same hive when dumped down in front of it.

TAKING OFF SECTIONS.

As fast as supers are filled they are taken off. I do not think I could be bothered to take off each section as fast as finished, putting in an empty one to take its place. It would take too much time. Neither do I like to wait till every section in a super is entirely finished. Unless the bees are crowded very much, there will be some uncapped cells in the outside sections which the bees will be very long in sealing. If these are waited for, the central sections may lose a little of their snowy whiteness—the thing which, perhaps, helps most to sell them.

A super is, then, taken off when all but the outside sections are finished. This can be pretty well told by glancing over the top of the super, although sometimes the sections may be all sealed at the upper part and hardly filled below. A look at the under part of the upraised super will decide it. The sharp, circular end of the hive-tool is thrust under the supers to pry apart the attachment of bee-glue.

Fig. 64—Load of Forty Supers.

Unless care is taken, bees will be killed when a super, which has just been taken off, is put back again. Sometimes there may be so few bees in the way that the super can be put on quickly without danger. Oftener too many bees are in the way for this, so I put one end on its place, and with a series of rapid-up-and-down motions gradually lower the other end to its place. This gives the bees time to get out of the way, and there are seldom any crushed by it.

CLOSE OF CLOVER HARVEST.

Formerly I took off all supers at the close of the white-clover harvest. Of late there has been a tendency to leave them on for the later flow. I am not sure whether this is wise, except in the few years in which from some unknown source some exceptionally white sections were secured at the Hastings apiary. In other years at the Hastings apiary, and in all the years at the other apiaries, the honey stored during the cucumber flow is rather dark in color, and is likely to have an unpleasant appearance on the surface, as if lightly varnished with bee-glue. But of late years the late honey has been improving, both in color and flavor. I don't know why. Possibly a greater proportion of sweet clover may have improved the flavor. Possibly, also, the increase of heartsease may have something to do with it. Although I think my bees get no inconsiderable quantity of honey from cucumbers, I confess I don't know what pure cucumber honey tastes like, but I am afraid it does not rank very high in flavor.

LATE HONEY.

As I said, I am not sure that it is ever wise, except in the Hastings apiary, to allow supers to stay on after the white-clover harvest is over. True, a considerable amount of honey may be got in sections from the late flow, but it is not all of it of the best, and if it were stored in brood-combs and saved as extra combs to be crowded into the brood-chamber the next year before the beginning of the harvest, there might be nearly or quite as many more sections of white-clover honey stored to offset what was lost in sections in the fall.

OBJECTS TO PORTER ESCAPE

For the purpose of getting bees out of sections I have tried pretty thoroughly the Porter escape and other escapes which work on the principle of allowing the bees to go down out of the supers without the chance of returning, but they do not work fast enough to suit me. When I go to an out-apiary, I always want to bring home with me all the honey taken off that day. Even at home I want it all taken in the same day that it is taken off. I may want to go elsewhere the next morning, and I don't want to be hindered from an early start by having to get it in before starting. Besides, I am just a little afraid that if I should make a practice of leaving honey out over escapes till the next day, some one none too scrupulous might learn the trick and by a night visit save me the trouble of taking off some of the honey. So whatever honey is taken off any day is got into the house before we go to bed that night; for sometimes it happens that when we have a big day's work at an out-apiary we do not get home till 8 o'clock or later.

Fig. 65—One-cent Queen-Cage.

SMOKING BEES DOWN.

When a super is to be taken off, smoke is blown down into it until a sufficient number of bees have gone down out of it. What that sufficient number is depends upon circumstances. If it is early in the day, and we do not care to take the honey home till late, there is no need to drive out so many bees. Other circumstances may also make a difference, and we "cut our coat according to the cloth."

SUPERS STANDING OPEN.

Suppose the honey flow is in full blast, and we commence to take off supers early in the day, or at least in the forenoon.

At such a time there is little need to be very careful about robbers, and it may be that honey may stand exposed for hours without being troubled by them. So when the super has been smoked it is taken off and set on the ground leaning against the hive, the hive-cover is put on the remaining supers, and then our removed super is set on its end on top, so as to project a little over the side of the hive. After a time, perhaps half an hour, the bees are likely to start a trail from the super over the side of the hive to join the bees of the colony below.

A number of supers may be thus standing at a time on their respective hives. Sometimes two supers are taken from the same hive, and, in rare cases, especially late in the season, three.

WATCHING FOR ROBBER BEES.

These supers, left standing on the hives, however, are never left entirely out of mind, and a glance is given toward them every few minutes. If at any time bees are seen flying with their heads toward a super, immediate attention is given to the matter, and the supers hustled off the hives. When the bees are nearly out, or at any time when it is not desirable to leave supers standing on the hives, they are put in piles, preferably not more than ten high.

WHEN ROBBER BEES TROUBLE.

If fear of robbers does not allow the supers to stand exposed, the super is still put on top of the hives, and a good many of the bees are at once driven out by smoke. The smoker is held on the side toward the wind, so that the wind will help drive the smoke between the sections, and from time to time the bees are brushed off. The bee-brush generally used is the Coggshall, but if it were not for the trouble of preparing one fresh every day, I think I would prefer a good-sized bunch of asparagus, sweet clover, goldenrod, or something of the kind tied together.

MILLER TENT-ESCAPE.

In piling the supers a sunny place is preferred, to entice out the bees. A deep bottom-board is put on the ground, a super placed on it, and the entrance closed with wire cloth somewhat as a hive-entrance is closed for hauling (Fig. 72). Then over the super is thrown what Root's "A B C of Bee Culture" has been pleased to call the Miller tent-escape (Fig. 73). (Later on I'll tell you how it's made.) When a second super is brought to the pile, the escape is kicked off, the super placed on the pile and the escape thrown over it. When the pile becomes too high to kick off the escape, it is shoved off with the hand, but still allowed to fall to the ground, and afterwards picked up.

Fig. 66—Colony at left treated for swarming.

The bees can now make their exit through the top of the escape at their leisure, and from time to time those that have gathered on the wire cloth below are allowed to escape. Matters may be hurried up a little by blowing in smoke below. But this is hardly advisable, for the smoke, being more or less confined, is likely to give an unpleasant flavor to the sections. When there is abundance of time for the bees to get out without being hurried, or if the pile is only five or six high, it is better not to have any opening at the bottom of the pile, but to set the first super on a flat surface that admits no light, or right on the grass.

KEEPING TALLY OF SECTIONS.

The number of the colony from which each super is taken is marked in pencil on one of the middle sections, perhaps when the super is first taken from the hive, certainly before it is taken from the hive entirely. A board or a slip of paper is kept where the supers are piled, and as each super is taken to the pile the number of the hive and the number of sections in the super are taken. Occasionally the number of supers in the pile is counted, so as to see whether it tallies with the number taken on the memorandum, for without this there is danger that some super might be forgotten, and the colony not have proper credit. When convenient, possibly while we sit resting a little while after the supers are all piled, possibly not till the next morning, the numbers on the memorandum are used to give each colony its proper credit in the record book.

CREDITING COLONIES.

The credit to each colony is entered *over* the first line that belongs to that colony, so that it may easily be seen at a glance, and so that it may be convenient to have all the credit on one spot. If a super containing 24 sections is taken from a colony, the number 24 is entered over its first line. Then when another 24 sections is taken from that colony, +24 is written after the first 24, and whatever number is taken each time, that number is put down with the plus sign preceding. Sometimes it happens that a super partly filled is taken from one hive and put on another. Suppose it is estimated that the super contains the equivalent of 7 sections, and that it is taken from No. 21 and given to No. 45. At No. 21 will be entered +7, and at No. 45 will be entered —7. At the end of the season the whole will be summed up. In an extra-good year, an average colony may have some such account as this: 24+48+48—7+16 +24 equals 153. But the minus sign very seldom occurs.

WHEELING SUPERS IN.

At the home apiary, the piles of supers are generally left till nightfall, so the bees will have abundance of time to be fully out. Then they. are taken on a wheelbarrow to the honey-room (Fig. 74).

You will notice that the wheelbarrow is innocent of any box or tray. It is a common railroad barrow, with the tray removed. In this shape it is very convenient for wheeling supers or stove-wood, the principal uses to which it is put. When desired the tray can be replaced to be used for other purposes.

Fig. 67—Jumbo Hive (at right).

HAULING SUPERS FOR OUT-APIARY.

At the out-apiaries the supers must be loaded on the wagon, and sometimes at the close of the season that is a rather ticklish job. When we go to the apiary in the morning, we drive pretty close to the place where the piles of supers are to be—much closer than it will be safe to take the horses at the close of the day's work when the bees are thoroughly stirred up—and after the horses are unhitched the wagon is taken by hand to the most convenient spot for loading on the supers.

LOADING SUPERS ON WAGON.

Unfortunately, although the wagon was built especially for the purpose, some irons prevent a perfectly level floor on which to put the supers, so strips of thin board or lath are laid so the supers will be level. The size of the wagon-box is such as to take on one side three supers running crosswise, and on the other side two supers running fore and aft. Great care is taken to build up the piles true, and when all are on they are fastened together by laths with nails driven partly in, so the nails can easily be drawn upon reaching home. Each pile has a lath vertically; across the top, laths are braced in both directions, so that the whole load is practically one solid pile (Fig. 64). As the load comes mainly on the hind axle, 40 supers are as many as we like to haul at one load. We seldom take so large a load.

As I have said, putting the load on the wagon at the close of the season is something of a ticklish job, and is mostly done under cover of smoke, my assistant playing the smoker wherever it will do the most good. The character of the tent-escape comes into fine play here, for it can so quickly and surely be thrown into the right place that the robber bees have little chance at the piles, so the smoking is mostly done at the wagon. A robber-cloth (Fig. 75) is even a little better than the tent escape.

When the load is all on, the wagon is drawn away to a distance safe for the horses. This may be 8 or 10 rods, or it may be more than twice that distance. Fortunately, at each out-apiary the ground lies in such a way that after the first few rods the ground is descending, making it easy to draw the load the longer distance. Then the horses are hitched on as speedily as possible.

HONEY-ROOM.

Generally, Philo will be ready to take off the load when we get home, unless we get home too near bedtime and Philo has gone home, in which case I am not always a good enough fighter to keep the women from helping to carry the supers to the honey-room. This is an addition built on to my dwelling house. It is 20 x 15 feet, and the floor timbers are blocked up with stones so that it will sustain a great weight without breaking.

When the supers of sections are taken in, they are piled up near the center of the room with no very great precision,

Fig. 68—Pile of Stories.

usually being piled crosswise, that is, each super placed across the one under it, for the double purpose of ventilation and to make it easier to lift the supers off the pile than they would be if piled straight and stuck together with bee glue.

PUSH-BOARD.

Perhaps the sections will be taken out of the supers the next day, possibly not for a week or more. A push-board

(Fig. 76) is used to push the sections out of the super. This is made as follows:

Take a board 16⅝ inches long and 11 inches wide. Take boards 12 inches long and ¼ inch thick and nail them across the first board so as to cover just its length, and project ½ inch at each side. This makes a surface 16⅝ x 12 inches. If this board be now put inside an empty T super, and the T super raised, it will be seen that the board will easily drop through the super, except where it is upheld by the three T tin supports on each side. Places must be cut out of the board so that the supports will present no hindrance. In order to make these places abundantly large, I cut them 1½ x ½ inch. When cut out, the measure will be, from the corner of the board to the first place or hole, 3¼ inches, then 1½ inches for the hole, then 2 13-16 inches to the next hole. Measure the same way from each of the other three corners, and you will have on each side three holes that will allow the supports of the T tins to pass through without obstruction.

Occasionally, after pushing sections out with the push-board, I found at the lower part of some of the central sections some of the cells looking watery, showing that the push-board had crowded down a little too hard at the central part. To obviate that I put a little cleat about ¼ inch wide and ⅛ thick at the outer edge of the board on all sides, giving the pressure right where it is needed. If the outer part of the sections comes out, there is no danger that the rest of the sections will not keep company. Unfortunately, the picture does not contain the little cleats.

TAKING SECTIONS OUT OF SUPER.

Being now ready to take out the unfinished sections, the first thing is to see whether there are any to take out. If a careful inspection shows that all sections in a super are sealed down to the bottom, it goes directly to the pile of finished sections. If any sections are seen that are not finished, the super is placed on the table, and the little sticks removed that were crowded between the ends of the sections on top. A flat hive-cover, or a board a little larger than the super, is placed upon it. Then super and board are both turned upside down, the board being firmly held on the super by one hand while reversing. If the super should be reversed without this board being held on it, there might be a possibility of sections tumbling out and breaking. (The board is needed under the reversed super in any case.) The super is now lying upside down on the board, the board even with the edge of the table. The side of the super having the follower is nearest, and I slide the super toward me enough so that I can push the follower down

Fig. 69—Swarm dumped before No. 32.

and let it drop out. Then I push the super back on the board and lay the push-board on the bottoms of the sections. Before putting the push-board on the sections, however, I remove any bits of wax that may be on the bottoms of the sections, otherwise the push-board coming down hard upon them will crush the comb enough to make the sealing on the lower part of the sections look watery, if it does no greater damage.

As the super now lies, the sections are not resting on the board beneath, there being ¼ inch space there. I push the push-board down till the sections rest on the board below,

EXCEPTIONALLY TROUBLESOME CASES.

The sections may fall that quarter of an inch with their own weight, and they may not go down at all without urgent coaxing. If the honey was stored with a rush in the early part of the season, there will be very little gluing, and the sections will come out easily. The later in the season, and the slower the storing, the more gluing, and the more trouble. If there is a lot of glue, and if it is warm, stringy, and sticky, it must be humored a little. It can hardly be jerked loose suddenly any more than if were nailed; but if it is allowed time enough the weight of the sections may be enough to bring them down. Of course a little insistence will hasten matters to some extent, but it seems to be a matter of principle with that kind of glue not to let go too suddenly. Sometimes I take a super of that kind and place it low enough to sit down on the push-board, and then let it take its time. When I feel it give way under me, I give up my seat, unless I continue matters a little longer by taking hold of the super at each end and lifting up while still sitting on the push-board.

WHEN THE GLUE IS BRITTLE.

Sometimes the glue is brittle, especially if quite cold. The case is then quite different. Sitting on it all day would do no good, unless one is heavy enough to bring down the whole thing suddenly. If pushing down with the hands on the push-board produces no effect, I pound with the fist at each corner enough to make the start. Then lifting on the super at each end with the fingers, I push the sections out of the super by pushing down on the push-board with the thumbs (Fig. 77).

After the first start is made, perhaps the super is at once lifted off without any trouble, and perhaps further coaxing is needed, and the super must be treated somewhat as one treats a refractory bureau drawer. I lift on each end alternately, holding down the push-board with one hand and lifting with the other, then with both hands lift off the super (Fig. 78).

This sounds a little as if were hard work getting sections out of supers, because I have spent so much time talking about the troublesome cases, but these are the exceptional cases, and in general the work is easy enough to be done rapidly.

The empty super being set down and the push-board removed, the unfinished sections are picked off, and the super is put back on the sections as it was before. Then the super and the board under it are reversed, and the board lifted off. Finished sections from another super used for that purpose

Fig. 70—Bee Working on Red Clover.

are put in to take the places of the unfinished sections that were removed, and the super with its 24 finished sections is put on the pile.

BLOCKING UP SUPERS OF SECTIONS.

The piles of finished sections are 20 supers high, the piles being about 6 inches from each other and from the wall. Four blocks 7⁄8 of an inch thick are placed under the corners of the first super in the pile, and four are put on the corners of each super before the next super is placed over it. This for ventilation (Fig. 79). The sun has a fair chance to make this room a pretty warm place, and screened doors and windows allow free passage for the air.

FUMIGATING SECTIONS.

Years ago it was very important to fumigate these sections, or else a good many of the larvae of the bee moth would disfigure them. The trouble gradually faded away until for several years I have done no fumigating whatever, and no harm has come from the omission. I do not know why there should be so much change except a change in the character of the bees that stored the honey. Years ago black brood was present in my bees to a larger extent than now. The weeding out of bees too lazy to fight away the wax moths may have much to do with it.

"GO-BACKS."

The unfinished sections that were taken out are to be disposed of. They are filled into supers and returned to the bees to be finished up, and these supers of sections that are to *go back* to the bees for finishing are called "go-backs," for short. In filling up these supers of "go-backs," no very great care is taken as to assorting them, although it is desirable so far as convenient to have all in the same super at nearly the same stage toward completion.

ARRANGEMENT OF SECTIONS IN "GO-BACKS."

All *except* the two outside rows. In these two rows are put the sections that are the least advanced, the four corner sections often containing only foundation.

There are two objects in having these outside rows different from the others. The bees will not make as rapid work finishing them as the others, and if all were alike the super would have to be left on too long before all would be finished. So there is no expectation of their being finished, and it is not worth while to put in the outside row any that are near completion. There is another reason. Toward the close of the season, especially, there will be no other supers on a hive that has "go-backs," and these outside rows are needed to give them a chance to do some storing while finishing up the sealing of sections that allow little or no room for storing.

COLONIES FOR "GO-BACK" WORK.

Being more convenient, the "go-backs" are all given to colonies in the home apiary. When the first are given, the

honey harvest is usually still in full blast, and a good many
colonies in the apiary will have "go-backs," each colony having
only one, that being placed on top of its other supers. We keep
watch to see which colonies make the best work on "go-backs."
Some seal faster than others, some seal sections with extra
whiteness. In order to help keep track of the rate of progress,
each "go-back," at the time it is put on, has marked on one of
the middle sections the word "go-back" and the date. If the
super were not thus marked, the colony would get more credit
than it deserved when the super was removed.

A little later in the season the number of colonies chosen
for this work is limited, only those which do the best being
continued at it, and these are not allowed to have any other
supers. Generally two supers at a time will be enough for a
colony to have, but sometimes three will be given. As fast as
one super is ready to come off another takes its place.

ROBBER-CLOTH.

Before fulfilling my promise to describe the tent escape,
I must describe a robber-cloth (Fig. 75), which forms an essential part of the tent-escape. I take a piece of stout cotton
cloth (sheeting) or burlap large enough to cover a hive and
hang down four inches or more at both sides and at each end.
This must be weighted down at the side with lath, and for this
purpose I take four pieces of lath about as long as the hive. I
lay down one piece of lath with another piece on it, and one
edge of the cloth between the two pieces of lath. I then nail
the two together and clinch the nails. I use the other two
pieces of lath for the opposite edge of the cloth. This makes a
good robber cloth as it is, but it is better to have the ends also
weighted down, especially on a windy day. For this purpose
I make a hem in each end, and put in it shot, nails, pebbles,
or something of the kind, stitching across the hem here and
there so the weighting material will not all run together at
one side or the other.

QUICK COVERING WITH ROBBER-CLOTH.

In any case where one wants to cover up a hive quickly
against robbers, as when opening and closing the same hive

frequently for the sake of putting in or taking out combs, this robber-cloth will be found a great convenience. No careful adjustment is needed, as in putting on a regular hive-cover, but one can take hold of the lath with one hand, and with a single throw the hive is covered securely, with no killing of bees if any should happen to be in the way.

Fig. 71—Shop (looking South).

MILLER TENT-ESCAPE.

Having made the robber-cloth, an escape, not in the shape of a cone, but in the shape of a pyramid, is fastened centrally upon it(Fig. 73). Take three triangular pieces of wire cloth, each of the three sides measuring alike. Put them together in the form of a tent, sewing the edges together at the three sides by weaving fine wire through. At the top, however, let each of the pieces be folded out, so that a hole large enough to push your finger in will be left. Lay the tent centrally on the robber-cloth and mark where the three corners of the tent come. Now starting at each of these points, cut the cloth to the center. Cut away the three flaps of cloth all but about 1¼ inches, and turn this 1¼-inch margin up on the outside of the tent and sew there with heavy thread.

Another way is a little easier to do, and it is a little better. although a little harder to describe. Take a piece of wire cloth $2\frac{1}{3}$ times as long as it is wide. Mark a point at the middle of one of the longer sides, and on the other side mark a point half way from each end to the middle, as shown in the figure. Make a fold at each of the dotted lines. The wire cloth may be cut away at the two outside dotted lines, or, what is better, the end pieces may be folded over and sewed down. Now bring the two parts of the upper margin together and sew with wire, and then proceed to fasten the tent in place as before. In this latter case, of course, a hole must be cut in the top of

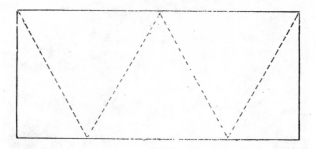

the tent. Before the tent is sewed together, cut a slit about an inch deep in the two dotted lines at the top, and then fold out the three points.

When one of these tent-escapes is placed on a pile of supers, or on a hive containing bees, the bees will pass out freely at the top, but the bees that try to get in attempt to make the entrance further down. Once in a great while there will gather a bunch of the outgoing bees at the top so as to clog the exit, and then the robbers will settle on this bunch of bees and work their way in, but a little smoke will scatter the bunch of bees.

But bees are persevering creatures, and are not likely to stay scattered. In that case it is a good thing to put two escapes over the pile, a larger one over a smaller one. The piece of wire cloth used in making some of mine is 22 x 9½ inches, and in others it is 14 x 6. The smaller ones seem to work just as well as the larger, and it is a convenience to have the two sizes when a case such as I have mentioned occurs. But it does not often occur.

"ONCE A THIEF" NOT "ALWAYS A THIEF."

For many years I believed what perhaps is generally believed, that the saying, "Once a thief, always a thief," is true of any bee ever guilty of robbing. There is, no doubt, some ground for such belief, for a bee that has spent today robbing from a certain hive will very likely start in on the same business tomorrow, if any more plunder is to be had in the same place; but it is not true that a bee that has been engaged in one robbing scrape will never after return to honest labor.

Indeed, so far as the bee is concerned, getting honey out of another hive probably seems just as honest work as to gather nectar from the flowers. And the more active a bee is when engaged in the field, the more active might we expect to find it in trying to rob when there is nothing more to be found in the field.

Many a hive is robbed out in the spring, and many a bee is engaged in the robbing; yet the first day in which an abundance of stores can be had in the field, every bee of sufficient age gleefully joins in the quest abroad, and the fact that honey may be exposed with little danger shows that the bees that were formerly so intent upon robbing are now afield with the others.

LEAVING SOMETHING FOR ROBBERS.

A practice that is just as far from right as the theory about which we have been talking is the practice of taking away whatever the robbers are working upon, without leaving any thing in its place. If by carelessness I have left a section of honey on a hive, and find the robbers at work upon it, I can hardly do a worse thing than to take it away.

If I leave it, the bees will stick to it, and clean it out, and for some time a number of robbers will stick to it after the honey is all gone, but they stick to that one spot, and if the empty comb is left there, they keep hunting it all over and over, and by and by conclude the honey is all used out of it and go about their business. If the section is taken away and nothing left in its place, they seem to think they have made a mistake as to the place and hunt all around for the missing section, until they force their way into the nearest conquerable colony.

If a weak colony is attacked, I may sometimes take it away, but if I do, I immediately put in its place an empty hive in which I put some scraps of comb containing a little honey.

Fig. 72—Hive, No. 12, Closed for Hauling.

They will rob this out and that will be the end of it. It is possible that dry comb without any honey might answer.

ROBBING FAULT OF BEEKEEPER.

Except in case of queenless colonies, I am somewhat of the opinion that most cases of robbing have been through my own carelessness. When there is nothing to do in the fields, the bees may be seen busily trying to enter cracks about hives so small that there is no possibility of their entering, and they are sharp to observe any change. If, at such times, a fresh opening be left anywhere about a hive, it is sure to be discovered. An entrance at the top of the brood-chamber, at the back end, may be left open all the season without being disturbed by robbers. But if it has been kept closed until a time when robbers are troublesome, and then opened, whether it be that the robbers are stirred up by seeing the change, or whether the bees of the colony are not in the habit of protecting themselves in that quarter, the robbers are pretty sure to give the new entrance especial attention; and if the colony be not very strong there may be serious results.

STARTING ROBBING BY FEEDING.

As feeding is done only in a time of scarcity, it is one of the most common causes of robbing among careless beekeepers. When general feeding is done with Miller feeders, there is little danger, no matter what time of day the work is done; but if some weak colony is short of stores I try to be somewhat careful to do nothing to attract especial attention to it. I have sometimes fed at night, and so far as convenient prefer to feed late in the day, but convenience does not always allow it.

One time I found a colony at the close of the honey harvest, by some means about at the point of starvation. With more carelessness than was excusable, I gave them, I think in the forenoon, two or three combs filled with sugar syrup. Some time after, I happened to look toward that end of the apiary, and saw what looked to be a swarm. The bees had become excited over their new-found stores; the robber-bees had joined in, and the bees of the colony seemed to think forage was so plentiful that it wasn't worth while to be mean about it, there was enough for all; so the robbers were doing a land-office business without let or hindrance.

STOPPING ROBBING WITH WET HAY.

I closed the entrance of the other hives in the immediate neighborhood, so that only two or three bees could pass at a time, and then threw a lot of loose wet hay at the entrance of the besieged hive.

Not only did I put hay at the entrance, but piled it up all around to the top of the hive. For some time I kept every thing very wet around the hive by pouring on pails of water, then left them till next day.

No other hives were attacked. I somewhat expected to find the queen killed, but she was all right next day, and no further trouble occurred, as the colony was a strong one, and, when in its right mind, capable of taking care of itself.

DO ROBBED BEES JOIN THE ROBBERS?

One of the venerable traditions that is perhaps generally accepted without question is that when a colony is being robbed it is a quite common thing for the bees that are robbed to join

Fig. 73—Miller Tent-Escape.

the robbers and help carry off the stores. I am very skeptical as to there being any truth in the tradition. I do not say such a thing never happened, but I never saw such a case, and I have seen from first to last a number of cases in which all the stores were emptied out of the combs by robbers, and the bees of the colony seemed to be all left, and generally by taking the right kind of pains I have succeeded in re-establishing such a colony. In such cases there was certainly no joining the robbers.

I have found other cases in which the bees were entirely gone, and I could only guess what had become of them. My guess was that after being robbed of all their stores, and having used up all the honey in their honey-sacs, perhaps some time after the robbers had ceased to pay any attention to them, they had swarmed out as any hunger-swarm will do, and had united, or tried to unite, with some other colony. Would they not be likely to join some colony other than the one that had treated them so unkindly?

SUPERS ON HIVES SELDOM ROBBED.

Piles of four or five stories with abundant ventilation at each story are in no danger from robbers under ordinary circumstances; but if you ever have such piles, and are so unfortunate as to get the robbers once started at them, you "better watch out." Even if there should be a dearth for some time, robbers are not likely to attack a pile; for they have probably got into the habit of thinking that such a pile is not to be meddled with; but just you do something to call particular attention to the pile, such as letting a comb of honey stand by it exposed, and there are so many exposed places to defend that the robbers are likely to have things their own way.

A BAD CASE OF ROBBING.

One time George W. York was here when bees were not busily at work in the fields, and I opened up a pile of four stories, for what purpose I do not now remember; very likely I was trying to show off in some way. At any rate I showed him a fine case of robbing, for the robbers pounced down upon every exposed point, and before I had noticed what was going on they were having a gay time. Of course I couldn't build a haystack about the four stories, but I had to do something, for although the colony was a powerful one it was utterly inadequate to the protection of four exposed stories, and without any interference on my part its doom was sealed. I closed all entrances except the lower one, and then applied the hay and water to the lower story successfully.

WHEN SUPERS ON HIVES MAY BE ROBBED.

During the usual working season there is need of some foolishness on the part of the beekeeper to start robbing at a pile having a strong colony; but after the weather becomes quite cool toward fall, the case is different. Of course, all but the lower entrance should be closed before cold nights come, but sometimes there is a case of neglect. In a cold night the colony shrinks down into the lower or the lower two stories— all the more because there is a current of air right through the hive—and the two or three upper stories are left without any bees.

Fig. 74—Wheeling Load of Supers.

In the following morning they do not go up again into the upper stories till some time after the day has warmed up. The robbers, however, do not wait so long, but finding an upper entrance unprotected go to work in lively style.

As late as October 6, in the year 1902, a pile was left with an upper entrance or ventilating space still open, and on the forenoon of that day I observed lively work at that place, while all was quiet at the lower or regular entrance. I shoved the cover back so as to close the space, and then took a snapshot of the bees trying to get in, as shown in Fig 81. Only two stories show in the picture, although the pile was four stories high. Fortunately no other place was open except the regular lower entrance, and it was so far from top to bottom that the robbers made no attempt below—indeed I suppose they would have been promptly repulsed if they had—so after trying for a time to get in the place I had closed, they gave up and left the hive.

PLAYING BEES AND ROBBERS.

I think I can tell by carefully looking at bees when flying with unusual commotion at the entrance of a hive whether it is a case of robbing or bees at play, but I am not sure I could tell some one else the difference in appearance. Looking at bees at play in Fig. 82, and comparing with Fig. 81, there appears little difference. In actual life there will be seen the same excited eagerness in each case.

The time of day helps to decide. During the middle of the day, say from noon till the middle of the afternoon, playing is common; earlier or later than that time, if there is big excitement at the entrance of a weak colony, the likelihood is that robbing is going on.

SIGNS OF ROBBING.

One pretty sure sign of robbing, when there is a good deal of stir at the entrance, is to see bees working frantically to force an entrance under the cover or at some other part of the hive. Just why they should do this at times when they seem to have plenty of chance to get in at the regular entrance I do not know. It seems to be a way they have.

A sure sign of robbing is to find the bees entering the hive with empty sacs and coming out with their sacs full. The contents of the sac can be told by killing the bee, pulling it in two and squeezing out the contents of the sac. Indeed, the squeezing is hardly needed.

BEES STICK TO SAME ENTRANCE.

A glance at the hive shown in Fig. 81 would show that it is a case of robbing, for the flying is at an opening never used for an entrance. It is a somewhat curious fact that bees are very persistent in continuing to use the same place for an entrance.

After the bees have become used to going in and out at the regular place, if I make an opening at the back end of the hive, no matter if it be as large as the front entrance, that back opening will never be used as an entrance. One would think that young bees taking their first play-spell would be as likely to use the back as the front opening; but when I have had ventilating openings at the backs of the hives I do not remember to have seen bees playing at the back. Perhaps the noise of the regular traffic in front attracts them there.

Fig. 75—Robber-Cloth.

LOSING THE ROBBERS.

I make it a rule to stop operations usually when robbers are very bad, but sometimes it seems necessary to fight it out. I have sometimes taken advantage of the plan of making cross bees or robbers lose themselves or, rather, lose the object they are after by rapidly changing the base of operation. One day at the Wilson apiary I had taken off some wide frames of sections and wanted to take them from the place where they were piled up, so as to put them on the wagon. The robbers were so fierce and persistent that it seemed impossible to open a crack without their immediately forcing their way in. My wife was provided with a smoker in full blast, and a big bunch of goldenrod or other weeds. A robber-cloth covered the pile. With one hand I lifted the cloth and with the other took out a frame of sections, then quickly dropped the robber-cloth in its place, my wife keeping a cloud of smoke in the way of any robbers which should attempt to enter the pile while the cloth was raised. Instantly the frame was out of the super, the robbers made for the frame of sections. I made for the wagon and my wife made for me. Running in a zigzag, circuitous course, my wife followed me, puff ng and switching at every step, and by the time we got to the wagon the robbers were lost, the frame was slipped quickly into the super on the wagon, and the robber-cloth dropped over it. The Scotch folks at the house had a good laugh at the crazy couple chasing one another through the orchard, but we beat the bees. Under ordinary circumstances it would be better to take an easier plan or wait till dark.

PROTECTION FROM STINGS.

I have been a beekeeper since 1861, and since 1878 I have made the production of honey my sole business, aside from writing about bees, and yet I have not reached that point where I care nothing for protection from stings. When I first commenced keeping bees, a sting on my hand was a serious affair, swelling to the shoulder, and troubling fully as much the second day as the first. Now, if I receive a half-dozen stings or more, I cannot tell an hour or two later where I was stung, except as a matter of memory. Yet I think that a sting gives me fully as much pain for the first minute now, as it did fifty years ago. Sometimes the pain is so severe that it literally makes me groan, especially if no one is within hearing. I sometimes wonder at those who scout any sort of protection, and query whether there may not be just a little of a spirit of bravado about it. I think I *could* go through a year without any sort of protection, but I do not think I ever shall. A bee inside my clothing makes me very nervous, and I cannot go on in comfort at my work with a feeling of uncertainty as to where and when its little javelin shall pierce my flesh. If I felt it crawling on me, and then cease to feel it because it is on the clothing and not on the skin, I am in momentary dread as to where it shall turn up next; and it is a real relief when it stings me, for I know then the precise spot where it is, and have no further expectations from it.

BEE-VEIL.

So I seldom go among the bees without a veil. I may not have it over my face, but it is on the hat, ready to be pulled

Fig. 76—Push-Board.

down at any time. The veil is made of inexpensive material, called by milliners cape-lace or cape-net. It is 21 inches wide. A piece is cut off as long as the circumference of the brim of a straw hat, and both ends sewed together. Shirr a rubber cord in one end of this open bag, thoroughly soak or wash out the starch, and sew the other end on the edge of the hat brim. It is important for the eyesight that the stuff of the veil be black; but the black coloring crocks one's clothing. So of late years a border of white cloth is sewed on the veil to receive the rubber cord.

The rubber cord holds the veil close about one's neck, yet

not close enough but that a bee sometimes gets under it. Although a bee is not at all likely to sting when it gets inside a veil, it is just as well to have it remain outside. So my assistant devised the plan of drawing the veil down *very* tightly in front, and pinning it to her waist with a safety pin. Seeing it work so well with her, I have also adopted the plan, pinning on to my suspenders on one side, or to my vest if I have one on.

Sometimes a face-piece of silk net is sewed in the veil. Instead of having the veil sewed to my hat, so that the bee-hat must be taken along when we go to the out-apiary, I sometimes have in my pocket a veil made with a rubber cord shirred into each end, and when I reach the apiary the veil is slipped on over the hat I am wearing.

BEE GLOVES AND OTHER PROTECTION.

The openings at the wrist and neck of my shirt are small, the cloth lapping over so as to give a bee little chance for entrance. If bees are likely to be on the ground I put my pants inside my stockings, or, still better, put on a pair of trouser guards such as bicyclists wear. I get a great many stings on my hands, but the inconvenience and discomfort of gloves are so great that for many years I felt the stings to be the lesser of the two evils. But after working for years to get bees that would give the most honey, without paying any attention to the temper of the bees, I finally had bees so cross that in spite of the inconvenience I felt obliged to wear gloves.

My assistant prefers to wear gloves, not only to avoid the stings, but to avoid the bee glue. I may say in passing that I am not always very particular about getting the bee glue off my hands, but when I do clean them I usually give the bee glue a good rubbing with butter or grease, and then wash off with soap and water. I confess I don't very much mind having bee glue on my hands unless there is so much of it that it sticks to the bedclothes at night. But I do abhor the sticky feeling of honey on my hands; and when they get daubed, if I have no water I pick up some soil to rub them with. That at least takes away the sticky feeling. Perhaps you think the soil is worse than the sticky feeling. I don't.

BEE-GLOVES.

For some time Miss Wilson wore a kind of cheap white glove that I think was made of pigskin. She dislikes the smell of oiled canvas gloves, although to me the smell is not very bad, and the smell of the pigskin is horrid. Latterly she wears

Fig. 77—Pushing Sections out of Super.

light buckskin, which are free from smell, and wash well, or else a pair of kid gloves with a pair of 10-cent pickle gloves over them. The latter are rather bungling.

GETTING OUT STINGS.

I like to get a sting out of my skin as soon as possible, if not too busy. A little trick in this direction is, I think, not known to all beekeepers. I am not sure whether I learned it by instinct, or from the writings of G. M. Doolittle. If a bee stings my hand I instantly strike the hand with much force upon my leg, with a .sort of quick, wiping motion. This mashes the bee, generally, and rubs out the sting at the same time.

SCOLDING BEES.

If one thinks of the thousands or millions or bees in a large apiary, it will be seen that comparatively few bees make any attack. Sometimes a single bee will threaten and scold me by the hour, perhaps finally stinging me by getting into my hair or whiskers, and for aught I know the same bee may keep up the same thing for days—I mean the scolding, not the stinging. It is sometimes worth while to get rid of the annoyance by stepping to one side and knocking it down with a stick by a few rapid strokes back and forth in front of my face. I often mash it by slapping my hands together.

CROSS COLONIES.

Sometimes the bees have seemed very cross, and a little observation has shown these bees to proceed from a particular part of the apiary, and really from only one hive. A careless observer might have said all the bees in the apiary were cross. I have had a few colonies so cross that merely walking by the hive was the signal for a general onslaught. Truth obliges me to say that I have sometimes been so badly stung by one of these, when working at them, that I have taken refuge in inglorious flight, glad to get a respite and scrape out the stings. Just why there should be one or two of these in a year in such marked contrast with others I cannot say. The only remedy I had was to kill the queen.

DRESS FOR THE HOTTEST WEATHER.

During the principal part of the honey flow, a prominent element of hardship is the endurance of the heat. Sometimes the heat really has made me sick, so that in spite of a press of work I have been obliged to give up and lie down for an hour or more. At such times you may be sure I am not very warmly clad. One straw hat and veil, one cotton shirt, one pair cotton overalls, one pair cotton socks and one pair shoes comprise my entire wearing apparel (Fig. 83). Before noon, shirt and pants are both thoroughly wet with perspiration.

Fig. 78—Lifting off the Super.

SPONGE-BATH AT NOON.

In this heated condition, I sponge myself off with cold water before dinner, put on dry pants and shirt, and hang up the wet ones in the sun to be put on next day. I am sure that, by this refreshing change, I am able to do more work. It might be thought that applying cold water all over the body when every part is dripping with perspiration might make me take cold. I have never found it so, even if followed up every day. The body is so thoroughly heated that it easily resists the shock, and a brisk rubbing leaves one in a fine glow.

My overalls are white, such as painters or masons use. I do not enjoy being so conspicuous when I happen to be on the street clad in white; but I would rather be conspicuous than to be stung; and I feel sure that I do not get so many stings as I would with darker clothing.

WOMAN'S BEE-DRESS.

My assistant is not dressed so coolly as I. Her desire to keep her dress clean makes her warmer than she otherwise would be, for she wears an apron that covers all the dress except the sleeves (Fig. 84). This apron is made of denim, and has two large pockets. It is made after pattern 3696 of the Butterick Publishing Co. To cover the sleeves of her dress, she uses a pair of white sleeves fastened together by a strap sewed to each sleeve across the back, a similar strap in front being sewed to one sleeve and buttoned to the other. The wrists of these sleeves are sewed to the wrists of her gloves, and ripped off whenever it is necessary to wash either gloves or sleeves. For convenience, several pairs are kept.

QUEEN-REARING—BREEDING FROM BEST.

My sole business with bees being to produce honey, I am not particular to keep a popular brand of bees, only so far as their popularity comes from their profitableness as honey-gatherers. I am anxious to have those that are industrious, good winterers, gentle, and not given to much swarming. For some years I got an imported Italian queen every year or two. Then for a good many years I preferred to rear from queens of my own whose workers had distinguished themselves as being the most desirable. The chief thing considered was the amount of honey stored. Little or no attention was paid to color, and unfortunately no more to temper. So I had bees that were hybrids, hustlers to store, but anything but angels in temper. Then, beginning with 1906, I introduced quite a number of Italian queens, in the hope that among them I might find one as good as my hybrid stock without so much ill tem-

per. By the time of the year 1913 most of the black blood was
worked out, and in that year, when I obtained the world's
record for the highest average of sections from as many as
72 colonies, it had come to pass that my best yields were from
colonies having three yellow bands.

IMPORTANCE OF SELECTION.

The queen being the very soul of the colony, I hardly consider any pains too great that will give better queens. The first

Fig. 79—Supers of Sections Blocked Up.

thing is to select the queen from which to rear, for generally
all rearing will be from the same queen, whether for the home
apiary or for an outside apiary. The records are carefully
scanned, and that queen chosen which, all things considered,
appears to be the best. The first point to be weighed is the
amount of honey that has been stored. Other things being
equal, the queen whose workers have shown themselves the best
storers will have the preference. The matter of wintering will
pretty much take care of itself, for a colony that has wintered
poorly is not likely to do very heavy work in the harvest. The
more a colony has done in the way of making preparations for

swarming, the lower will be its standing. Generally, however, a colony that gives the largest number of sections is one that never dreamed of swarming.

BREEDING FROM BEST.

I am well aware that I will be told by some that I am choosing freak queens from which to rear, and that it would be much better to select a queen whose royal daughters showed uniform results only a little above the average. I don't know enough to know whether that is true or not, but I know that some excellent results have been obtained by breeders of other animals by breeding from sires or dams so exceptional in character that they might be called freaks. I know, too, that it is easier to decide which colony does best work than it is to decide which queen produces royal progeny the most nearly uniform in character. By the first way, too, a queen can be used a year sooner than by the second way, and a year in the life of a queen is a good deal. I may mention that a queen which has a fine record for two successive seasons is preferred to one with the same kind of record for only one season. At any rate, the results obtained in the way of improvement of stock as a result of my practice have been such as to warrant me in its continuance at least for a time.

The danger from inbreeding must not be lost sight of entirely. With two or three hundred colonies kept in three different apiaries it is perhaps not great. Should signs of degeneracy at any time appear, it will not be difficult to introduce fresh blood.

CONDITIONS FOR QUEEN-REARING.

Having chosen the queen from which to rear, I have kept in mind that unless conditions are favorable the royal progeny of the best queen in the world may be very poor. Queen-cells must be started when the weather is sufficiently warm, when bees are gathering enough to make them feel that there is no need to stint the royal larvae in their rations, and until near the point of emergence it is much better that the cells shall be in the care of a strong colony. So I do not begin operations for queen-rearing until about the time that bees inclined to swarming would begin to make preparations therefor.

REARING QUEENS IN HIVE WITH LAYING QUEEN.

It would be too long a story to enumerate all the plans I have used in queen-rearing. I have reared excellent queens, and many of them, by the Alley plan and by the Doolittle cell-cup plan, together with is modifications by Pridgen, and others.

Fig. 80—Cleated Smoker.

I think I was the first one to report rearing a queen in a colony having a laying queen; and I have reared them in stories under as well as over the story having the laying queen. Neither is it absolutely necessary to have a queen-excluder between the stories. In lieu of an excluder I have used a cloth with room for passage at the corners. Neither excluder nor cloth is absolutely necessary; distance is enough. That first reported case was on this wise:

Upon a hive containing a colony had been piled four
stories of empty combs for safe-keeping. To make sure that
the bees would not neglect the care of the most distant combs,
I put a frame of brood in the upper story. A few weeks later
I found a laying queen in the upper story with the old queen
still below. The bees that had gone up to that frame of brood
were so far from the queen that they had reared a queen of
their own. A hole in the upper story had allowed the flight of
the young queen without invading the domains of her mother.
For those who produce extracted honey this plan might be
used to advantage.

UNQUEENING COLONIES TO START CELLS.

I have reared good queens by the old and simple plan of
taking away the queen of a strong colony. Of course this must
be a choice queen. Previous to the removal of the queen the
colony is strengthened. Frames of well-advanced brood are
from time to time given from other colonies until it has two—
perhaps three—stories of brood. None of this brood, however,
is given less than five or six days before the removal of the
queen. The queen is taken with two frames of brood and adhering bees and put on a new stand in an empty hive, an
empty comb and one with some honey being added.

TIME TO START NUCLEI.

In nine or ten days from the removal of the queen it is
time to break up the queenless colony into nuclei. It might
generally be left till a day or two later before a young queen
would come out to destroy her baby sisters in their cradles, but
it is best to take no chances. If it were true, as formerly believed, that queenless bees are in such haste to rear a queen
that they will select a larva too old for the purpose, then it
would hardly do to wait even nine days. A queen is matured
in fifteen days from the time the egg is laid, and is fed
throughout her larval lifetime on the same food that is given
to a worker larva during the first three days of its larval existence. So a worker larva more than three days old, or more
than six days from the laying of the egg, would be too old for

a good queen. If, now, the bees should select a larva more than
three days old, the queen would emerge in less than nine days.
I think no one has ever known this to occur.

Fig. 81—Robber Bees.

BEES DO NOT PREFER TOO OLD LARVAE.

As a matter of fact bees do not use such poor judgment as
to select larvæ too old when larvæ sufficiently young are present, as I have proved by direct experiment and many observations. It will not do, however, to conclude from this that all
queen-cells started by a queenless colony left to themselves will
be equally good. Bees have a fashion of starting cells for a
number of days in succession, and will continue to start them
when larvæ sufficiently young for good queens are no longer

present. So some means must be taken to make sure that no nucleus has for its sole dependence one of these latest cells. If several cells can be afforded for each nucleus, there is little danger they will all be bad. Neither is there great danger if a cell is chosen which is large and fine-looking. Perhaps the safer way is to give the queenless colony a frame with eggs and young brood three or four days after the removal of the queen, and then they will not be obliged to use the old larvæ of the other comb.

PLACING QUEEN-CELLS.

Two or three frames of brood with adhering bees are taken for each nucleus. If one of the frames has a cell or several cells in a good location, well and good. If not, the lack must be supplied. But the cells must be where they will be sure to be well cared for. They must not be on the outer edge of a comb, with the chance to be chilled, neither must they be on the outer side of the comb, but on the side of the comb that faces the other comb. Any cells that are not just where they are wanted must be cut out. For this purpose I like a tea-knife with a very thin and narrow blade of steel.

STAPLING CELLS ON COMB.

A staple, such as is used to fasten a bottom-board to a hive, is used to fasten a cell in place. The cell is placed where it is wanted, then the staple is placed over it, one leg of the staple close to the cell, and the other leg is pushed deep into the comb (Fig. 85).

MAKING BEES STAY IN NUCLEI.

Each nucleus is put upon a stand of its own, and the entrance is plugged up with leaves so that no bee can get out. One of the nuclei, however, is left without having its entrance closed, and this is put in the place of the hive which contains the queen, and the hive with the queen is put back on the old stand from which the queen was first taken. The entrances may be left closed until the shrinking of the leaves allows the bees to make their way out, but I generally open them in about twenty-four hours, first pounding on the hive to make the bees

mark their location upon emerging. Although queenless bees
are much better than others at staying wherever they are put,
there will be still fewer bees return to the old place if the
nucleus is fastened in twenty-four hours or longer.

LOOKING FOR EGGS.

Twelve or fourteen days after forming the nuclei I look
to see if the queens are laying. I might find eggs in less time,
but not always, and at any rate not in considerable number,

Fig. 82—Bees Playing.

and it saves time on the whole not to be in too much of a hurry.
If no eggs are found a comb of young brood is given as an
encouragement to start the young queen to laying, and a day
or two later, if queen-cells are started on this young brood, a
mature queen-cell is given.

KEEPING BEST QUEEN IN NUCLEUS.

Instead of having my best queen in a strong colony, as in
the plan just given, she is usually kept in a two-frame nucleus
throughout the summer, the nucleus being strengthened into a

full colony in the fall for wintering. One object of this is to make the queen live longer. It is generally understood that a worker lives a longer time if it has little work to do, and probably the same is true of a queen. As laying eggs is her work, the less the number of eggs she lays the longer she ought to live, and in a nucleus she lays a smaller number of eggs than in a strong colony.

There is another reason for keeping her in a nucleus. Some who have tried to have comb built in the colony containing their best queen complain that they can get only drone-comb built. This may be avoided by filling the frame with worker-foundation, but the better way is to keep the colony with the queen so weak that only worker-comb will be built. In a nucleus only worker-comb will be built.

STARTING BROOD FOR CELLS.

Having my breeding queen in a two-frame nucleus, I take away one of the combs, and in its place put a frame in which are two small starters four or five inches long and an inch or two wide. One of these starters is put about four inches from each end (Fig. 86). The nucleus must be strong enough in bees so that a week later this frame will have a comb built in it that will fill most of the frame, the comb being fairly well filled with eggs and young brood (Fig. 88). It is taken away, and another frame with two small starters put in its place as before. Thus this nucleus will furnish once a week a frame of comb with brood of the best sort for queen-rearing. It will be a day or two after the frame is given before the queen lays in it, so that the brood will not be too old even if the bees were so foolish as to prefer it.

The comb being new and tender makes it probably an easier job for the bees to build queen-cells upon it; at any rate they always show a preference for such comb, and start on it a larger number of cells than they would on older comb.

BEES FOR CELL-BUILDING.

Having now arranged for the right kind of brood and eggs to be ready on the same day of each week, the next thing is to find the right kind of bees to start the cells, not only to start them, but to take the very best care of them. We can probably find no bees better fitted to produce good queen-cells than those that of their own accord have already engaged in the business. So a strong colony is chosen which has already started queen-cells in preparation for swarming. All queen-cells already started are destroyed, the queen is removed, and

Fig. 83—Bee-Dress.

one of the frames is taken away, leaving a vacancy in the center of the hive. Most likely the colony has one or more supers. but these are not to be taken away.

BROOD FOR QUEEN-CELLS.

We now go to the nucleus containing our best queen, take out the frame with the virgin comb, and replace it with an empty frame with its two starters, brushing back into the hive the bees from the comb taken out, and closing the hive. Looking at the comb taken out, you will see that, instead of the oldest brood being in the center, it will be in two places where the two starters were put. It was for this purpose the two starters at the sides were given rather than a central one. For by this means the waving contour will give opportunity for a larger number of queen-cells on the edge of the comb than would otherwise be the case.

TRIMMING THE BREEDING-COMB.

For a little distance at the edge, the comb contains eggs only. This part is trimmed away, leaving the youngest of the brood at the edge of the comb (Fig. 89). One reason for this is that, other things being equal, the bees show a decided preference for building on the edge of a comb. Another reason is that I decidedly prefer to have cells on the edge, thus making them easier to cut out when wanted. The part cut away would only be in the way of both of us.

BEES USING YOUNG LARVAE ONLY.

When a queen is taken away from a full colony, the bees start cells from young brood, and, as I have already said, they continue to start fresh cells for several days, and until after there is no longer brood of the proper age, so that the last cells started would contain larvæ too old to make good queens. But on these combs prepared as I have described, they do not do so. Rarely, if ever, will a cell be found elsewhere than on the edge of the comb, and I have never known the bees to start a cell after the larvæ were too old. I do not know why there is this difference. I know only the fact. But it is a very convenient fact.

AGE OF LARVAE FOR QUEENS.

Scientists tell us that a worker larva is fed for three days the same as a queen larva, and then it is weaned. Theoretically, then, up to the time a larva in a worker-cell is three days old, it ought to be all right to rear a queen from. Practically, I do not believe a larva three days old is as good as a younger one. The only reason I have for so believing is the expressed preference of the bees themselves. Give them larvæ of all ages from which to select, and they always choose that which is two days old, or younger. Indeed, it will be seen that in the comb from which I have trimmed the edge (Fig. 89) the larvæ on

Fig. 84—Woman's Bee-Dress.

the edge of the comb have been out of the egg but a short time, for I merely trimmed away the eggs, and possibly not all of them.

PLACING THE BREEDING-COMB.

The breeding-comb, thus properly trimmed, is taken to the queenless colony, and put in the vacancy that was left for it. On the top-bar of the frame is penciled the date on which the cells are to be cut out, allowing ten days from the time of putting in. Thus, if the frame be given June 27, the number 7 is put on the top-bar, July 7 being ten days later than June 27. No need to put the month on. Besides giving the date, that figure marks the frame, so I can know at a glance which frame to take out. At the same time a memorandum of this date is put in the record book to remind me when to cut the cells.

Some one may ask, "But if you leave nearly all the old brood in the hive, will the bees not start cells on them, with

Fig. 85—Queen-Cell Stapled on Comb.

only the smaller part on your breeding-comb?" So I thought at first, and took some pains to have no very young brood of the old stock left. But I found upon trial that when I left all the young brood of the old stock, the bees ignored this, at the most starting upon it one, two, possibly three cells, confining their attention to the prepared frame I had given. Probably the hardness of the old combs and the lack of convenient places in which to build cells convince the bees that it is better to use the soft comb where room is abundant. Of course a cell or two on the old combs can do no great harm, for they will not be used.

MORE THAN ONE NUCLEUS IN HIVE.

The frames for nuclei are the regular full-sized frames, and a full hive may be used for each nucleus, but it is economy to have the hive divided up into two or three compartments for as many nuclei. Three nuclei in one hive are mutually help-ful in keeping up the heat, and thus it is possible to have the nuclei weaker than if each nucleus were by itself, while results are as good with the three weaker nuclei in the one hive as with three stronger nuclei in three separate hives.

NUCLEUS HIVE.

For many years I have had hives divided into two or more compartments, and have had much trouble from the bees find-ing a passage from one compartment to another, but my latest nucleus hives have not troubled in that way. They are made from ordinary 8-frame hives together with the 2-inch-deep bot-tom-board. First, two pieces are nailed on the inside of the bottom-board, each piece $18\frac{1}{4}$ x $1\frac{3}{4}$ x $\frac{7}{8}$. One piece is nailed $4\frac{1}{2}$ inches from one side, the other $4\frac{1}{2}$ inches from the other side. These pieces do not lie flat in the bottom, but stand on edge, with $1\frac{3}{8}$ inches between them. Then the hive is fastened on the bottom-board with the usual four staples. Two division-boards, each $18\frac{1}{4}$ x $9\frac{3}{4}$ x 5-16, are now put in place and crowd-ed down tight upon the two pieces in the bottom-board. These two division-boards are $4\frac{5}{8}$ inches from each side, leaving $2\frac{1}{4}$ inches between them. The four spaces at the top, at the ends of the division-boards, are closed by blocks $\frac{3}{4}$ x $\frac{1}{2}$ x 5-16, whittled enough to allow them to be wedged into place. Light $1\frac{1}{4}$-inch wire nails are driven through from the outside to hold the division boards in place. A block 10 x 2 x $\frac{7}{8}$ is pushed into the entrance centrally, and held there by a nail lightly driven in front of it. That leaves an entrance at each end of the block for the two side compartments, but no entrance for the middle compartment. For this purpose an inch hole is bored in the back end of the hive midway between the two cor-ners, its center being about three inches from the upper sur-face of the hive. Three boards of half-inch stuff cover the three compartments, and over this is an ordinary hive-cover.

At Fig. 90 will be seen a bottom-board for a nucleus hive. You will notice that the two pieces that run lengthwise through the center of the bottom-board are a quarter of an inch shallower than the rim of the bottom-board. If they were 2 inches deep instead of 1¾, the bottom-bars of the frames would rest directly on them. Of course the division-boards are deep enough to come clear down upon these two pieces.

Fig. 86—Starters in Breeding-Frame.

Two nucleus hives will be seen at Fig. 91. The one at the right faces us, showing the entrance at each side. The back of the left hive is toward us, showing the round hole near the top, which serves as an entrance to the middle compartment.

LARGE SPACE FOR MIDDLE FRAME.

In one of these side compartments there is abundant room for two frames and a dummy, and three frames without the dummy can with care be crowded in. The central compartment will, of course, take only one frame. It seems as though 2¼ inches is quite too much space for one frame, but I use that space advisedly. Many years ago I made a nucleus hive with six compartments; and at that time, not having had much

experience, I made each compartment 2¼ inches wide. Years
afterward I made another nucleus hive; and, smiling at my
former ignorance and congratulating myself upon the superior
knowledge I had gained with the passing years, I made the
compartments more nearly in accord with the usual space occupied by each frame in a hive, making each compartment—
I'm not sure whether it was 1⅝ or 1¾. At any rate, the bees
swarmed out of these limited quarters to such an extent that
I could not use them, whereas they had not swarmed out of the
2¼ compartments; neither have they swarmed out of these
later ones. Having so much room in these central compartments, the bees sometimes build pieces of comb on the sides
which I must clean away, but that is better than to have them
swarm out.

CONTENTS OF NUCLEUS HIVES.

A nucleus hive is tenanted by a two-frame nucleus on each
side and a one-frame nucleus in the middle. Care is taken to
choose one of the best frames of brood for the middle nucleus,
and perhaps a few extra bees are brushed in. A third comb
may be put in each of the side compartments, or a dummy, the
same as the dummies used in the regular hives.

MAKING THE BEES STAY.

When populated, the entrances of the nuclei are plugged
up with green leaves. These are generally taken away twenty-
four hours later, after the hives are pounded to stir up the
bees, but if they are neglected the leaves will dry and shrink so
the bees can make their way out. It is better to form nuclei
with queenless bees, for they are not so much inclined as others
to go back to their old place.

BABY NUCLEI.

There has been much interest in the matter of having
queens fertilized in small nuclei containing only 200 bees or
so. About the year 1863 I had seen miniature nuclei in the
apiaries of Adam Grimm, but they had not so few bees as the
so-called baby nuclei of today. Of course, I had a number of
queens fertilized in baby nuclei, but I did not go to the trouble

of having hives specially built for them. I merely used an 8-frame dovetailed hive, putting in it sometimes a 1-pound section nearly filled with honey, and sometimes two such sections side by side. A frame of brood ·with its adhering bees was taken from some colony, the bees shaken or brushed into the nucleus hive quickly, a virgin not more than a day or two old dropped into the hive among the bees, and all hastily closed, the entrance having been closed in advance. Of course, the frame of beeless brood was returned to its old place. Three days later the entrance was opened, and in due time the queen was laying.

However it may be for the commercial queen-rearer, for the honey-producer there seems no great advantage in baby nuclei. He generally needs to make some increase, and it is more convenient for him to use 2 or 3 frame nuclei for queen-rearing, and then build them up into full colonies.

REGULAR HIVES FOR NUCLEI.

One year I tried rearing queens on a commercial scale, producing them for Editor G. W. York, of the American Bee Journal. I may say, parenthetically, that one season was enough to convince me it was best to stick to honey-production, rearing queens only for my own use. But I had 50 three-compartment hives left on hand; and in spite of that, truth compels me to say that latterly they generally lie idle, and I use a full hive for each nucleus, merely putting 3 or 4 frames in one side of the hive, with a dummy beside them. To be sure, it takes more bees than to have three nuclei in one hive, but it is a good bit more convenient to build up into a full colony a nucleus that has the whole hive to itself.

QUEEN-CAGE.

When we go to give queen-cells to the nuclei, we are provided with introducing queen-cages. The first introducing-cage I devised was the Miller introducing-cage, listed in the catalogs of supply-dealers. Then I got up one I liked better, three of which are shown in Fig. 92, the blocks containing the candy being separate from the cages. This may be called Miller cage No. 2. Two blocks 3 inches by $\frac{1}{2}$ by $\frac{1}{4}$ and a piece of wire cloth 6½ x 1⅞ form the material for the cage. Lay the two blocks parallel on their edges, and nail on these one end of the wire cloth, the end of the wire cloth corresponding with the ends of the blocks. Fold the wire cloth around the ends of the blocks and nail it on the other side, and you have a cage 3 x 1⅞ x ½, outside measure. The plug to close

Fig. 87—Putting Foundation in Sections.

the cage is not so simple, for the cage is to be provisioned, and the plug holds the candy. Two blocks 1¼ x ½ x ¼, a piece of tin and a piece of section stuff each 1¼ inches square form the material for the plug. Lay the two blocks parallel on their sides, with ¼-inch space between them. On these nail the piece of tin, turn over and nail on the section stuff. Near one end drive a tack partly in to prevent the plug going too far into the cage. That makes all complete.

After using these for some years, I got up another that in some respects I like still better. This is shown in Fig. 87½, and may be called Miller cage No. 3. Make a block 3¾ x 1⅛ x 5-16. From one side of the block, at one end, cut out a piece 1½ x ⅜, making the block as shown at No. 1, Fig. 87½. Cut a piece of tin 1 x 2 inches. Stand the block on edge with the cut-out place uppermost, and in this cut-out place lay a lead pencil or similar object 11-32 in diameter. Over this bend the tin, letting it come out flush with the end of the block. Then laying the block on its side, still keeping the pencil in place, drive two ½-inch wire nails through tin and wood, clinching on the opposite side. When the pencil is withdrawn there is left a tube to be filled with candy. That completes the plug (No. 2, Fig. 87½). The cage itself is made of a piece of wire cloth 4 inches square, if one edge is a selvedge. If there is no selvedge, it must be 4 x 4½ and ½ inch folded over as a selvedge to prevent raveling. A block must be made, not to be part of the cage, but to be used to form the wire cloth over. It must be a little larger than the first block, say 5 x 1 3-16 x ⅜. If the block were the same size as the first, there would be too tight a fit, and if the fit be loose it is easy to wedge in a thin slip, as a piece of wood separator. The wire cloth is wrapped around the block and allowed to project at one end about ½ inch. A light wire is wound twice around, about ½ inch from the selvedge end (which is the part that does not project) and fastened. Another wire is similarly fastened about 1¾ inches from the first wire. Now the projecting part of the wire cloth is bent down upon the end of the block, and hammered down with a hammer. That completes the cage (No. 3, Fig. 87½), but for convenience in hanging it between brood-frames one end of a light wire 7 or 8 inches long is fastened into one side of the cage about ½ inch from the open end. To put it in a hive, I shove the frames apart, and holding the end of the wire lower the cage where I want it, and then shove the frames together. That leaves 3 inches or more of the wire above the top-bars, and when I want to take out the cage I take hold of

the wire, draw the frames apart, and lift out the cage.   The
wire serves also to mark the spot where the cage is.

When the tube is filled with candy, it may be pushed so
far into the cage that the bees can not get at the candy.   Then
when it is desired that the bees shall get at the candy, the
plug is drawn out until the candy is exposed (No. 5, Fig.
87½). This is more reliable as to time than to have the usual

Fig. 87½—Miller Cage No. 3.

cage with the candy covered with cardboard. With the cardboard there is no certainty as to whether the queen will be re-
leased in 24 hours or much longer. Sometimes it may be several days. With the No. 3 cage you know just how long the
bees have the cage before they get to the candy, and after the
candy is exposed you may count on the bees clearing out the
candy in about 24 hours.

It may be objected that it is troublesome to open up the
hive to change the position of the plug in the cage. That is

true, and often, if not generally, the cage is not put between the combs, but thrust in the entrance, making sure that it is where it will be protected by the bees. After being there about two days, it is only the work of a minute to take out the cage, expose the candy, and put the cage back in the entrance.

Sometimes, if I want to have the work done automatically, I use a device that delays the work about as much as the cardboard, but is more uniform in the time it takes. I thrust into the center of the tube of candy its whole length a wooden splint about 1-16 of an inch square, and that delays the bees at gnawing out the candy.

When a queen-cell is to be caged, the No. 2 cage allows more room for the cell.

For making queen-cages, instead of the common painted wire cloth that is used for screen doors, I like better extra-heavy bright wire cloth. It is more substantial. But E. R. Root says queens have been poisoned in such cages, so have a care, although I have had hundreds of queens in them without noting any harm. Perhaps all tinned wire cloth is not alike.

DISTRIBUTING QUEEN-CELLS.

When the queen-cells are to be distributed, the first thing is to provision a number of queen-cages of the No. 2 style, with the usual queen-candy, tacking a piece of pasteboard on the end of the plug. Then we go to the nucleus where the cells are stored, cut out the cells, rejecting any that do not appear satisfactory, and put the cells in the cages. Some cells, however, are left uncaged. When we come to a nucleus that has had no queen for a day or more, there is no need of caging the cell. It is put against the comb in a good place, and fastened there with a hive-staple (Fig. 85). Coming to a nucleus with a queen which we wish to remove, we put the queen in a cage, and give the nucleus a caged cell, laying the cage against the comb and nailing it there with a 1½ or 1¾ wire nail (Fig. 93). This nail is slender so as to push easily through the meshes of the wire cloth. Then the young queens that we have removed are used wherever needed.

BRUSHING BEES OFF QUEEN-CELLS.

Before cutting cells from the comb the bees must be removed, and it would mean the ruin of the cells to shake the bees off. Brushing with a Coggshall brush, although it might do with extreme care, would be likely to result in torn cells. Even something no stiffer than goldenrod or sweet clover needs much care. I like best a bunch of long and soft June grass—a very flimsy affair to use as a brush, but it is safe.

Fig. 88—Comb for Queen-Cells.

ADVANTAGE OF CAGING CELLS.

Of course the object of caging the cells is to prevent the bees from tearing them down. At the time of taking a queen out of a nucleus, if a cell were merely stapled on, the bees would be pretty sure to destroy it; for, not yet realizing that their young laying queen has been taken from them, they feel no need of anything like a queen-cell. So the cage saves the time and trouble of waiting and making a second visit another day.

There is, however, another advantage in using the cage, making it somewhat desirable to use it in all cases. We often want to know what has been the fate of a cell, and can generally tell pretty well by its appearance. If it has the appearance of most of those in Fig. 94, we know that a young queen has emerged and must be in the nucleus. If it is torn open in the side, like the one at the extreme right, the capping being still perfect, we are sure that the young queen in it was destroyed by the bees.

If the cells have merely been stapled on, the bees are so prompt about removing them as soon as they are no longer of any use that scarce a vestige of them is left, so we have nothing to judge by. But when a cell is enclosed in a cage, the bees are very slow about removing it, so the cage gives us a better chance for judging.

APPEARANCE OF VACATED CELLS.

In Fig. 94 the first three cells at the left have the cap still adhering by a neck, showing that it has been only a short time since the queen emerged, provided the cell has not been caged; if it has been caged the queen may have been out some time. The fourth cell looks entire, as if it yet contained a young queen. But it is deceptive. The bees have a trick of fastening the cap back again as if it were a great joke, sometimes thus imprisoning one of their own number. A very close look will generally show a little crack, and a very little force will be needed to pick the cap loose. The next six cells show plainly that a young queen has emerged from each, and finding a cell of that kind is just as good evidence as a sight of the queen; only I would a little rather see the queen for the bare chance that she may not have perfect wings. As already mentioned, the cell at the extreme right shows by the hole in its side that no queen ever came out of it alive.

MILLER QUEEN-NURSERY.

Whatever the advantages of using queen-cells instead of virgin queens, there are also advantages in having the young queens hatch out in a queen-nursery. So I have made considerable use of a nursery of my own devising, Fig. 88½. It may take the place of a brood-frame in any hive, in the lower story or in an upper story, and it does not matter whether a laying queen is in the hive or not.

For this nursery I use a regular Miller frame, which lends itself to the purpose admirably, top-bar, bottom-bar, and end-

bar being all of the same width, 1⅛ inches. If you haven't a
Miller frame, you can easily make a frame having all parts
the same width, 1⅛ inches; only be sure the end-bars are at
least ⅜ thick, and have the outer dimensions of the frame the
same as the frames you have regularly in use. I'll give instructions for making a nursery with a frame of the Langs-

Fig. 88½—Miller Queen Nursery.

troth size, and if your frames are of different size you must
act accordingly.

Make 7 pieces, each long enough to reach from top-bar to
bottom-bar (with top-bar ⅞ and bottom-bar ¼, which makes
the length 8 inches), 1⅛ wide, and ⅜ thick. Saw-kerfs must
be made on each end of these 7 pieces. Beginning 1¼ inches
from one end, on one side of the piece, with a very fine saw,
make a saw-kerf by sawing about halfway through. Make a
similar kerf 1¼ inches from the first, and then, each time
measuring off 1¼ inches, make 3 more kerfs, making five in all.
(Your last kerf will be more than 1¼ inches from the end,

but that's all right.) Do the same thing on the opposite side, beginning at the opposite end. Make similar kerfs in each end-bar, measuring from the top-bar for one end, and from the bottom-bar for the other end. Of course these kerfs are to be made on the inside of the end-bar, and none on the outside. Now distribute these 7 pieces at equal distances from one end of the frame to the other, and if you are exact about it the distance between each two will be 1 25-32 inches. Fasten these 7 sticks in by driving one nail down through the top-bar into each, and two nails through the bottom-bar. Before nailing, make sure that each stick faces right, as mentioned further on. Nail upon one side of your frame a piece of wire cloth to cover it (17⅝ x 9⅛). Have the nails not more than 2 inches apart all around and on each stick. I use bright wire cloth, extra heavy, with meshes of the usual size in screendoors.

You now need 40 pieces of tin, 2 x 1⅛ inches to go into all the saw-kerfs. Each piece of tin serves as a shelf, thus dividing the whole into 48 compartments. You will now see the necessity of having the sticks face each other so as to have the kerfs correspond, as mentioned a minute ago. Look out for this before you nail the sticks in place.

To close these compartments, you need 8 pieces of tin, each 10 x 2 inches. That's ⅞ inch longer than the depth of the frame, allowing the ⅞ to be bent over at right angles on the top-bar. To hold these covers in place I use heavy pins bent over. Small screw-hooks of straight pattern might do better. Three are needed in each end-bar, and 6 in each upright. Of course these tin covers are put in at the top and slide down.

You will see that each of the compartments furnishes a large amount of room, 40 of them being 1 25-32 x 1¼ x 1⅛, and the remaining 8 being larger. This gives abundance of room to put in the largest kind of queen-cell. With each cell is given a ball of candy the size of a pea.

ADVANTAGES AND DISADVANTAGES OF A QUEEN-NURSERY.

If a ripe queen-cell is given to a nucleus or colony, there is no way to be sure that a queen that is all right will issue from it. She may be imperfect as to her legs, and, what is still worse, her wings may be so deficient that she never can fly. If she can not fly she can never be fertilized, and so is worthless. Indeed she is worse than worthless, for she is wasting the time of the nucleus. Sometimes, indeed, it happens that the occupant of the queen-cell is dead. All of this is avoided by having the virgins hatch out in a nursery. If a cell is cut into, and is given to a nucleus, the bees will at once destroy it, but in the nursery it will hatch out all right.

One may have a lot of queen-cells on hand with no immediate use for them. It will not do to leave them without cutting out beyond a certain time, for the hatching out of the first one means the death of all the rest. But if they are put into a nursery they are safe, and may be left stored in the nursery for some days after hatching out.

Over against these advantages stands the one disadvantage that in the nursery the bees are not allowed to come in immediate bodily contact with the cells, nor with the young queen after she issues from the cell. Some think this so serious a disadvantage as to overbalance all the advantages of the nursery. It is claimed that the clustering of the bees about the cells and the young queens does more than merely to keep up the temperature to a certain point, and that when this close contact is lacking something will be lacking in the resulting queens. Also that the young queens thus isolated and imprisoned are in a frightened condition, and that a young queen reared in such an atmosphere is not the same as one that has the feeling that she is all the while closely surrounded by friends.

So whether it be wise to use a nursery or not, it will certainly be wise not to put cells into it before it is necessary for their safety, nor to leave a virgin in a nursery any longer than necessity demands.

QUALITY OF QUEENS.

The question has been raised whether queens reared in the way I have described are as good as those reared by the latest methods. I think I can judge pretty well as to the character of a queen after watching her work for a year or two; I

have kept closely in touch with what improvements have been
made in the way of queen-rearing, and have reared queens by
the hundred in the latest style; and I do not hesitate to say
that the simple method I have given produces queens that can
not be surpassed by any other method.

BEGINNER IMPROVING STOCK.

I have been asked whether I would advise a beginner with
only half a dozen colonies, one of them having a superior
queen, to use the plans I have given to rear queens from his
best queen. I certainly should, if he intends to give much attention to the business and increase the number of his colonies.
The essential steps to be taken are simple enough; and even a
beginner can easily follow them. But in a few words, here is
what I would advise him:

Take from the colony having your best queen one of its
frames, and put in the center of the hive a frame half filled or
entirely filled with foundation. If small starters are used in a
full colony the bees are likely to fill out with drone-comb. A
week later take out this comb, and trim away the edge that
contains only eggs. Put this prepared frame in the center of
any strong colony after taking away its queen and one of its
frames. Ten days later cut out these cells, to be used wherever
desired, giving the colony its queen or some other queen.

Now there's nothing very complicated about that, is there?

ITALIANIZING WITH NATURAL SWARMING.

Yet still there are some who don't want to take even that
much trouble. A man says: "All I care to do with the bees is
to hive the swarms that come out, and to put on the surplus
boxes and take them off when filled. I never take a frame out
of a hive any more than if they were all box hives. But I have
Italians in one hive, and if I could I'd like to have more of that
stock."

For such a one I would advise after this manner: Suppose
we call your Italian colony A, the strongest of the other colonies B, the next strongest C, the next D, and so on. When A
swarms, hive the swarm and set it on the old stand, put A in
place of B, and put B on a new stand. All the field-bees of B

will return to A, making A quite strong again. In 8 or 10 days a young queen will be ready in A to go out with a swarm. Hive the swarm, put it in place of A, put A in place of C, and put C in a new place. The field-bees of C will again strengthen A, and in a day or two another swarm will issue. Put the swarm in place of A, put A in place of D, and put D in a new place. Continue this as long as A continues to swarm, and each one of your swarms will have for its queen a daughter of your Italian queen. If you have only five or six colonies, the whole lot may be thus Italianized.

QUEENS FOR OUT-APIARIES.

On any day when we are going to an out-apiary and expect to use young queens, we take them from any nucleus that will furnish them, never putting any escort bees in the cage with the queen, and generally one or more extra queens are taken along, for we are never sure that they may not be needed.

Care is taken that the record book shall always show the condition of each nucleus; so that we always have some idea as to which nucleus will furnish a laying queen, which one needs a cell, and so on.

INTRODUCING QUEENS.

A queen may be introduced in a No. 2 provisioned cage, the cage being nailed directly over the brood, as in Fig 93, or she may be introduced in a No. 3 cage let down between the combs or thrust into the entrance as already described. Often, however, when it is convenient, I take from the nucleus the frame on which the queen is found, and put frame and all in the queenless hive. If this is done at a time when honey is yielding, there is little or no danger, provided the colony has been queenless long enough to be fully conscious of its queenlessness. Indeed, I have introduced many queens during the harvest into a colony conscious of its queenlessness, by merely taking out a frame of brood and dropping the queen among the bees on the middle of the comb. If I wish to run no risk whatever, as in the case of a valuable imported queen, I put in a hive without any bees several frames with no unsealed brood, but with plenty of sealed brood, some of it just emerging, and then closing the hive bee-tight put it where there is no danger of the brood being chilled. One way to do this is to put it over a strong colony, wire cloth preventing the passage of the bees from one hive to the other. At the end of five days the hive can be set on its own stand, and these five-day-old bees, under stress of necessity, will soon be seen carrying in pollen.

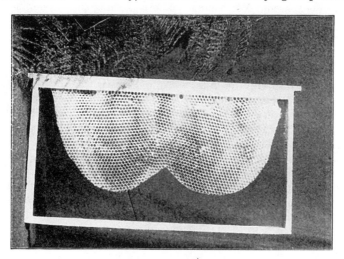

Fig. 89—Comb for Queen-Cells, Trimmed.

ARTIFICIAL INCREASE.

Fighting so bitterly against all increase by swarming, I would run out of bees entirely if I did not resort to artificial increase. Without pretending to give all the ways by which increase has been made, I may tell just a little about it.

One can make increase by drawing brood or bees, or both, from colonies that are working for honey, and thus keep all the old colonies storing, and at the same time make the desired increase. In that way the largest number of colonies possible are kept at work on the harvest, and one might have a feeling that all the increase was clear gain. But the feeling is a delusive one. It is not the number of colonies at work storing, but the number of *bees,* that counts. And 60,000 bees in one hive will store more honey that will the same number of bees equally divided in two hives. So in planning for increase I generally count that the colonies that are drawn upon for increase shall make that their business without being expected to be called upon to store surplus, while those at work for surplus are to be left in the fullest strength possible throughout the season. You cannot make something out of nothing, and if increase is to be made you may as well devote a certain number of colonies to that business.

INCREASING BY TAKING TO OUT-APIARY.

The case may be different in a locality where there is a long and late flow, but I am talking about this locality with white clover as the dependence for a harvest. In the year 1880 I took 1200 pounds of honey from twelve colonies and increased them to eighty-one; but the honey taken was extracted buckwheat, and I never knew such a buckwheat harvest before or since. Perhaps it will be well to tell more explicitly how that increase was made. The success achieved will be somewhat diminished when I say that the bees were supplied with ready-built combs, so they had no combs to build. But they had no help from other colonies in the way of bees or brood except a few eggs from which to rear queens.

The twelve colonies were taken from the home apiary to the Wilson apiary, and were prepared in advance for dividing. From part of them the queens were taken and queen-cells thus secured. Ten-frame hives were used at that time, and by some help from others of the twelve a hive would contain ten frames of brood and bees without any queen, a sealed queen-cell on each frame of brood. After standing a day or so this hive would be taken to the out-apiary, and the ten frames put in ten different hives. Of course every bee stayed just where it was put. To each of these was added another frame of brood and adhering bees that had been brought along, and whether these bees were queenless or not there was nothing for them but to stay where they were put. In the course of time these first-formed nuclei were strong enough to help others, and the latest nuclei were built up at once into fair colonies.

INCREASING 9 WEAK COLONIES TO 56.

In the year 1899, at the Hastings apiary, I increased nine colonies to fifty-six, making them rear their own queens, and building up mostly on foundation. No advantage was taken in the way of hauling colonies from home to divide, and the same plan would work just as well if I had had only one apiary. The increase was very satisfactory, considering how weak the colonies were at the start. May 29 there were only forty-one

Fig. 90—Nucleus Bottom-Board.

combs containing any brood in the nine colonies, counting each comb with brood, even if the patch of brood were no larger than a silver dollar. I doubt if the nine averaged any more than three and a half good frames of brood each. On the other hand, the year was unusually favorable for increase, for there was a continuous though not strong flow right through until, I think, in September.

No attempt could be made at increase until the colonies were stronger, and the first step looking in that direction was not made until June 12. On that date No. 237 with its seven frames of brood and bees was taken from its stand, and a hive of empty combs set on the stand. The queen was found and put in the hive of empty combs, which by this time had a good many bees returning from the field. The queen of No. 237 was considered the best in the apiary. No. 237 was now set on the stand of No. 235, and No. 235 was set in a new place. Please understand that the stand holds its number, and that when the hive that was on stand 237 is moved as stated it is now No. 235. We now have on 237 a hive full of brood and bees without any queen; and while it will lose the old flying force it had it will get the flying force that belongs to its present stand. The colony that was moved from 235 will, of course, lose its flying force, and will take its time to recuperate.

The bees on these two stands—235 and 237—were the principal actors throughout the season, the other colonies in the apiary merely serving as feeders from which to draw brood from time to time. On 237 were left the hive of empty combs, the queen, and the constantly increasing flying force. We now go to the other colonies and draw from them what brood they can spare without depleting them unwisely, leaving foundation in place of the brood. Looking at the record I find this was only four frames of brood. No bees were taken with this brood. An upper story was put on 237 and these four frames of brood put in it with four empty combs. Of course the queen and bees would soon be up in this upper story.

Matters were left in this shape for nine days, the plan being to visit the apiary every nine days throughout the summer. A stormy day, however, might extend the time to ten days, or Sunday coming on the ninth day might shorten the time to eight days.

At the expiration of the nine days, June 21, we returned. We took the brood with queen-cells and all bees from 235, and formed two nuclei. Just why we did not start three I don't know, for usually we started a nucleus with two frames of brood, and we must have had more than four frames of brood. No measures were taken to make these bees stay where they were put; it was not necessary with such queenless bees.

Then we took the upper story of 237, with all its brood and bees, and put it on 235, taking out the queen and putting her back in the lower story on 237. Then we looked to see what brood we could get in the seven colonies that acted as feeders, without reducing any of them to less than four or five brood. This time we found six brood, which we took without any bees, and put on 237.

This was the regular program each time: forming nuclei with the brood, bees, and cells on 235; putting all brood and

Fig. 91—Nucleus Hives.

bees from 237 on 235, always leaving the queen at 237; and then getting for 237 a fresh stock of brood wherever it could be spared.

As none of the assisting colonies were overdrawn, they would be getting stronger, so that up to a certain point more brood could be drawn each time. July 18, for the first time, more brood was drawn than it was thought wise to give to 237, there being twenty frames in all. Sixteen of these, or two hives full, were taken for 237, the other four were used to strengthen some of the nuclei. Not the weakest nuclei were strengthened, but the earliest and strongest, for by being helped these would become strong enough to be helpers in turn. In fact, toward the last of the season, when there was little time for nuclei to grow up, the earlier nuclei rendered substantial aid to the later ones, at least one of them yielding as many as nine frames of brood. The first nuclei were formed June 21, as already mentioned; the last were formed August 23.

I have gone thus fully into details because I believe this plan can be used successfully by any one who has only a small number of colonies and is desirous of increase. The first nuclei are formed early enough in the season so that they have more than time enough to become strong colonies, and the latest must be formed only in sufficient numbers so that they can be strengthened up as soon as the queen gets to laying.

NUCLEUS PLAN OF INCREASE.

With nucleus hives for queen-rearing, as already described, it is easy to carry out the nucleus system in the strictest sense. I go to a nucleus with a laying queen, preferring a nucleus with two or three frames, take all the frames with queen and adhering bees, put them in an empty hive, and set the hive on an empty stand. A week later a frame of brood may be added. It will be better if it can be given with adhering bees, and still better if the bees can be queenless. Still, there is no great danger to the queen in any case, although the weaker the nucleus when strange bees are given, the greater the danger to the queen. A week later on, two frames of brood and bees may be added, and the queen will be safer if these two frames are taken from two different colonies. The colony will then be strong enough to be left to its own devices.

NUCLEUS BUILDING UP WITHOUT HELP.

Indeed, it is not necessary to do anything more than to let a nucleus stand without any help in a fair season, if it can stand *long enough*. My assistant is inclined to be quite

optimistic in some things, and one August she expressed her
belief that a nucleus of two frames with a laying queen would
be able without any assistance, if started on that date, Aug. 6,
to build up into a colony strong enough to winter. I said that
would be asking too much, and we would put the matter to the
test. So two frames of brood with adhering bees were put in a
hive on a new stand, and two days later a laying queen was
given. The two frames of brood were rather better than the average, for I wanted her to see that even with an extra cnance it
was too late in the season for any such growth. I don't know
whether she watched that colony on the sly or not, but I did.
Looking at it every few days, I could see no gain—if anything
it grew weaker. Then I thought I could see a little gain, and
in twelve days from the time it was started the two frames of
brood had increased to two and a half. Five days later there
were three brood, and from that on it walked right along to
a fair colony, although it had to be fed up for winter. But
I would not want to count on starting for a full colony so
late as that in all seasons, especially if the frames of brood
were not the very best.

INCREASE WITHOUT NUCLEI.

These different ways are all on the nucleus plan. Just one
more way I want to mention, and it is not on the nucleus plan,
but if queens are on hand I think I like it is well as any. We
take four colonies, and the first thing is to have all four
strong before anything is done. Then we take an empty hive-
body without any bottom-board, and into it we put two frames
of brood without any bees from the first hive (a few bees will
do no harm), the same from the second, and the same from
the third, filling out the hive with two empty combs or combs
with some honey. In the middle of the hive is a provisioned
introducing-cage containing a laying queen. Upon the fourth
hive we put a queen-excluder, and on this we set our hive full
of brood, and cover it up. Very soon bees enough will go up
through the excluder to take care of the brood. Three or four
hours later, or twenty-four hours later if more convenient,
this hive is set upon a bottom-board on a new stand, and the
work is all done. A way that is easier, and nearly as good,

is to set the hive, with the six brood immediately in place of the fourth hive, setting the fourth hive in a new place. The returning field-bees will populate the new hive. Ten days or two weeks later the performance may be repeated if the season is prosperous, and this may be repeated a number of times. Of course empty combs or foundation will take the place of the two frames of brood drawn from each hive. An advantage of this plan is that it makes a strong colony at once, and there is no danger of being caught with a number of weaklings

Fig. 92—Miller Cage No. 2.

on a sudden cessation of the harvest. Each new colony formed will in its turn soon be able to take its part in the game to start still others.

SHAKING BEES OFF COMBS.

In this last plan, since the frames of brood are taken without bees, there is a good deal to be done in the way of cleaning bees off the combs. While it does not matter if a few bees should be left on the combs, it does matter greatly that care be taken to make sure that the queen is not among the bees taken. So it is well to *brush* the combs tolerably clean, and then one can easily see whether the queen is present.

Before brushing, however, most of the bees should be *shaken* off, for if this is rightly done it will be a saving of time.

FINAL TAKING-OFF OF SECTIONS.

When the time comes that the bees are expected to do no more work in the sections, whether that be immediately at the close of the clover harvest or later, the supers with their sections are all brought home and piled up in the honey-room. On some accounts it is better if the sections can be taken out of the supers at once and taken care of, and on other accounts

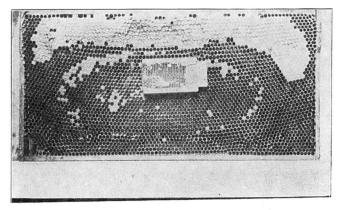

Fig. 93—Caged Queen-Cell.

it is better they should stand for some time. It is a very difficult thing to scrape the bee glue from sections while the weather is still hot, and as disagreeable as it is difficult. There may be some unsealed cells of honey in the outer cells of some sections, and this will have little chance to evaporate if it is thin, after the sections are in the shipping-cases. So the sections are likely to stand for some time in the supers after all are taken off, being blocked up as in Fig. 79.

FUMIGATING SECTIONS.

Formerly it was necessary to fumigate the sections with sulphur after they were brought into the house, the fumigation being repeated two or three weeks later. I suppose I should now prefer bisulphide of carbon to sulphur for fumigation, but for several years I have not found it necessary to fumigate. Formerly the larvæ of the bee moth would make bad work if fumigation were omitted, and sometimes in spite of it, but now there is no trouble. I don't know what makes the difference, unless it be that formerly there was so large a per cent of black blood in my bees.

When the time does come for taking the sections all out of the supers, the work is gone at in earnest and continued until all the marketable sections are in their shipping-cases ready for market. It will be understood that all supers taken off before the last have been handled as heretofore mentioned, the marketable sections having all been piled up in the honey-room and the others returned as "go-backs," and the last lot taken off will consist of every sort, from foundation untouched by the bees up to sections entirely filled and sealed.

SORTING THE SECTIONS.

Philo sorts the sections into four classes as he takes them out, although some supers are assigned to one class or another without being taken out, because all in the super are of one kind. One lot consists of dry sections, or those in which the foundation either has not been touched by the bees, or else has been drawn out so little that not a drop of honey has been put in it. These are put in a pile by themselves.

FEEDER SECTIONS.

The second lot consists of those which have just a few drops of honey in them, up to those which are not more than half filled. Some entire supers will be assigned to the first or second lot without being taken out of the super at all. When a super feels pretty light, it is inspected with some care by looking through it from the under side. If it is found that there is no honey in any section in the super, it goes to the dry pile without any taking out. If there is honey in the super, but no section in it more than half filled, it goes to the second pile without being emptied, even if there is only one section in the super containing any honey, and that section having only a few drops.

BEES EMPTYING SECTIONS.

The supers of sections in this second pile are called "feeders," because the honey in them is to be fed back to the bees (Fig. 96). Usually this feeding is not done until all the "feeders" are ready for the bees. They are taken into the shop cellar, and if there are only a few of them they are put in

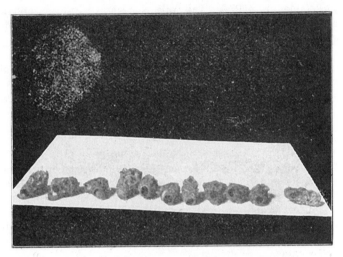

Fig. 94—Vacated Queen-Cells.

piles bee-tight with an opening at the top and another at the bottom only large enough for one or two bees to pass at a time. If the number of supers is sufficiently large, say half as large as the number of colonies in the home apiary, then the supers are set singly all around against the wall of the cellar so as to make them as easily accessible to the bees as possible. When there are only a few sections, if the bees have free access to them they will tear the comb to pieces.

When all the "feeders" are in the cellar, then the door is opened wide, and the bees help themselves. The reasons for having these "feeders" in the cellar rather than outdoors are, first, that I want to keep the bees away from them until the whole of them are ready for the attack; second, that in the cellar they are safe from the rain. The best of these emptied "feeders" furnish "baits" for the following season.

UNMARKETABLE SECTIONS.

The third pile Philo makes consists of those which are more than half filled with honey, but not good enough to be marketable (Fig. 97). This pile is never very large, and is easily gotten rid of at home, together with some help from relatives. Some of it will make as fine appearance as any honey when placed on the table, although the under side on the plate may have too many unsealed and unfilled cells to admit it into the marketable class. There may also be some broken sections, for sections have a fashion of falling with half a chance.

BEES CLEANING DAUBY SECTIONS.

Sometimes it happens that a section otherwise good is spoiled, and badly spoiled, in appearance, by having honey from some sections above leak all over one or both of its faces. Miss Wilson hit upon a plan for having such sections cleaned up in short order, and with very little trouble. She puts them in a super, puts the super over a colony of bees, and an hour later, if the bees are active, they are taken from the hive as good as new.

The rest of the sections that do not go into one of these three piles are merchantable sections. That makes four kinds into which Philo sorts them, and you will see that it is possible out of one super to take sections that will go into all four of the piles. Of course there is always standing a super ready for any odd sections of each kind, that is, a super for dry sections, another for "feeders," etc.

FIRST PART OF CLEANING SECTIONS.

Having now told how Philo sorts the sections, let me further tell what he does with them. When he comes to a super that does not go entire to the first or the second pile, the sections are taken out in the manner described on previous pages, leaving the contents of the super upside down on a board. The T tins are lifted off, and any sections that are not marketable are picked off and their places supplied with those that are marketable. Then the super that was taken from them is replaced by a box without top or bottom, that is, it is much like the super, only it is perhaps an inch longer, an inch wider,

Fig. 95—Miller Frame.

and an inch shallower than a T super, the exact size not being important. A piece of board is wedged into one side, and another into one end, so as to hold the sections firmly in place (Fig. 98). A case-knife with the whole length of its edge held at right angles to the sections sweeps back and forth, and when this has made the surface fairly clean, No. 2 sandpaper is used. A cabinetmaker's scraper is better than a case-knife while it is sharp, but is harder to keep sharp. Then a board similar to the one under the sections is laid on top, and with

one hand under the under board and the other over the upper
board he turns the whole upside down, the super resting on one
end on the table as he turns it over. The knife and sandpaper
now do their work on the tops of the sections. Then the
wedges are taken out, the box removed, and the boardful of
sections is slid along the table to the one who is scraping.
This table, which is very convenient, is 8 ft. long and 3 ft.
9 in. wide.

<h3 style="text-align:center">FINAL SCRAPING OF SECTIONS.</h3>

Miss Wilson generally does all the scraping; that is, all
the scraping besides what Philo has done, and sometimes his
part, as in Fig. 98. She sometimes scrapes on a board on her
lap, but usually on one of the small tables heretofore mentioned (Fig. 99). If the section should rest upon the table, the
knife used in scraping could not freely reach the lowest parts,
so a loose block lies on the board, on which the sections rest.
Another advantage of the block is that the accumulation of
propolis is not so much in the way. The size of this block is
not material; it may be an inch thick, four inches long or
longer, and two inches wide or wider. The block could be
nailed down, but it is more convenient to have it loose, so as
to scrape the propolis off the table from time to time. The
scrapings have generally been thrown away, but with a steam
wax-press it may pay well to get the wax out of it. Possibly
propolis may yet be a marketable commodity.

The knife used is a steel case-knife kept very sharp. The
sides and edges of the sections are to be scraped, and, if necessary, sandpaper follows the knife. The finishing touches are
put on Philo's work, knife marks, pencil marks, and any dis-
colored spots being carefully removed.

If it is cool enough, so that the bee glue is brittle instead
of being sticky, then sandpaper replaces the knife. The sandpaper is not rubbed upon the section, but the section is rubbed
upon a sheet of sandpaper lying flat. This makes more rapid
work than the knife, especially in scraping the edges, for four
edges are sandpapered at one operation.

A scraper should be a careful person, or in ten minutes'
time he will do more damage than his day's work is worth.
Even a careful person seems to need to spoil at least one sec-

tion before taking the care necessary to avoid injuring others. But when the knife makes an ugly gash in the face of a beautiful white section of honey, that settles it that care will be taken afterward.

PACKING SECTIONS IN SHIPPING-CASES.

The scraper has in easy reach two shipping-cases. 'In one, as fast as they are scraped, are put all sections that are not in any way faulty, such as appear in Fig. 100. In the other are put any which are a little off color, either as to comb or honey, or which have some cells unsealed. These must be sold as second-class at a reduction of about 2 cents a pound. In Fig. 101 are shown six such sections, the upper three having the best side out and the lower three having the poorest side out.

KIND OF SHIPPING CASES.

For some years I used double-tier shipping-cases holding twenty-four sections each, the upper tier resting on a little board supported by two other little boards, so that no weight came upon the lower tier. A pile of such cases showed a greater proportion of honey in its surface than a pile of single-tier cases, and for this reason I liked it, but it was odd goods, and so I changed to single-tier cases. I have used mostly the twelve-section case, as shown in Fig. 102. But please do not think that all my honey looks as well as that in Fig. 102. The specimens in Fig. 100 are fair samples, although they are possibly a little below the mark.

I have used some single-tier cases holding twenty-four sections (Fig. 103). These are not so nice and firm to handle as the smaller cases, but it costs less to pack a ton of honey in the larger than in the smaller cases. Grocers who sell by the case are inclined to prefer the larger case, for they say a customer who buys a case at a time will as readily buy a twenty-four-section case as a twelve-section case.

I have used several hundred safety shipping-cases, but am none too sure they are worth the extra cost.

The most difficult thing about the packing is to prevent veneering. It seems to come so natural, when a particularly white and straight section goes into the case, to put it next the glass, best side out at that. But it is especially desirable that the outside shall be a fair index of the entire contents of the case. In the long run there is money to be made by it, to say nothing of the feeling of satisfaction.

HONEY SHOW.

When the cases are filled they are stacked up in piles, and these piles are mostly—perhaps always—so arranged as to make the best show possible. There is no object in this beyond

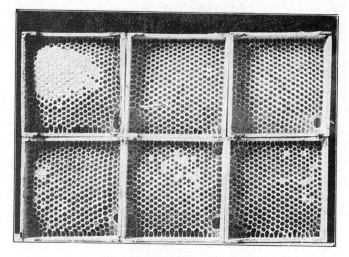

Fig. 96—Feeder-Sections.

the pleasure it gives the family to see it for a few days, perhaps only for a day. But the sight is a beautiful one so long as it lasts, as I think you will agree with me if you look at Fig. 104.

PLACE TO KEEP HONEY.

I have sold a crop of honey before it was off the hives and sometimes I have kept part of a crop over till spring.

In any case the honey for home use in spring must be kept over. It is not the easiest thing in the world to keep it through the winter in good shape. If kept cold it is apt to granulate, or candy, as it is usually called. If allowed to freeze, the combs crack and look bad, and in time the honey oozes out of the cracks. Honey is deliquescent, absorbing from the atmosphere a large amount of water if conditions are favorable. Try putting some common salt in a place where you think of keeping honey; if the salt remains dry, so would honey. But a place that is suitable at one time may not be at another. Years ago I filled the back end of the honey-room with honey. It was a good place for it; the outside walls were thin and the heat of the sun made it a hot place. When cold weather came, however, it was a bad place, and the lower sections at the back part—beautiful, snowy-white, when first put in—became watery and dark-looking. A fire for cooking was kept in the adjoining room, and although there seemed but very little steam in the air, by the time it got to the back end of the room, and settled to the lower part, there was enough to spoil hundreds of sections. You see, warm air is like a sponge to take up moisture, and cold squeezes the moisture out of it. The point to see to, then, is to have no air coming from a warmer place to the place where the honey is. I would sooner risk honey in a kitchen with a hot fire and plenty of steam than in a room without fire and with a door partly opened into a sitting-room where no water or steam is ever kept. Indeed, a kitchen is quite a good place to keep honey, the higher up the better.

KEEPING HONEY IN GARRET.

It is well known that a cellar, except in particularly dry localities, is about the worst place in which to keep honey; but it is not so well known that the place the furthest removed from the cellar—the garret—is one of the very best places. My mother kept some sections throughout the latter part of summer in a garret, and after enduring the freezing of the following winter they were as fine as when first put there. The roasting heat of the summer in that garret had so ripened the honey as to make it proof against injury from freezing.

HONEY IN CELLAR WITH FURNACE.

I just spoke of a cellar as a poor place for honey except in very dry climates. But a furnace in a cellar makes a big difference. In 1902 a furnace was put in my cellar. Several winters since then I have piled up sections beside the furnace, at a distance of 1 to 4 feet from it, and anything better could hardly be desired.

GRANULATED HONEY.

If comb honey becomes granulated or watery, I know of no way to restore it. If for home use, or if one happens to have a market where extracted honey sells for a good price,

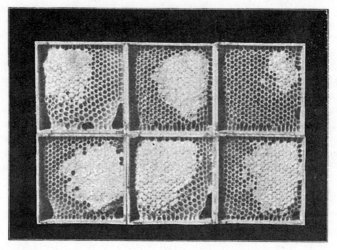

Fig. 97—Unmarketable Sections.

the sections may be put in stone crocks, *slowly* melted, being sure it is not overheated; and then when cool, the cake of wax may be lifted off the honey.

The best place to keep comb honey is also the best place to keep extracted; but if extracted honey becomes granulated or watery. it may be restored to its former, or even a better condition. If thin and not granulated, by setting it on the reservoir of a cook-stove and letting it remain days enough, it will become thick. I suppose you may have known this, and also that extracted honey, when granulated, may be liquefied by slowly heating, but did you know that when thin honey is warmed for a long time the flavor is improved? I have had the flavor improved and could attribute it to nothing but remaining a couple of weeks on the reservoir. I do not mean by this that if fine-flavored honey in good condition is placed on the stove reservoir it will be improved. Most people, however, who have had much to do with honey, must have noticed that when extracted honey becomes thin from attracting moisture from the atmosphere, it seems to acquire a different flavor—perhaps I might say it has a sharp taste—and the slow heating seems to restore it partly if not wholly to its former condition.

RIPENING HONEY.

The same thing is true of honey which is taken thin from the hive, not yet having been brought to proper density by the bees.

There is a difference of opinion as to whether honey, or perhaps nectar, evaporated outside of the hive, is equal to that which remains in the hive till thick. Of course, no large amount could be evaporated on a stove reservoir. Some beekeepers have large tanks in which to evaporate honey by the sun or other heat. The general opinion, however, is that the best place for ripening honey is on the hives.

It must not be understood that when honey has really soured it can be made good by the process mentioned. The only thing is to use it for vinegar; and fine vinegar it will make.

DRAINING EXTRACTED HONEY.

There is another plan which I have used to secure some extra-fine extracted honey for our private use. Whether it could be used profitably on a large scale, I cannot say. There are, however, always people who are ready to pay a high price for an extra article. After a crock of clover honey has granulated, I turn it on its side or upside down, and let it remain days enough to drain off all the liquid part. If drained long enough, the residue—and this will be nearly all the crockful—will be as dry as sugar, and when this is liquefied by slow heating it makes a delicious article. It will, however, granulate very easily a second time. On a large scale, the liquid might be drained off by boring a hole at the lower part of a barrel of granulated honey. I spoke of treating clover honey in this way; I do not know what other kinds may be treated the same way, but I have had some granulated honey of smooth, even

Fig. 98—Sections Wedged for Scraping.

texture, from which no liquid part could be drained. When set to drain, the whole mass would roll slowly out.

MARKETING HONEY.

I have had no uniform way of marketing honey. I should prefer in all cases to sell the crop outright for cash, if I could get a satisfactory price; but some years I can do better to sell on commission. Judgment must be used as to limiting commission men to a certain price. Some commission men will sell off promptly at any price offered, and when sending to such men it is best to name a certain figure, below which the honey must not be sold. I have sold in my home market, as well as in towns near by, and have shipped to nine of the principal cities, and it would be an impossibility for me to say what would be my best market next year. Prices vary according to the yield in different parts of the country. If shipping to a distant point in cold weather, I keep up a hot fire to warm the honey twenty-four hours before shipping. If very cold I wait for a warm spell.

LOADING SECTIONS WHEN SHIPPING.

On a wagon, the length of a section should run across the wagon—on a car, lengthwise of the car. Convenience of packing in a wagon, however, is of first consideration, for with careful driving it matters little which way the sections are placed. On the other hand, no matter what the inconvenience, I would have the sections in a railroad car so that when a heavy bump comes the sections must take it endwise. I always prefer, if possible, to load the honey directly into the car myself. Then I know that it will carry well unless the engine does an unreasonable amount of bumping.

PACKING SECTIONS IN A CAR.

Very likely a number of cases of honey packed in a crate do not need any special care in loading; but if I can make sure that the honey will go through to its destination without any reloading, I prefer to put the cases in the car one by one. If the number of cases is so small that there is no need to pile one case on another, then the cases are put in one end of the car and kept in place by a strip of common inch lumber nailed on the floor. If there are enough cases so they must be tiered up, then the lower tier has a strip nailed on the floor as before, but each of the upper tiers is fastened differently. On each side of the car is nailed a cleat to support a fence-board which runs across the width of the car, resting flat like a shelf on these cleats. Another cleat is nailed on the side of the car over the board, so it can move neither up nor down. The board is up tight against the cases, perhaps a little above their middle. Then a third cleat is nailed on each side of the car against the board to prevent the board from moving in the least.

If there is a space at the side of the car, straw is packed hard into it beside the cases. If the space is very small, pieces

Fig. 99—Scraping Sections.

of old wooden separators may be wedged in. Newspapers are laid on the bottom of the car under the cases, and newspapers tacked on top of them.

HOME MARKET.

Much has been said about cultivating a home market, but there are two sides to the matter. If beekeepers from neighboring towns come in and supply my home market at 2 cents per pound less than my honey nets me when shipped to a distant market, about all I can do is to leave the home market in their hands. I suspect, however, that it would have been to my advantage to have paid more attention to developing my home market for extracted honey.

HOME VERSUS DISTANT MARKET.

In deciding between a home and a distant market, there are more things to be taken into consideration than are always thought of. There is breakage in transportation, and the greater the distance the greater the risk. If I can load my honey into a car myself, and it goes to its destination without change of cars, I do not feel very anxious about it. On this account a car-load is safer than a small quantity, for a full car-load may be sent almost any distance without reshipping. If reshipped, it is not at all certain how it will be packed in a car. I once sent a lot of honey to Cincinnati, and when it arrived at its destination the sections were actually lying on their sides! I suppose the railroad hands who packed it in the car at the last change, thought the glass was safest from breakage if the case was put glass side down. The strangest part about it was that I lost nothing by the breakage. The dogged persistence of a German consignee obliged the railroad company to pay all damage! for the consignee was that staunch German and genial friend of beekeepers—the late C. F. Muth.

There is less danger of breakage by freight than by express. Besides danger of breakage, there is risk of losing in various ways. You may not be able to collect pay for your honey. If sent on commission, the price obtained may be less than the published market report. You have no means generally to know how correct the claims for breakage may be. In fact, unless you know your consignee to be a thoroughly honest man, you are almost entirely at his mercy.

PRICES IN HOME AND DISTANT MARKET.

Taking all these things into consideration, together with the cost of freight and shipping-cases, it must be a good price that will justify a man to ship off honey to the neglect of his home market. If shipped to be sold on commission, provided he ships to a near market, the price should be at least 2½ cents per pound more than he can get in his home market, to justify his shipping. If he ships to a distant market the difference should be still more, as the additional freight may make a difference of 1 cent per pound or more, and the risk of breakage becomes greater.

Fig. 100—Sections Ready for Casing.

Not always, however, must I be willing to sell in my home market for less than I can get abroad. If there is a year of dead failure in my locality, or so nearly a failure that the home market must be at least partly supplied from elsewhere, then I should get more for my honey than the grocers will have to pay in the large city markets, for they must add freight to the price they pay there.

FALL FEEDING.

Some seasons are so poor that the bees do not get enough throughout the whole season to carry them through the winter.

One year I took no surplus, and fed 2800 pounds of granulated sugar for winter stores. Some years the clover crop will be a failure, but plenty of stores will be gathered later in the season to carry the bees over winter. It is not always easy to tell in advance just what will be, but it is best to err on the safe side; and it is no harm to have more stores on hand than are actually needed. It is also better to have the feeding done early. If the feed is given so early that it can be given thin enough, the bees make chemical changes in it that make it better for winter.

FEEDING SYRUP.

Formerly I did not take this into account, and syrup was prepared that approached the consistency of honey. Water was put in a vessel on the stove, and when at or near the boiling-point granulated sugar was slowly stirred in at the rate of five pounds of sugar to a quart of water. When the sugar was about dissolved, an even teaspoonful of tartaric acid for every twenty pounds of sugar, previously dissolved in water, was stirred into the syrup, for without the acid the syrup is likely to turn into sugar in the combs when fed so thick. If I were to feed late in September, or in October, I think I should prefer the same syrup now.

FEEDING EARLY FOR WINTER.

But by feeding in August or early in September the work can be made much easier, and at the same time the food will be better for the bees. For they will so manipulate the thin feed given them that no acid will be needed, making their winter stores much more like the stores they obtain from the flowers. There is nothing complicated about the feeding, and there is not the same trouble with robbers as when syrup is made. First, the feeders are all put on, and left standing uncovered. Then the amount of sugar needed in each feeder is put in dry, whether that be two pounds or fifteen pounds. Then I go around to each feeder, and, making a depression in the center of the sugar, put in half a pint or more of water. I do this rather than to put in the full quota of water at first, because in the latter case it is possible that the water would force its way into the reach of the bees without having much sweetness in it, for I forgot to say that I use the Miller feeder. I am not sure that this precaution is necessary, but it can do no harm. I now go around and put in each feeder about as much water as will balance the sugar, counting either by pints or pounds. Of course, if twelve pounds or more of sugar should be in the feeder, it will be impossible to balance the sugar with water. In that case I put in all the water I can. Next

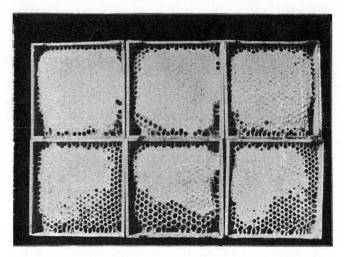

Fig. 101—Second-Class Sections.

day or so the liquid will be used out, and I can fill up again. Indeed, in many cases where equal parts of sugar and water are given, the water will be mostly out by the next day, leaving only damp sugar in the feeder, and more water must be added. Practically, this is giving the feed very thin, and I suspect it is all the better. I have never had any trouble from robber bees while leaving the feeders open in the way mentioned, of course covering up as soon as the water is all in; although I have had trouble by leaving a cover on a feeder that was not bee-tight, and with such a cover it is better first to put on a cover of cotton cloth that hangs down all around.

SELECTING COLONIES TO FEED.

I have spoken as if a feeder was put over each colony lacking stores. That is by no means always the case—indeed, not often the case. There are reasons why it is better to have a comparatively small number of colonies do the storing, taking sealed combs from these to give to the weaker ones. It is a good deal less trouble, when the feeding is begun in good season, to have one colony store enough for five or ten others besides itself than it is to have feeders on all the five or ten colonies. Some colonies will store better than others, and the best can be chosen.

FEEDING IN FALL FOR SPRING.

For some reason, bees seem to store from a feeder much better late in the season than they do before the harvest time. The greater strength of the colonies and the warmer weather would make one expect a difference, but it has always seemed to me that there was more difference than could be accounted for without some other reason. So it is desirable at this time to have not only enough combs filled to bridge over the winter, but to supply any possible deficiency up to the harvest time.

An upper story of empty combs is put on, possibly two. As fast as combs are completely filled and sealed they can be removed and replaced by empty ones. If it is desired to have combs filled out upon foundation, beautiful work will be done upon them in these upper stories. It will easily be seen that it is less trouble to add sugar from time to time as needed, also to add water as needed, than it is to apportion the smaller amounts to a number of colonies. No great matter if too much or too little of one or the other is present; the thing will regulate itself. For with cold water there is no danger of the feed being too thick, and all the harm of too large a proportion of sugar is that the bees will have to wait for more water when it is too dry to give down. On the other hand, they will continue taking it down when it is much thinner than half-and-half, and perhaps it is all the better manipulated when very thin.

Perhaps it would do as well to feed as described under wholesale feeding in spring, but in that case I should want the feed quite thin, and there would be more danger from robbers, and more danger of having thin feed left in the feeders to sour.

DIFFICULTY IN DECIDING ABOUT STORES.

It is not an easy thing to determine just what amount of stores is needed to carry a colony through to the next harvest. Some colonies use more than others under apparently the same conditions. Experience will enable one to judge fairly well by inspection as to the amount of stores present, but one can be more exact about it by actual weighing. Besides, with proper conveniences for it, the weighing takes less time. But two colonies may weigh exactly the same, and one may have abundance and the other may starve, because, although weighing the same, one had much more honey than the other. One had much pollen, the other little. Or, the combs of one were new, and the combs of the other were very old and heavy. The only safe way is to have all so heavy that under any and all circumstances there will be no danger. So we aim to have each hive with its contents, its cover, and its bottom-board weigh as much as fifty pounds. Some will weigh so much more than this that hefting will show that there is no need of weighing. Even a strong colony that stored well throughout the season in a prosperous year may have had the brood-chamber so stocked with brood that not enough honey was in the brood-chamber; so it is well to heft and weigh even in the best seasons, and to do this late enough so that storing from flowers need no longer be taken into account, and so early that there will be abundance of time for the bees to arrange matters to their liking in the brood-chamber.

WEIGHING COLONIES.

A common spring balance with a capacity of eighty pounds is used for weighing (Fig. 105). An endless rope passes around the hive under the cleat at each end, then the hook of the spring balance passes under the two parts of the rope over the hive, and the slack is taken up by tying a string around the two parts under the hook. A hickory stick used as a lever passes through the ring of the upper part of the spring balance, the short end of the lever being supported by a light framework that stands on the adjoining hive. When all is properly adjusted, the long end of the lever is raised, and the weight is read, and then taken down, so that a comb or combs may be added to bring up to the desired weight. If no precaution is taken, the spring balance, when first raised, will slide on the lever down against one's hands or shoulders. To prevent this a stout string has one end tied to the short end of the lever, and the other end tied to the ring of the balance, so as to keep it within bounds. When once adjusted, rope,

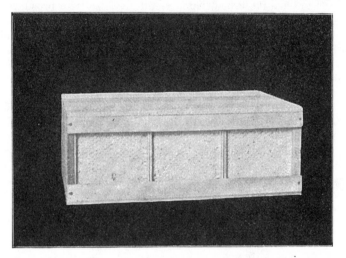

Fig. 102—Twelve-section Shipping-case.

balance, and lever are left fastened together, the rope being slipped on each end of the hive for weighing, and slipped off when the hive is weighed.

RESERVE COMBS OF HONEY.

After all I have said about feeding, I am happy to say that since about the time of the coming in of the 20th century very little feeding has been done. Most years not a feeder is put on. This is partly due to the increase of fall pasturage, and perhaps in some degree to the fact that the present stock of bees are more provident than they were some years ago.

In spite of the better fall feed, some colonies in eight-frame hives might be short of stores before the white-honey harvest. To meet such cases, combs filled with sealed honey are kept in reserve from the previous fall. These reserve combs are valuable for another purpose. Left to themselves the bees would have very little honey in the hives at the opening of the honey-harvest, and all vacancies in the brood-chamber must be filled before honey goes into the supers. Now if we have reserve combs on hand from the previous fall, so as to have the brood-chamber entirely filled with brood and honey at the opening of the harvest, then there is nothing left for the bees to do but to tote the first honey upstairs, instead of waiting for the brood-chamber to be filled. You may ask what is gained by merely swapping last year's honey for honey in the sections. There would be nothing gained if the honey in the reserve combs were white-clover honey. But it is fall honey; and for every pound of fall honey we put in the brood-chamber we get back a pound of white honey in sections.

So I like to have one or two reserve combs on hand for each colony in the spring. These reserve combs may be obtained by taking them in the fall from colonies that are over-heavy, giving in place of them empty combs to be again filled, or upper stories may be given filled with combs.

NUCLEI IN FALL.

When the time for rearing queens is over, the nuclei will be in various conditions. Some will be weak, some strong, some queenless. Here will be a nucleus hive containing three strong nuclei with a good laying queen in each nucleus. Nothing is to be done in such a case but to leave the three nuclei as they are, to be carried into the cellar without any further preparation, unless it be to give some honey if it be needed. In the case of the middle nucleus, that will mean exchanging their comb for one as much as two-thirds or three- quarters full of honey. In the nuclei at the sides of the hive, the heaviest frames of honey will be toward the center of the hive. This will encourage the bees to cluster in that direction, thus concentrating the warmth of the three nuclei.

UNITING NUCLEI.

But the hives with three strong nuclei and three queens will be exceptional. Some will have only two queens, some one. If a nucleus hive has in it only one queen, it may be that a full hive is set in place of the nucleus hive, the contents of the three apartments of the nucleus hive put into this full hive, and, if necessary, enough nuclei added from elsewhere to make a fair colony. If none of the nuclei in any one nucleus hive be sufficiently strong where there is only one

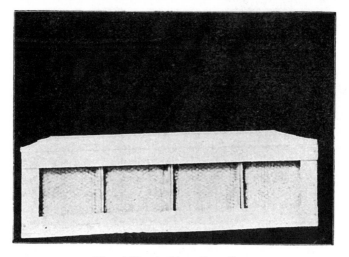

Fig. 103—A 24-section Case.

queen in the hive, then the nucleus with the queen is likely to be put in some nucleus hive that has contained only two queens. In some cases one of the division-boards is taken away, making one of the compartments large enough to receive five frames, besides the other with the three frames. Thus the nucleus in the larger compartment may be built up to a tolerably fair colony.

Thus you will see that there is little or no destroying of queens, the effort being to have each queen supported by a good force of bees, considering the size of her compartment. No attention is paid to the matter of trying to make bees stay where they are put. If they don't like to stay they don't need to; they'll count somewhere. But as they are mostly queenless bees that are moved, they are not bad about returning.

DOUBLE HIVES FOR WINTER.

Not only have I wintered nuclei two and three in a hive, but a few years ago I had considerable experience in wintering full colonies in double hives. If I had not changed from ten-frame to eight-frame hives I should have continued the

Fig. 104—Honey Show.

practice, but an eight-frame hive makes too cramped quarters for two full colonies, even in winter. Still, I approximate it with five frames on one side and three on the other, and of course the hive could be divided to take four frames on each side.

There is nothing new or original about two colonies in one hive, among others Dzierzon's twin hives having been highly esteemed by him and others for many years. These, however, are used the same all the year around, and my use of them is only during the time of year when bees can be crowded into a less space than a full hive.

From the time the bees are fed in the summer or fall,

till perhaps the middle of May, most of my colonies would
have room enough in one half of a ten-frame hive. I am not
sure that any of them ever need more room through the fall
and winter, and in the spring they need no more till more than
four frames are needed for brood. With some, this may come
quite early, but I think I should be well satisfied if I could
get all my colonies to contain four combs well filled with

Fig. 105—Weighing Colonies.

brood by the middle of May. Some of them may have at that
time brood in nine or ten frames, but more of them could have
all their brood crowded into three or four combs.

ADVANTAGE OF DOUBLE HIVES.

Now if, during the time I have mentioned, we can have
two colonies in one hive, we shall, I think, find it advantageous
in more than one direction. It is a common thing for beekeepers to unite two weak colonies in the fall. Suppose a beekeeper has two colonies in the fall, each occupying two combs.
He unites them so they will winter better. If they would not
quarrel and would stay wherever they were put, he could place
the two frames of the one hive beside the two frames in the
other hive, and the thing would be done. Now, suppose that

a thin division-board were placed between the two sets of combs, would he not see the same result? Not quite, I think, but nearly so. They would hardly be so warm as without the division-board, but nearly so; and both queens would be saved. In the spring it is desirable to keep the bees warm. If two colonies are in one hive, with a thin division-board between them, they will be much warmer than if in separate hives. The same thing is true in winter. I have had weak nuclei with two combs come through in good condition during a winter in which I lost heavily, these nuclei having no extra care or protection other than being in a double hive. You would understand the reason of all this easily if in winter you would look into one of these double hives in the cellar. On each side the bees are clustered up against the division-board, and it looks exactly as if the bees had all been in one single cluster, and then the division-board pushed down through the center of the cluster.

Now suppose we have 100 colonies that are all fed up for winter and they are then put into double hives. Please understand that there is little or no extra expense for these double hives. They are just the regular hives, only we take special pains to see that the division-board is perfectly bee-tight. If the hives are to be hauled home, as I haul mine each fall, there are only 50 instead of 100 to haul; just half the bulk, and a much less weight than the 100 would be. Just half the hives are to be handled in taking in and out of winter quarters; just half the room is occupied in winter quarters; and I think, although I do not know, that the bees will winter better than if only one colony in a hive. If they are to be taken, in the spring, to a distant apiary, there is the advantage of hauling only 50 hives instead of 100. If, in the spring, any colony be found queenless it is in fine position to be united with its fellow colony.

CHANGING FROM SINGLE TO DOUBLE HIVES.

Possibly you may be ready to agree with me so far as to say, "Certainly, the thing looks desirable, but is it feasible? Will not the trouble counterbalance all advantage?" I know it is usually a matter of some trouble to change a colony from one location to another in the same apiary. I think, however, that I have reduced the trouble to a minimum. I will give you my plan and you can judge for yourself.

As I have already told you, my hives stand in pairs, and I kept them so, years before I thought of double hives. Some time before the change is made to double hives, the entrances of the hives are closed at one side, so that the bees become accustomed to using the same side of the entrance that they will use when thrown into the double hive, that is, the right-hand colony will use the right-hand side of its entrance, and the left-hand colony will use the left-hand side of its entrance. Each colony will have four of its combs so solid with honey that it will be well provisioned.

Remembering that the two colonies of a pair are on the same stand, we now remove both hives from the stand and set the double hive on the middle of the stand. Then the four combs from the right-hand hive will be put with their bees in the right-hand side of the double colony and the rest of the bees brushed from the other combs. The left-hand side is treated the same way. Some bees will still be left in the de-populated hives; so these hives can be set at each side, the entrance of the empty hive at the proper entrance of the double hive, and left there long enough for the bees to crawl in and join their companions.

The matter is now accomplished and it has been no long or difficult job. The bees use the new entrance *almost* as readily as the old. To them their hive seems moved less than its width to one side, and there is no possible danger of their entering the wrong place. I have tried it, and watched the result, therefore I speak of not what the bees *ought* to do, but what they *do* do.

CHANGING FROM DOUBLE TO SINGLE HIVES.

Can we as easily get them back into two hives in the spring when they become crowded in this double hive? Just exactly as easily. We simply reverse the operation. Take the double hive from its place and replace it with the two hives, then remove the contents of the double hive and put them in the proper single hives and the bees will go every time to the right place. I speak again from personal observation as to what the bees actually do.

BRINGING BEES HOME IN THE FALL.

In the fall the bees must be brought home from the out-apiary so as to be wintered in the cellar.

There are always a few things upon which bees can work till quite late; so it is desirable to be as late as possible bringing them home. They must, however, be brought home early enough so they will be sure of a good flight after being brought home and before being put in the cellar. Some say they may

Fig. 106—Colonies Home from Out-apiaries.

be safely put into the cellar without the flight, but one winter part of mine were put in without a flight, and that part wintered distinctly worse than the others. At the latest, I want them home before Nov. 1. When brought home they are placed conveniently near the cellar door (Fig. 106).

WHEN TO PUT BEES INTO CELLAR.

It is a thing impossible to know beforehand just what is the best time to take bees into the cellar. At best it can be only a guess. Living in a region where winters are severe,

there are some years in which there will be no chance for bees
to have a flight after the middle of November till the next
spring, and I think there was, one year without a flight-day
after the first of November. One feels bad to put his bees
into the cellar the first week in November, and then two or
three weeks later have a beautiful day for a flight. But he
feels a good deal worse after a good flight-day the first week
in November to wait for a later flight, then have it turn very
cold, and after waiting through two or three weeks of such
weather to give up hope of any later flight and put in his
bees after two or three weeks' endurance of severe freezing
weather. So it is better to err on the side of getting bees in
too early.

Theoretically, the right time to cellar bees is the next day
after they have had their last flight for the season, and one
must do the best he can to judge after any flight-day whether
it is the last or not. More than one reason can be given for
taking in next day after a flight. The hives are dry; there are
no accumulations of frost or ice inside; and the bees are unusually quiet. All the better if the next morning is cool as it
is likely to be. Sometimes, however, one cannot have everything as he wants it, and I have been caught taking in bees in
a snow-storm. Better take them in during the storm than after it is all over and constantly growing colder. But it seems
to do no harm for them to be taken in covered with snow.

PREPARING THE CELLAR.

For twenty-four hours before taking in—perhaps for several days—doors and windows of the cellar are kept wide
open, so as to air it out thoroughly, and perhaps the walls are
whitewashed and the floor limed, although this is generally
done after taking out in the spring. Strips of board are placed
on the ground so that the bottom hive has its bottom-board
an inch or two above the ground at the front end, and an inch
more at the back end.

CARRYING IN HIVES.

Hives are carried in just as they are, because before the
time for hauling bees home all false bottoms were removed,
and the bottom-boards fastened to the hives where necessary.

With the large ventilating space at the entrance, and with abundance of stores, there is no need to loosen the gluing of a cover from before the time a colony is hauled home till after the time for hauling back in spring.

PILING HIVES IN CELLAR.

The hives are piled five high, each pile independent of the others, so jarring one hive can jar only four others. First a row of piles is put at the further side of the cellar, the hives

Fig. 107—Dripping-pan Wax-extractor.

close side by side, entrances facing the wall, with a space of about two feet between them and the wall. Then another row is placed back to back close up against this row. Then comes a space of about two feet, and another row facing the space, so that entrances face each side of the space. Then comes another row, back to back, and so on. That makes the hives in double rows, back to back, with a two-foot space in which to get at the entrances.

As far as convenient, the heavier hives are put at the bottom, and lighter at top. It is easier work to do so, and the lighter ones have perhaps the advantage by being higher up, where it is a little warmer.

CARRYING IN BEES WHEN ROUSED UP.

Often the bees get so warmed up by the middle of the forenoon, that they fly out when their hive is lifted to be carried into the cellar. In this case the hive is put back on its summer stand, and another colony, less wide-awake, is taken. But if the rousing up becomes general, operations must cease until the after-part of the day or the next morning. If for any reason, as the lateness of the season, or the fear of an approaching storm, it is thought best to carry in a hive whether the bees are willing or not, the entrance must be stopped. For this purpose—as there is no danger of suffocation from stopping for a short time—I know of nothing better than a large rag or cloth which will easily cover the entire entrance. The rag must be dripping wet. In this condition it can be very quickly laid at the entrance, and being cold and wet the bees seem to be driven back by it, and when the rag is removed in the cellar, few if any bees come out. If dry, the bees would sting the rag, and upon its removal in the cellar a crowd of angry bees would follow it.

WARMING THE CELLAR.

There is a furnace in the cellar where my bees are kept, which has been there since the winter of 1902-3. But let us go back to the time before that, when the chief difficulty was to keep the cellar warm enough. Some think it a bad thing to have fire in cellar. I would rather have the right temperature without the fire. So I would in my sitting-room. But when the temperature in the sitting-room without a fire gets down in the neighborhood of zero, I would rather have the fire. Same way in the cellar. In this latitude, 42 degrees north, I have known the mercury to reach 37 degrees below zero, and some winters there is very little of the time when my cellar is warm enough for the bees. A thermometer hangs centrally in the cellar, and I try to keep it at about 45 degrees. Sometimes it goes to 36 degrees, but not often, and not for long. Oftener it reaches 50 degrees, but that is neither often nor long.

STOVE IN CELLAR.

Whenever the thermometer appears to have any fixed determination to stay below 45 degrees, a fire is started. I would not think of using an oil stove, nor any thing of the kind that would allow the gases to escape in the cellar. A chimney

Fig. 108—Screwing Down Wax-press.

goes from the ground up through the house, and a hard-coal stove is used. For many years I used a common small cylinder stove, having an inside diameter of about 8 inches between the fire-brick. Then I used a low-down open or Franklin stove, and I think I like it as well or better. With either stove there is the open fire, and one might fear that the bees would fly into it, but they do not appear to do so. Neither does any harm come to the hives that stand within two feet of the stove, for the stove is right in the same room as the bees. A few minutes' attention each morning and evening will keep the fire going continuously, in case it is needed continuously. There have been winters when fire was kept going nearly all the winter through, and other winters when little was needed. The winter of 1901-2 was one of the mild ones. A fire started Dec. 21 was kept for three days. Another, Jan. 27, lasted one day. A third started Feb. 3 lasted seventeen days. I think the outer temperature was at no time more than 15 degrees below zero.

HEAT FOR DIARRHOEA.

I do not know for certain, but I *think* I have had good results at a time when diarrhoea began to trouble the bees in the cellar, by making a hot fire and running up the temperature above 60 degrees. The bees would become very noisy, but after the cellar cooled down to the normal 45 degrees they were quieter than before, and I suspect the bees felt better.

VENTILATION OF CELLAR.

I believe heartily in the doctrine of pure air and plenty of it for man, beast, and bee. So I consider ventilation a very important affair. With a two-inch space under the bottom-bars and a 12 x 2 entrance, there is no trouble about the ventilation of the *hive;* but no matter how well ventilated a hive may be, if the cellar in which it is placed contains nothing but foul air, how can the air in the hive be sweet?

FIRE FOR VENTILATION.

I am not sure but I should want a fire in a cellar for the sake of ventilation even if not needed for heat.

For the purpose of ventilation alone, the warmer the weather the more the fire in the cellar is needed. Of course there must be some limit to this, for when the temperature of the cellar goes above 60 degrees, the bees show signs of uneasiness.

WARM SPELLS IN WINTERING.

The most difficult time to keep the bees quiet in the cellar, is when a warm spell comes in the fall soon after taking them

in, or early in the spring. At such times I open up the cellar
at dark. If very warm, all doors and windows are opened
wide and by morning generally all are quiet. I leave all open
as long as possible in the morning; sometimes till noon; when
the bees begin to fly out all must be darkened. Very likely it
would be better if there were a way to admit air in abundance
without admitting light.

COOLING AND AIRING CELLAR.

Years ago, when the temperature became too high in the
cellar in spring, and I wanted to keep the bees in the cellar still
longer, I tried cooling down with cakes of ice. But it was not
satisfactory. The trouble was not so much with the *temperature* as the *quality* of the air. Then I learned that opening the
cellar was more effectual.

OPENING CELLAR AT NIGHT.

The first time I tried that trick I got a pretty bad scare.
It was in the spring, and there came a warm spell, lasting perhaps two or three days. It kept getting warmer in the cellar,
and the bees kept getting noisier. At the same time I kept
getting more uneasy, not knowing just what the end would be.
After the trouble got pretty bad, I thought I would venture
to open the cellar wide in the evening, hoping that it might
become cooler through the night. I think it was 50 or 60 degrees outside, and not far from that in the cellar. The bees
were quite noisy when the cellar was opened, and I listened
closely for the quieting down. It didn't come. On the contrary, the noise increased to a roar that could be heard some
distance from the cellar, and the bees were running all over
the hives, some of them hanging out in great clusters as if
getting ready to swarm. I felt afraid they would all leave
their hives and make a wreck. I assure you I was badly frightened; but I didn't know of any thing to do, so I didn't do any
thing. As nearly as I now remember, I did not go to bed till
I could recognize a little subsiding, and in the morning the
bees were back in their hives as quiet as mice. More than
once since then I have gone through the same performance
without being troubled by it; only the cellar is not allowed to
get so bad before it is opened.

LETTING LIGHT IN CELLAR.

Here is a memorandum written March 14, 1902: "During the past eight days the weather has been unusually warm for the season, varying from 29 to 65 degrees. The doors have been wide open day and night except on the two warmest days, and the (east) window part of the time. Three days ago it was 65 degrees in the afternoon. Within twenty-four hours the ground was covered with snow, and yesterday morning the mercury stood at 29 degrees. At 7 A. M. to-day, it was 35

Fig. 109—Emptying Out Slumgum.

degrees without and 44 degrees in the cellar, doors and window having been open all night. At 9 A. M. it was 46 degrees outside and 45 degrees in the cellar. The sun shone directly into some of the entrances near the window without disturbing the bees. At 10:30 A. M. it was 52 degrees outside and 47 degrees in the cellar; the bees still quiet. At 11 A. M. it was 53 degrees without and 48 in the cellar. In five minutes by the watch I counted fifteen bees which flew to the window. I then closed the window, leaving the doors wide open. At 12 o'clock it was still 53 degrees without and 49 degrees in the cellar. In five minutes I counted five bees flying to the door. The light does not shine directly into the room where the bees are, they being in an inside room. I can see to read easily at the hives nearest the door. At 3:20 it was 55 degrees outside and 50 degrees in cellar. In five minutes I counted three bees flying to the door. It was then getting cloudy, the sun having been shining most of the day. I opened the window for five minutes and twelve bees flew to it. At 6 P. M. the window was opened again, leaving all wide open till it should again become bright enough on the next or some following day to make the bees fly out, or cold enough to bring the mercury down too far in the cellar."

I have not given this as an example of the perfection of wintering. It is far from that. But it shows that after 119 days of confinement the bees will stand a good deal of light and warmth without showing much insubordination, provided they have an abundance of good air. It must be higher than 45 degrees to induce them out when in good condition.

SUB-EARTH VENTILATOR.

Some years ago I put in a sub-earth ventilator of 4-inch tile, 100 feet long and 4 feet deep. It was of common porous draintile, and becoming a little skeptical of the quality of the air admitted I allowed it to become filled up. I am not sure that I did wisely. I am strongly of the opinion that an airtight pipe large enough and deep enough would be a great aid to successful cellaring.

MICE IN BEE-CELLARS.

Mice are troublesome denizens of cellars in winter. Even if a cellar should be entirely free from them, they are likely to be brought into the cellar with the bees when the hives are brought in. Some winters I have closed the entrances with heavy wire-cloth having three meshes to the inch. This shuts out mice without hindering the free passage of bees. Even if a mouse is shut up in a hive, it will not be so bad as to let it have the free run of the cellar. Other winters traps have been used and various poisons, perhaps the most satisfactory poison being strychnine thinly spread upon very thin slices of cheese, the cheese being then cut into tiny squares.

CLEANING OUT DEAD BEES.

Aside from attending to warming and ventilating my cellar, and waging war against the mice, I think of no other attention given to the bees through the winter, except cleaning out the dead bees. For cleaning them out of those hives which have them—for some reason of which I am not yet sure, there are some hives which contain scarcely a dead bee—I have a very simple tool. It is a piece of round, ¼-inch or smaller iron rod, with one end hammered flat for about two inches and bent at right angles, making something like a hook. With this hook I can reach into the hive under the frames and scrape out the dead bees.

I have a common kerosene hand-lamp with a sheet-iron chimney having a little mica window on one side—such as is used for heating water on lamps. This serves as a dark-lantern, making little light except in one direction. Holding the lamp in my left hand, I look in to see whether any live bees are in sight. Often I see the cluster near the front of the hive, oftener at the center or back part of the hive, the bees looking as if dead, so still are they; but in a few seconds some one will be seen to stir. Sometimes the cluster will come clear down so as to touch the bottom-board, and sometimes not a bee will be seen below or between the bottom-bars. When the cluster comes clear down, there may or there may not be bees on the bottom-board. In any case, all the dead bees are cleaned out that can be got without disturbing the living. There is, as has been said, a difference as to the number of dead bees in different colonies, and there seems also a difference in different winters. In some cases perhaps the dead bees all reach the cellar bottom, in others staying in the hive.

SWEEPING UP DEAD BEES.

It is very unpleasant to have the dead bees under foot on the cellar bottom. Some fasten them in the hive. Some sprinkle sawdust on the floor. In either case they are left in the cellar to foul the air. It seems much better to sweep out the cellar. During the first part of the winter very few bees will be on the floor, and sweeping once a month will be enough, or more than enough. Toward spring the deaths will be very much more frequent, and the sweeping must be more frequent. As giving a more definite idea with regard to this, I find by referring to the record that in the winter of 1901-2 the cellar was not swept till January 29—seventy-five days after the bees were taken in. Then it was swept again after respective intervals of twenty-one, nineteen, and five days, the quantity swept out each time being about the same. That gives some

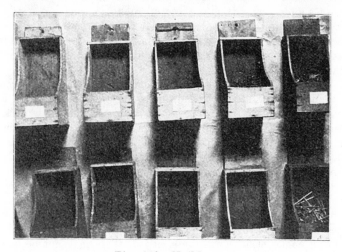

Fig. 110—Nail-boxes.

idea of the greater mortality as spring approaches. One winter, when the bees were confined 124 days, the dead bees for each colony amounted to four-fifths of a quart or three-fifths of a pound, which made about 2130 bees for each colony I think the mortality is usually greater than that.

FURNACE IN CELLAR.

In the year 1902 the coal famine following the great anthracite strike caught me with four hard-coal stoves and no coal to put in them—indeed, no prospect of getting any, and winter close at hand.

About that time my friend E. R. Root happened to be here, and strongly advised as the best way out of the dilemma

to have a furnace put in—one big enough to heat the whole
house, and of such character as to burn wood, green or dry,
coal, hard or soft, and indeed any thing having any inclination toward combustibility. I followed his advice, or rather I
outran it, for I got a larger furnace than he thought advisable,
the firepot being 27 inches in diameter. I am not sorry the
furnace is so large so far as heating the house is concerned,
for it makes a delightful summer temperature in any part of
the house, no matter how cold the weather, without any of
that unpleasant and unwholesome burnt-air effect. But it
made a matter of impossibility for me to think of keeping
the temperature of the bee-room down to 45 degrees; and since
that time, instead of having to make an effort to keep the cellar warm enough, the problem has been to keep it cool enough.

UNFAVORABLE CONDITIONS.

Conditions for successful wintering were by no means
the best.

The workmen that set up the furnace were late in finishing up the last part of the work in the cellar, so that the bees
were not put in till the 8th of December. On that day the
temperature was 8 degrees below zero. It would have been
much better to leave them out for another flight if I had been
sure of a day warm enough without waiting too long. But I
was not sure of that, and I thought it better for them to be
taken in in rather bad condition than to run the risk of leaving them out longer. The sequel showed I was wise in so
doing, for no day warm enough for a flight came until February 26.

A thin partition of lath and plaster is all that separates
the bee-room from the room in which the furnace is located,
and the thermometer in the bee-room generally showed a temperature of 50 degrees. Some of the hot-air pipes pass
through the bee-room overhead; and a thermometer laid on one
of the two hives directly under one of these pipes nearest the
furnace showed a temperature of 70 degrees. The pipe is covered with asbestos paper, but there was only a space of about
three inches between the pipe and the top of the hives. There
was plenty of room to set these colonies in a cooler place, but

they were allowed to stay right where they were to see what
the result would be. They wintered beautifully—until they
died. They starved to death, and that not so very late in
winter, although I think they were well supplied with stores.
No doubt the heat kept them so active that they used up their
stores with unusual rapidity.

BAD WINTERING.

Under the circumstances I figured on considerable loss.
The loss went beyond my figuring. Not that the deaths all
occurred in the cellar. They were largely after the bees were
taken out in the spring; none the less, however, they were
chargeable to bad wintering. By the 12th of May there were
left only 124 colonies out of 199 put in cellar, and many of
them were mere nuclei. A loss of 37 per cent was not gratifying; but, beekeeperlike, I looked forward hopefully to the next
winter.

Alas for my hopes! Instead of 37 per cent, the loss for
the winter of 1903-04 was 47 per cent, leaving 150 colonies
alive out of 284. And the loss was mainly due to lack of
sufficient stores. Some of them had died in the cellar, and
more would have died there if they had not been taken out a
little earlier than was well, so they could be fed. But feeding very early in spring is not so well as having an abundance
of stores in the fall, and the mortality continued well along
in spring. The fact that after so many years of experience,
and after advising others always to have abundant stores for
winter, I should have lost colonies by the score through starvation, was humiliating indeed.

But conditions were new and I needed to learn that in a
cellar with the thermometer generally ranging from 50 to 60,
and sometimes going higher, bees consume stores much more
rapidly than at a lower temperature, and to the increasing
number of those who are putting furnaces in cellars, I would
say, "Look out for starvation."

But along with the disadvantage mentioned, there are not
lacking advantages. Perhaps I ought to say advantage rather
than advantages, for the one great advantage is that of an
abundant supply of pure, fresh air. Except in the very

severest weather, the outside cellar door is more or less open, and the air in the cellar is sweeter than in many—perhaps most—living-rooms. That's good for the people living over the cellar, and it must be good for the bees. Inside the hives the combs are just as dry and nice as in summer. No dampness, no mould, no musty smell.

It seems nice to look into a hive and find so few dead bees lying on the bottom-board, often none. When a bee wants to die, it is warm enough so it can come outside, just as in summer.

It would be better if it was so arranged that fresh air could enter without the light. During the first part of the winter, the bees do not seem to mind the light at all, and not very much till toward spring, when the door must be closed in daytime. But there is no need to be unduly frightened by a few bees coming out; for bees will get old and die off, no matter how dark the cellar is kept; and there may be some question whether a little light is as bad as the fouler air when the cellar is closed.

GOOD WINTERING.

Having had such a severe lesson, you may be sure that in succeeding years I took pains to see that before the bees went into the cellar they had enough stores to stand a winter temperature of 50 or 60 degrees. The result has been very gratifying. I no longer have anxiety about wintering, and do not expect any colonies to die unless it be from queenlessness.

Some one may say, "But why don't you make sure that no queenless colony goes into the cellar?" Possibly that might be better; but I doubt. The queenless colony is not worth very much at that time of year, and anything that would be done with it would hardly pay for the trouble of hunting through a number of colonies causing them no little disturbance.

On the whole I am quite in favor of a furnace in cellar. To be sure, it does away with one argument in favor of cellaring, for there may be as heavy consumption of stores as on the summer stands, but that is greatly overbalanced by having the bees practically outdoors all winter in a very mild climate. For with the abundance of fresh air allowed, are they not practically outdoors? Besides that, I think the bees are

stronger—I mean each individual bee is stronger—when well
wintered outdoors than when wintered in the usual close cellar, and I think there will be that same strength when wintered
in a cellar with a furnace and a full supply of outdoor air.

EUROPEAN FOUL BROOD.

In the year 1907 a number of cells of dead brood were
found in colony No. 13. I cannot now be certain of it, but I
think a few such dead brood had been seen a year or two previously. A large cherry orchard in easy range of my bees had
been sprayed before the blossoms had fallen, and it was easy
to believe that the poison sprayed on these blossoms was ac-
countable for the dead brood. Nothing was done about it, and
No. 13 turned out to be one of the best in the apiary. In 1908
I think some cells of dead brood were found in two colonies.
The season was good, and no attention was paid to it, the idea
still being that the poisonous spray was the cause of the
trouble.

Beginning with the year 1909 I decided to give up the
last out-apiary (the Wilson), and keep all colonies in the home
apiary. When I found out later what was before me I was
thankful that all were in a single apiary. Diseased brood was
found to such an extent and in so many colonies that I sent a
sample to Dr. E. F. Phillips at Washington. Back came the
report that European foul brood was the thing I had to deal
with. I do not know how many colonies were diseased at the
opening of the season, but I do know that we had been doing
our very best to spread the disease throughout the whole
apiary by indiscriminate exchanging of combs of brood.

It was fairly along in the season when I got the word
from Washington, and here is what I had to face: A season of
dearth, there being a dead failure of the early honey flow;
bees in about 150 hives, counting nuclei and all, and only 22 of
them that showed no sign of disease throughout the whole
season; with a disease that at that time was said to be ten
times worse than American foul brood. I felt like giving up,
but for only a little while. If others had fought the disease,
why couldn't I? Besides, I could now have some live experience
with a thing I had only previously read about.

I started in to use the McEvoy treatment, brushing the

diseased colonies upon foundation, after doing some breaking
up and doubling. In all, however, only 56 colonies were actually brushed upon foundation. When I came to look how
they were building up, I found, out of those first treated, that
nine had left, bag and baggage, leaving empty hives. That
was probably from starvation, so after that I gave to each
shaken colony one or more sections of honey taken from diseased colonies. So far as I know, this did not in any case
convey the disease. Later, to make more sure against deser-
tion, one of the diseased combs was left in the hive, and
beside it two empty frames—not even a starter in the two
frames, and the rest of the hive empty. When the bees made
a start at building in the empty frames, the old comb was
taken away, and the hive was filled up with full sheets of
foundation. Sometimes the comb the bees had built in the
empty frames was taken away after a good start was made
on the foundation, and sometimes not. The outcome seemed
to be all right either way.

Partly to please Editor E. R. Root, toward the latter part
of the summer I tried the Alexander treatment. The gist of
that treatment is to remove the queen and in 20 days give the
colony a ripe queen-cell of best Italian stock, or else a very
young virgin. Previous to the treatment, however, an important requisite is to make the colony *strong*.

I varied from the regular treatment by giving hybrid
virgins instead of Italians, as my bees were mostly hybrids.
It may be a question whether hybrids are not as good as Italians in carrying out the treatment, provided the hybrids are
of equal vigor.

I made the inexcusable blunder of understanding that Mr.
Alexander had given a *laying* queen at the end of 20 days of
queenlessness, instead of giving a virgin. So I gave a young
virgin after ten days of queenlessness, so that there would be
a laying queen present in about 20 days from the removal of
the queen. I now think that the blunder was a fortunate one,
since there is a gain of 8 or 10 days in the time of the treatment, always provided that continued trial of the plan by
myself and others should prove it to be reliable.

There were some cases of failure, but in each of these

cases the colonies had not been made very strong. Mr. Alexander had emphasized the point that in order to have the treatment effective the colony must be strong, either by uniting or giving frames of sealed brood. My experience leads me to think that not only must the colony be strong but it must be strong in *young* bees.

With the opening of the season of 1910 you may well suppose I was on the alert to see whether any colonies were diseased. In fact I was really hoping there would be some cases, for I had formed a theory and wanted to try some experiments. I was not disappointed. In 27 hives could be found the distinctive mark of the disease, in some only a cell or two, while in others as much as one cell in every ten was affected.

Some one may think it a difficult thing to detect the disease if only one or two bad cells are to be found in a hive. It is not difficult. The healthy brood is pearly white, while the diseased larva being distinctly yellow is quickly spotted, just as you would easily detect a yellow hen in a flock of white ones. It was impossible to say how many of the 27 cases were old offenders and how many of them were fresh cases brought in from outside; for there were diseased colonies all about me, and there was no law in Illinois to clean them up.

About that theory—the theory as to how the disease is continued in the hive and conveyed from one cell to another —it is well known that if a larva be broken open the bees will suck up its juices, and in a case of starvation the juices of the larvæ are consumed and the white skins thrown out of the hive. When a larva first becomes diseased, and has not yet become offensive, it is easy to believe that the nurse-bees will suck up its juices, and then when they feed healthy larvæ the healthy larvæ will become diseased. But in a little while a diseased larva will become decayed and offensive, so that it will no longer be eaten by the nurse-bees. If this supposition be correct, it will come to pass that if egg-laying should stop for 5 or 6 days (the time a larva remains unsealed in its cell) there will no longer be in the hive at the same time diseased larvæ fit for the nurses to eat and healthy larvæ to which the diseased food may be given, and thus the disease should come to an end.

It was not hard to make the test. I caged the queen of a diseased colony after strengthening it, and freed her after six days of imprisonment. No more diseased brood appeared in the hive. Of course, one swallow does not make a summer, and this might not work in all cases. Neither would I in any bad case recommend the continuance of the old queen after treatment. A queen that has been for some time in a foul-broody colony seems sluggish, and is better replaced by a vigorous young queen.

As between the McEvoy and the Alexander—or the Alexander-Miller treatment as it has been called—there is so much to be gained in the saving of combs that, even if the first plan always succeeds and the other sometimes fails, it may be cheaper to use the latter and treat over again the failures. But I may remark in passing that among the 27 cases of 1910 some of them were of those that had been brushed upon foundation the previous year.

With my present knowledge of the disease, here is the treatment that I believe well worth trying for European foul brood: Make the colony *strong*, preferably by giving sealed brood so as to have abundance of young bees; remove the queen and at the same time give a ripe queen-cell or a very young virgin, which cell or virgin shall be of the most vigorous stock, and trust the bees to do the rest.

In a mild case I do not think it necessary to take so much trouble: merely keep the queen caged in the hive for a week or ten days, and then free her. In the year 1913 about one in four of my colonies was slightly affected, and in nearly all cases all I did was to cage the queen for about eight days. The fact that in spite of the disease I averaged a little more than 266 sections per colony from 72 colonies, spring count, shows that good crops may be obtained even where European foul brood is present. Still, I am sure I could have done a little better without the disease.

In 1914, five cases showed up in the first week of June in 91 colonies. They were all mild, and were treated successfully by caging the queen.

Now please remember that I do not give this as a treatment well tried and thoroughly reliable. My theory is only a theory, and the plan of treatment needs confirmation, as the newspapers say. I only say that I think the treatment worth trying because it has worked with success so far; and if it proves successful with others it will be no small gain.

Remember, too, that it is European foul brood I am talking about. For American foul brood the plan would be worthless.

DRIPPING-PAN WAX-EXTRACTOR.

Before the introduction of the solar wax-extractor, the rendering of wax was generally reserved as winter's work, and indeed after the introduction of the solar it was often convenient to work up in winter some of the material saved up. A very simple arrangement on a small scale did excellent work on much the same principle as the solar extractor, only the heat of the stove was used in place of solar heat.

An old dripping-pan (of course a new one would do) had one corner split open, and that made the extractor. The dripping-pan is put into the oven of a cookstove with the split corner projecting out (Fig. 107). The opposite corner, the one farthest in the oven, is slightly raised by having a pebble or something of the kind under it, so that the melted wax will run outward. A dish set under catches the dripping wax, making the outfit complete. Of course the material to be melted is put in the pan the same as in the solar extractor.

SOLAR WAX-EXTRACTOR.

I do not know that the solar extractor has any advantage over the dripping-pan arrangement, except that the sun furnishes free heat. In either case, when old combs are melted a good deal of wax remains in the refuse or slumgum, because the cocoons act much like sponges. Especially is this the case if more than a single thickness of comb is placed for melting.

STEAM WAX-PRESS.

So when the German steam wax-press came, leaving the slumgum mostly free from wax, the solar extractor had to take a back seat, leaving wax-rendering again a proper thing for winter work.

The wax-press is placed upon the cookstove (Fig. 108), and the work is done according to the instructions sent out with the machine. I find that time is an important element in the work, and that there is nothing to be gained by trying to hurry up matters by screwing down very hard. If the screw be turned down as tight as can be done without sliding the can around on the stove, that is all that is necessary. Then when the wax ceases to run it can be turned down again. Continu-

Fig. 111—"Busy at the Typewriter."

ing in this way till no more wax runs, when the slumgum is turned out (Fig. 109) it is so free from wax that it is not worth working over again. The wax saved by using the steam wax-press will pay immense interest on the money invested in its purchase.

But the tendency to specializing has invaded the domain of wax-rendering, and now one can send off his old combs, cappings, and bits of wax, and have the rendering done by specialists without the bother and muss.

OTHER WINTER WORK.

The work of getting sections ready for the hoped-for harvest of the coming summer has already been mentioned, and the winter affords opportunity for making up hives,

supers, or any fixtures that may be needed. As these things
are bought mostly in the flat, the chief part of the work is nailing, and it is a great convenience to have the different kinds
of nails in their proper places ready for immediate use. A
set of nail-boxes, part of which are seen in Fig. 110, serves
the purpose excellently. The boxes are patterned somewhat
after a tin nail-box I saw at a tin-shop. When a box is taken
from its nail on the wall, laid flat and slightly shaken, the
nails are easily picked up from the shallow part of the box.

Truth compels me to say that so many different persons
find it convenient to use these boxes and inconvenient to return them, that of late the boxes are not always found in their
proper places, and when the picture was taken they were
assembled for that special occasion.

Most of the winter time, however, is occupied with reading and writing. There are some thirty or forty bee journals
to be read, and a large part of them are printed in the German
and French languages. I am a poor scholar in either German
or French, so it is not strange if I sometimes get behind in my
reading, to bring up in winter. I wish I could find the time
to read over again at my leisure in winter all the bee journals
that I read more or less hurriedly in summer. But I never
find the time. I used to think that if I ever lived to be fifty
years old I would take things very leisurely. But I am now
past fifty, and I never was more crowded in my life before.

WRITING FOR THE BEE JOURNALS.

Besides the reading, there is the writing. Some extra
writing usually to be done each winter, besides the regular
work in that line. I have written "Stray Straws" for *Gleanings in Bee Culture* ever since December, 1890, and four years
later I began writing answers to questions in the *American
Bee Journal*. The thought of keeping up that work year in
and year out, with never a vacation, summer or winter, would
be somewhat wearisome if it were not that I delight in the
work. If any one of my readers should hesitate about sending to me any question connected with beekeeping because of
the thought that it will be unpleasant to me, let him disabuse
his mind of any such thought. The receipt of such questions
is a real pleasure.

One thing, however, that gives pain instead of pleasure, is to find a stamp enclosed upon opening a letter, for then I know that the writer expects an answer by mail, and, in justice to others, answering bee-questions by mail is a thing I cannot do. If I should answer one by mail I must answer others, and the only fair way is to treat all alike. The request for me to answer a question in print will always be cheerfully complied with without any stamp accompanying the request.

IF BEGINNING AGAIN.

I am sometimes asked whether, if beginning afresh, I would take the same course I have already been over. That is not a very easy question to answer. There are some things that can be settled only by experiment, and about such things one cannot reply offhand. Likely, if I were beginning all over again not many things would be different from what they are. But it may be worth while to answer as well as I can about a few things.

CHOICE OF LOCATION.

If I were to start in afresh, I would take some pains to select a location as favorable for beekeeping as possible. I didn't choose a location. I just began beekeeping where I was, with no thought of doing any thing in a commercial way, and grew into the business. I certainly would not start in afresh in a location with only one principal honey plant, and that sometimes a failure. That was the condition here, clover the only dependence for a crop, and that with too many off years. Of late years, however, the fall crop is worth considering.

HIVE-STANDS.

I surely would not start in with such hive-stands as I now have. The bottom-board resting upon so large a flat surface makes a good place for moisture to lodge, and favors rotting both bottom-board and stand. It also makes a fine place for the large black ants to lodge and honeycomb the boards. Something would be better that allows a smaller area of contact. Tile or cement might fill the bill.

ITALIAN BEES.

Through years of selection I secured hybrids that were

hustlers. But they were cross. If I had it to do over again I would look out more for temper, and I think I would stick to pure Italian blood, even if occasionally a hybrid colony should store most honey. If I had persisted in breeding from pure Italian stock, I might have had just as good hustlers, with less tendency to change, and with better tempers.

As already mentioned, since 1912 I have mainly Italian stock that is excellent, but not as gentle as I should like. If, from the beginning, I had rigidly stuck to Italians, I might now have bees of best gathering qualities, and by attending to other qualities I might now have hustlers beautiful in appearance, mild in temper, and little given to swarming.

EIGHT VERSUS TEN FRAMES.

I changed from ten-frame to eight-frame hives, I think, more than for any other reason because at that time it was the fashion. I do not know that I got any better crops by changing. When it comes to moving hives about, the advantage is decidedly in favor of the smaller hive. The same may be said of the supers. I am not sure the smaller hives have any other advantage, unless it be that they occupy less space and cost a little less. But the larger hive has the great advantage that it can have a larger supply of stores on hand at all times, making less danger of starvation in winter and spring. That makes less trouble and less anxiety. An eight-frame hive is sometimes too small for a queen without a second story, where a single story with ten frames would answer. So if it were to do over again, very likely I might continue the ten-frame hive.

EXTRACTED HONEY VERSUS COMB.

I have learned the production of comb honey as a trade, and it would be a good deal like taking up an entirely different business to take up the production of extracted honey. Nevertheless I do not *know* that I can make more money with comb than with extracted honey. At one time there was so much adulteration of extracted honey that the price of the genuine article was affected thereby. Pure-food laws have changed that, so that comb honey has no longer that advantage.

There is another matter that deserves serious considera-

tion. If I were running for extracted honey I would undoubt-
edly produce more honey than by running for comb honey.
If more honey is produced, more of it will be consumed, and I
believe increased consumption of honey would be a fine thing
for the health of the nation. So if I were broad-minded
enough, very likely I would start in again as an extracted-
honey man.

Indeed, it is true that in 1913 I returned to the extractor
sufficiently to extract several hundred pounds, and it is not
impossible that I may do still more in that line.

"OFFICE."

Possibly some one of my readers might desire a picture of
the office in which I do my work. That would take a number
of pictures. According to circumstances, my office may be on
the back porch seen in Fig. 1, or it may be in any one of nine
different rooms inside. A look at the furnishings in Fig. 111
will show that it is no serious undertaking to move my "office"
whenever desired. I never like to be far from the rest of the
family, and when at work I enjoy the sound of their voices,
even though I may pay no attention to what they are saying.
They are generally quite considerate in refraining from inter-
rupting my work by remarks directed personally to me, but
sometimes they forget.

I count myself singularly blessed in having a home where
all the members of the family are so united in their tastes and
enjoyments. One of our chief earthly pleasures is the love of
flowers. At our quiet country home we have room unlimited
for producing summer roses by the bushel, and the bay window
of the sitting-room brightens the days of winter with its bright
colors and luxuriant green. If you were here, I am sure you
would enjoy a sight of that window, and then I would take
pride in displaying to you my set of china honey-dishes shown
in the last picture in the book. They were painted by my sister,
each dish showing a separate honey plant, one-half the dish
being covered by a honeycomb.

I desire to record my deep gratitude to a loving Heavenly
Father for giving me so busy and happy a life; and for you,
dear reader, I can hardly express a better wish than that your
life may be as happy, if not as busy, as mine.

Some years ago, at the instigation of Editor E. R. Root, I wrote a honey leaflet which has been circulated by hundreds of thousands. It has been thought well that it should be reproduced in more permanent form by having a place in the present work, and here follows:

HONEY AS A WHOLESOME FOOD.

About 80 pounds of sugar on the average is annually consumed by every man, woman, and child in the United States. Of course, many use less than the average, but to make up for it some consume several times as much. It is only within the last few centuries that sugar has become known, and only within the last generation that refined sugars have become so low in price that they may be commonly used in the poorest families. Formerly honey was the principal sweet, and it was one of the items sent as a propitiatory offering by Jacob to his unrecognized son, the chief ruler of Egypt, 3000 years before the first sugar refinery was built.

It would be greatly for the health of the present generation if honey could be at least partially restored to its former place as a common article of diet. The almost universal craving for sweets of some kind shows a real need of the system in that direction, but the excessive use of sugar brings in its train a long list of ills. Besides the various disorders of the alimentary canal, fatal disease of the kidneys is credited with being one of the results of sugar-eating. When cane sugar is taken into the stomach, it cannot be assimilated until first changed by digestion into grape sugar. Only too often the overtaxed stomach fails to perform this digestion properly, then come sour stomach and various dyspeptic phases. Prof. A. J. Cook says:

"If cane sugar is absorbed without change, it will be removed by the kidneys, and may result in their breakdown; and physicians may be correct in asserting that the large consumption of cane sugar by the twentieth-century man is harmful to the great eliminators—the kidneys—and so a menace to health and long life."

Now, in the wonderful laboratory of the beehive there is found a sweet that needs no further digestion, having been prepared fully by those wonderful chemists—the bees—for prompt assimilation without taxing stomach or kidneys. As Prof. Cook says: "There can be no doubt but that in eating honey our digestive machinery is saved work that it would have to perform if we ate cane sugar; and in case it is overtaxed and feeble, this may be just the respite that will save from a breakdown."

A. I. Root says: "Many people who cannot eat sugar without having unpleasant symptoms follow, will find by careful test that they can eat good, well-ripened honey without any difficulty at all.

HONEY THE MOST DELICIOUS SAUCE.

Not only is honey the most wholesome of all sweets, but it is the most delicious. No preparation of man can equal the delicately flavored product of the hive. Millions of flowers are brought under tribute, presenting their tiny cups of dainty nectar to be gathered by the busy riflers; and when they have brought it to the proper consistency, and stored it in the wondrously wrought waxen cells and sealed it with coverings of snowy whiteness, no more tempting dish can grace the table at the most lavish banquet; and yet its cost is so moderate that it may well find its place on the tables of the common people every day in the week.

IT IS ECONOMY TO USE HONEY.

Indeed, in many cases it may be a matter of real economy to lessen the butter bill by letting honey in part take its place. A pound of honey will go about as far as a pound of butter; and if both articles be of the best quality the honey will cost the less of the two. Often a prime article of extracted honey (equal to comb honey in every respect except appearance) can be obtained for about half the price of butter. Butter is at its best only when "fresh," while honey, properly kept, remains indefinitely good—no need to hurry it out of the way for fear it may become rancid.

GIVE CHILDREN HONEY.

Prof. Cook says: "We all know how children long for candy. This longing voices a need, and is another evidence of the necessity of sugar in our diet. . . . Children should be given all the honey at each mealtime that they will eat. It is safer, will largely do away with the inordinate longing for candy and other sweets; and in lessening the desire will doubtless diminish the amount of cane sugar eaten. Then if cane sugar does work mischief with health, the harm may be prevented."

Ask the average child whether he will have honey alone on his bread or butter alone, and almost invariably he will promptly answer, "Honey." Yet seldom are the needs or the tastes of the child properly consulted. The old man craves fat meat; the child loathes it. He wants sweet, not fat. He delights to eat honey; it is a wholesome food for him, and is not expensive. Why should he not have it?

HONEY BEST TO SWEETEN HOT DRINKS.

Sugar is much used in hot drinks, as in coffee and tea. The substitution of a mild-flavored honey in such uses may be a very profitable thing for the health. Indeed, it would be better for the health if the only hot drink were what is called in Germany "honey tea"—a cup of hot water with one or two tablespoonfuls of extracted honey. The attainment of great age has in some cases been attributed largely to the lifelong use of honey tea.

COMB AND EXTRACTED HONEY.

At the present day honey is placed on the market in two forms—in the comb and extracted. "Strained" honey, obtained by mashing or melting combs containing bees, pollen, and honey, has rightly gone out of use. Extracted honey is simply honey thrown out of the comb in a machine called a honey-extractor. The combs are revolved rapidly in a cylinder, and centrifugal force throws out the honey. The comb remains uninjured, and is returned to the hive to be refilled again and again. For this reason extracted honey is usually sold at a less price than comb honey, because each pound of comb is made at the expense of several pounds of honey.

DIFFERENT KINDS OF FLAVORS.

Many people think "honey is honey"—all just alike; but this is a great mistake. Honey may be of good, heavy body—what beekeepers call "well-ripened"—weighing generally twelve pounds to the gallon, or it may be quite thin. It may also be granulated, or candied, more solid than lard. It may also be almost as colorless as water, and it may be as black as the darkest molasses. The flavor of honey varies according to the flower from which it is obtained. It would be impossible to describe in words the flavors of the different honeys. You may easily distinguish the odor of a rose from that of a carnation, but you might find it difficult to describe them in words so that a novice smelling them for the first time could tell which was which. But the different flavors in honey are just as distinct as the odors in flowers. Among the light-colored honeys are white clover, linden (or basswood), sage, sweet clover, alfalfa, willow-herb, etc., and among the darker are found heartsease, magnolia (or poplar), horsemint, buckwheat, etc.

ADULTERATION OF HONEY.

In these days of prevailing adulterations, when so often "things are not what they seem," it is a comfort to know that *strictly pure honey*, both extracted and comb, can still be had and at a reasonable price. The silly stories seen from time to time in the papers about artificial combs being filled with glucose, and deftly sealed over with a hot iron, have not the slightest foundation in fact. For years there has been a standing offer by one whose financial responsibility is unquestioned of $1000 for a single pound of comb honey made without the intervention of bees. The offer remains untaken, and will probably always remain so, for the highest art of man can never compass such delicate workmanship as the skill of the bee accomplishes.

Extracted honey, however, is not incapable of imitation. Time was when a tumbler on a grocer's shelf labeled honey might contain honey, and it might contain glucose. If you were well enough acquainted with honey you might tell the difference by the taste; otherwise you had to trust to the honesty of the grocer. Always, however, you could be sure of the genuine article by getting it from the beekeeper himself. But the pure-food laws have changed all that, and nowadays you may trust that the label correctly represents what is under it.

CARE OF HONEY—WHERE TO KEEP IT.

The average housekeeper will put honey in the cellar for safe keeping —about the worst place possible. Honey readily attracts moisture, and in the cellar extracted honey will become thin, and in time may sour; and with comb honey the case is still worse, for the appearance as well as the quality is changed. The beautiful white surface becomes watery and darkened, drops of water ooze through the cappings, and weep over the surface. Instead of keeping honey in a place moist and cool, keep it dry and warm, even hot. It will not hurt to be in a temperature of even 100 degrees. Where salt will keep dry is a good place for honey. Few places are better than the kitchen cupboard. Up in a hot garret next the roof is a good place, and if it has had enough hot days there through the summer, it will stand the freezing of winter; for under ordinary circumstances freezing cracks the combs, and hastens granulation or candying.

GRANULATED HONEY—TO RELIQUEFY.

When honey is kept for any length of time it has a tendency to change from its clear liquid condition, and becomes granulated or candied. This is not to be taken as any evidence against its genuineness, but rather the contrary. Some prefer it in the candied state, but the majority prefer it liquid. It is an easy matter to restore it to its former liquid condition. Simply keep it in hot water long enough, *but not too hot*. If heated above 160 degrees there is danger of spoiling the color and ruining the flavor. Remember that honey contains the most delicate of all flavors—that of the flowers from which it is taken. A good way is to set the vessel containing the honey inside another vessel containing hot water, not allowing the bottom of the one to rest directly on the bottom of the other, but putting a bit of wood or something of the kind between. Let it stand on the stove, but do not let the water boil. It may take half a day or longer to melt the honey. If the honey is set directly on the reservoir of a cook-stove, it will be all right in a few days. In time it will granulate again, when it must again be melted.

HONEY COOKING RECIPES.

HONEY GEMS.—Two quarts flour, 3 tablespoonfuls melted lard, ¾ pint honey, ½ pint of molasses, 4 heaping tablespoonfuls brown sugar, 1½ level tablespoonfuls soda, 1 level teaspoonful salt, 1/3 pint water, ½ teaspoonful extract vanilla.

HONEY JUMBLES.—Two quarts flour, 3 tablespoonfuls melted lard, 1 pint honey, ¼ pint molasses, 1½ level tablespoonfuls soda, 1 level teaspoonful salt, ¼ pint water, ½ teaspoonful vanilla.

The jumbles and the gems immediately preceding are from recipes used by bakers and confectioners on a large scale, one firm in Wisconsin alone using ten tons of honey annually in their manufacture.

AIKIN'S HONEY COOKIES.—One teacupful extracted honey, 1 pint sour cream, scant teaspoonful soda, flavoring if desired, flour to make a soft dough.

SOFT HONEY CAKE.—One cup butter, 2 cups honey, 2 eggs, 1 cup sour milk, 2 teaspoonfuls soda, 1 teaspoonful ginger, 1 teaspoonful cinnamon, 4 cups flour.—*Chalon Fowls.*

GINGER HONEY CAKE.—One cup honey, ½ cup butter, or drippings, 1 tablespoonful boiled cider, in half a cup of hot water (or ½ cup sour milk will do instead). Warm these ingredients together, and then add 1 tablespoonful ginger and 1 teaspoonful soda sifted in with flour enough to make a soft batter. Bake in a flat pan.—*Chalon Fowls.*

OBERLIN HONEY FRUIT CAKE.—Half cup butter, ¾ cup honey, 1-3 cup apple jelly or boiled cider, 2 eggs well beaten, 1 teaspoonful soda, 1 teaspoonful each of cinnamon, cloves, and nutmeg, 1 teacupful each of raisins and dried currants. Warm the butter, honey, and apple jelly slightly; add the beaten eggs, then the soda dissolved in a little warm water; add spices and flour enough to make a stiff batter, then stir in the fruit and bake in a slow oven. Keep in a covered jar several weeks before using.

HONEY POPCORN BALLS.—Take 1 pint extracted honey; put it into an iron frying pan, and boil until very thick; then stir in freshly popped corn, and when cool mold into balls. These will especially delight the children.

HONEY SHORTCAKE.—Three cups flour, 2 teaspoonfuls baking powder, 1 teaspoonful salt, ½ cup shortening, 1½ cups sweet milk. Roll quickly, and bake in a hot oven. When done, split the cake and spread the lower half thinly with butter, and the upper half with ½ pound of the best-flavored honey. (Candied honey is preferred. If too hard to spread well it should be warmed or creamed with a knife.) Let it stand a few minutes, and the honey will melt gradually, and the flavor will permeate all through the cake. To be eaten with milk.

OBERLIN HONEY LAYER CAKE.—Two-thirds cup butter, 1 cup honey, 3 eggs beaten, ½ cup milk. Cream the butter and honey together, then add the eggs and milk. Then add 2 cups of flour containing 1½ teaspoonfuls baking powder previously stirred in. Then stir in flour to make a stiff batter. Bake in jelly-tins. When the cakes are cold, take finely flavored candied honey, and, after creaming it, spread between the layers.

HONEY NUT-CAKES.—Eight cups sugar, 2 cups honey, 4 cups milk or water, 1 pound almonds, 1 pound English walnuts, 3 cents' worth each of candied lemon and orange peel, 5 cents' worth citron (the last three cut fine), 2 large tablespoonfuls soda, 2 teaspoonfuls cinnamon, 2 teaspoonfuls ground cloves. Put the milk, sugar, and honey on the stove to boil 15 minutes; skim off the scum, and take from the stove. Put in the nuts, spices, and candied fruit. Stir in as much flour as can be done with a spoon. Set away to cool, then mix in the soda (don't make the dough too stiff). Cover up and let stand over night, then work in enough flour to make a stiff dough. Bake when you get ready. It is well to let it stand a few days, as it will not stick so badly. Roll out a little thicker than a common cooky, cut in any shape you like.

This recipe originated in Germany, is old and tried, and the cake will keep a year or more.—*Mrs. E. Smith.*

MUTH'S HONEY CAKES.—One gallon honey (dark honey best), 15 eggs, 3 pounds sugar (a little more honey in its place may be better), 1½ oz. baking soda, 2 oz. ammonia, 2 lbs. almonds chopped up, 2 lbs. citron, 4 oz. cinnamon, 2 oz. cloves, 2 oz. mace, 18 lbs. flour. Let the honey come almost to a boil; then let it cool and add the other ingredients. Cut out and bake. The cakes are to be frosted afterward with sugar and white of eggs.

OBERLIN HONEY COOKIES.—Three teaspoonfuls soda dissolved in 2 cups warm honey, 1 cup shortening containing salt, 2 teaspoonfuls ginger, 1 cup hot water, flour sufficient to roll.

HONEY TEA CAKE.—One cup honey, ½ cup sour cream, 2 eggs, ½ cup butter, 2 cups flour, scant ½ teaspoonful soda, 1 teaspoonful cream of tartar. Bake 30 minutes in a moderate oven.—*Miss M. Candler.*

HONEY GINGER-SNAPS.—One pint honey, ¾ lb. butter, 2 teaspoonfuls ginger. Boil together a few minutes, and when nearly cold put in flour until it is stiff. Roll out thin, and bake quickly.

HONEY CARAMELS.—1 cup extracted honey of best flavor, 1 cup granulated sugar, 3 tablespoonsfuls sweet cream or milk. Boil to "soft crack," or until it hardens when dropped into cold water, but not too brittle—just so it will form into a soft ball when taken in the fingers. Pour into a greased dish, stirring in a teaspoonful extract of vanilla just before taking off. Let it be ½ or ¾ inch deep in the dish; and as it cools, cut in squares and wrap each square in paraffin paper, such as grocers wrap butter in. To make chocolate caramels, add to the foregoing 1 tablespoonful melted chocolate, just before taking off the stove, stirring it in well. For chocolate caramels it is not so important that the honey be of the best quality.—*C. C. Miller.*

HONEY GRAPE JELLY.—Stew the grapes until soft; mash and strain them through cheese-cloth, and to each quart of juice add one quart of honey, and boil it until it is thick enough to suit. Keep trying by dipping out a spoonful and cooling it. If you get it too thick it will candy. Any other fruit juice just treat the same way.

MOORE'S HONEY GINGER-SNAPS.—One pint of honey, one teaspoonful of ginger, and one teaspoonful soda dissolved in a little water, and two eggs. Mix all, then work in all the flour possible, roll very thin, and bake in a moderately hot oven. Any flavoring extracts can be added, as you may wish.

MOORE'S HONEY JUMBLES OR COOKIES are made in the same way as the above, without any sugar or syrup, but add some shortening. In using honey for any kind of cakes, the dough must be as stiff with flour as possible, to keep them from running out of the stove.

TO SPICE APPLES, PEARS, OR PEACHES.—One quart best vinegar, 1 quart of honey, ½ ounce each of cloves and stick cinnamon. Boil all together 15 minutes, then put in the fruit, and cook tender. Put in a stone jar with enough of the syrup to cover the fruit. It will keep as long as wanted.

FOR SUGAR-CURING 100 POUNDS OF MEAT.—Eight pounds of salt, 1 quart of honey, 2 ounces of saltpeter, and 3 gallons of water. Mix, and boil until dissolved, then pour it hot on the meat.

MRS. BARBER'S HONEY CANDY.—One quart honey, 1 small teacup of granulated sugar, butter size of an egg, 2 tablespoonfuls strong vinegar. Boil until it will harden when dropped into cold water, then stir in a small teaspoonful of baking soda. Pour into buttered plates to cool. Without the vinegar and soda it can be pulled or worked a long time, and is just the thing for an old-fashioned candy-pull, as it is not sticky, and yet is soft enough to pull nicely.

SCRIPTURE HONEY CAKE.—One cupful of butter—Judges v. 25; 3½ cupfuls of flour—I Kings iv. 22; 2 cupfuls of sugar—Jeremiah vi. 20; 2 cupfuls of raisins—I Samuel xxx. 12; 2 cupfuls of figs—I Samuel xxx. 12; 1 cupful of water—Genesis xxiv. 17; 1 cupful of almonds—Genesis xliii. 11; little salt—Leviticus ii. 13; 6 eggs—Isaiah x. 14; large spoonful of honey—Exodus xvi. 31; sweet spices to taste—I Kings x. 2.

Follow Solomon's advice for making good boys, and you will have a good cake—Prov. xxiii, 14. Sift two teaspoonfuls of baking powder in the flour; pour boiling water on the almonds to remove the skins; seed the raisins and chop the figs. It makes one large or two small cakes.

MRS. BARBER'S HONEY COOKIES.—One large teacupful of honey. One egg broken into the cup the honey was measured in, then 2 large spoonfuls sour milk, and fill the cup with butter or good beef dripping. Put in one teaspoonful of soda and flour to make a soft dough. Bake in a moderate oven a light brown.

GOTHAM HONEY GINGER CAKE.—Rub ¾ of a pound of butter into a pound of sifted flour; add a teacupful of brown sugar, 2 tablespoonfuls each of ground ginger and caraway seed. Beat 5 eggs, and stir in the mixture, alternately, with a pint of extracted honey. Beat all together until very light. Turn into a shallow square pan, and set in a moderate oven to bake for one hour. When done, let cool and cut into squares.

MRS. AIKIN'S HONEY APPLE-BUTTER.—One gallon good cooking apples, 1 quart honey, 1 quart honey-vinegar, 1 heaping teaspoonful ground cinnamon. Cook several hours, stirring often to prevent burning. If the vinegar is very strong, use part water.

HOWELL'S HARD HONEY CAKE.—Take 6 pounds of flour, 3 pounds honey, 1½ pounds of sugar, 1½ pounds butter, 6 eggs, ½ ounce saleratus; ginger to your taste. Have the flour in a pan or tray. Pack a cavity in the center. Beat the honey and yolks of eggs together well. Beat the butter and sugar to cream, and put into the cavity in the flour; then add the honey and yolks of the eggs. Mix well with the hand, adding a little at a time, during the mixing, the ½ ounce of saleratus dissolved in boiling water until it is all in. Add the ginger, and finally add the whites of the 6 eggs, well beaten. Mix well with the hand to a smooth dough. Divide the dough into 7 equal parts, and roll out like gingerbread. Bake in ordinary square pans made for pies, from 10 x 14-inch tin. After putting into the pans, mark off the top in ½-inch strips with something sharp. Bake an hour in a moderate oven. Be careful not to burn, but bake well. Dissolve sugar to glaze over top of cake. To keep the cake, stand on end in an oak tub, tin can, or stone crock—crock is best. Stand the cakes up so the flat sides will not touch each other. Cover tight. Keep in a cool, dry place. Don't use until three months old, at least. The cake improves with age, and will keep good as long as you will let it. Any cake sweetened with honey does not dry out like sugar or molasses cake, and age improves or develops the honey flavor. This recipe has been used with unvarying success and satisfaction for 100 years in the family that reports. A year's supply of this cake can be made up at one time, if desired.

MARIA FRASER'S HONEY JUMBLES.—Two cups honey, 1 cup butter, 4 eggs (mix well), 1 cup buttermilk (mix), 1 good quart of flour, 1 level teaspoonful soda or saleratus. If it is too thin, stir in a little more flour. If too thin it will fall. It does not want to be as thin as sugar cake. Use very thick honey. Be sure to use the same cup for measure, and to mix the honey, eggs, and butter well together.

HONEY FRUIT CAKE.—Take 1½ cups of honey, 2-3 cup of butter, ½ cup of sweet milk, 3 eggs well beaten, 3 cups of flour, 2 teaspoonfuls of baking powder, 2 cups raisins, 1 teaspoonful each of cloves and cinnamon.

HONEY GINGER-SNAPS.—One pint honey, ¾ pound of butter, 2 teaspoonfuls of ginger, boil together a few minutes, and when nearly cold put in flour until it is stiff, roll out thinly and bake quickly.

MRS. MINNICK'S SOFT HONEY CAKE.—Put scant teaspoonful soda in teacup, pour 5 tablespoonfuls hot water on the soda; then fill the cup with extracted honey. Take ½ cup of butter and 1 egg and beat together; add 2 cups of flour and 1 teaspoonful of ginger; stir all together, and bake in *a very slow oven.*

HONEY CAKE.—One quart of extracted honey, ½ pint sugar, ½ pint melted butter, 1 teaspoonful soda dissolved in ½ teacup warm water, ½ of a nutmeg and 1 teaspoonful of ginger. Mix these ingredients, and then work in flour and roll. Cut in thin cakes and bake on buttered tins in a quick oven.

REMEDIES USING HONEY.

HONEY AND TAR COUGH CURE.—Put 1 tablespoonful liquid tar into a shallow tin dish, and place it in boiling water until the tar is hot. To this add a pint of extracted honey, and stir well for half an hour, adding to it a level teaspoonful pulverized borax. Keep well corked in a bottle. Dose, 1 teaspoonful every one, two, or three hours, according to severity of cough.

HONEY AS A TAPEWORM REMEDY.—Peeled pumpkin seeds, 3 ounces; honey, 2 ounces; water, 8 ounces. Make an emulsion. Take half, fasting, in the morning, remainder half an hour later. In three hours' time two ounces castor oil should be administered. Used with great success.—*Medical Brief.*

HONEY FOR ERYSIPELAS is used locally by spreading it on a suitable cloth and applying to the parts. The application is renewed every 3 or 4 hours. In all cases in which the remedy has been employed, entire relief from the pain followed immediately, asd convalescence was brought about in 3 or 4 days.

HONEY FOR DYSPEPSIA.—A young man who was troubled with dyspepsia, and the more medicine he took the worse he became, was advised to try honey and graham gems for breakfast. He did so, and commenced to gain, and now enjoys as good health as the average man, and he does not take medicine, either| Honey is the only food taken into the stomach that leaves no residue; it requires no action of the stomach whatever to digest it, as it is merely absorbed and taken up into the system by the action of the blood. Honey is the natural foe to dyspepsia and indigestion, as well as a food for the human system.

HONEY FOR OLD PEOPLE'S COUGHS.—Old people's coughs are as distinct as those of children, and require remedies especially adapted to them. It is known by the constant tickling in the pit of the throat—just where the Adam's apple projects—and is caused by phlegm that accumulates there, which, in their weakened condition, they are unable to expectorate.

Take a fair-sized onion—a good strong one—and let it simmer in a quart of honey for several hours, after which strain and take a teaspoonful frequently. It eases the cough wonderfully, though it may not cure.

HONEY FOR STOMACH COUGH.—All mothers know what a stomach cough is—caused by an irritation of that organ, frequently attended with indigestion. The child often "throws up" after coughing.

Dig down to the roots of a wild-cherry tree, and peel off a handful of the bark, put it into a pint of water, and boil down to a teacupful. Put this tea into a quart of honey, and give a teaspoonful every hour or two. It is pleasant, and if the child should also have worms, which often happens, they are pretty apt to be disposed of, as they have no love for the wild-cherry flavor.

HONEY AND TAR COUGH CANDY.—Boil a double handful of green hoarhound in two quarts of water down to one quart; strain, and add to this tea two cups of extracted honey and a tablespoonful each of lard and tar. Boil down to a candy, but not enough to make it brittle. Begin to eat this, increase from a piece the size of a pea to as much as can be relished. It is an excellent cough candy, and always gives relief in a short time.

SWISS REMEDY FOR A COLD SETTLING ON THE CHEST.—Boil a quart of pure spring water; add as much camomile as can be grasped in three fingers, and three teaspoonfuls of honey, and cover tight. The vessel is then to be quickly removed from the fire and set on table at which the patient can comfortably seat himself. Throwing a woolen cloth over the patient's head so as to include the vessel, he is to remove the cover and inhale the vapors as deeply as possible through the mouth and nose, occasionally stirring the mixture until it is cold, and then retire to a warmed bed. In obstinate cases the treatment should be repeated for three evenings.

HONEY CROUP REMEDY.—This is the best known to the medical profession, and is an infallible remedy in all cases of mucus and spasmodic croup; Raw linseed oil, 2 oz.; tincture of bloodroot, 2 drs.; tincture of lobelia, 2 drs.; tincture of aconite, ½ dr.; honey, 4 oz. Mix. Dose, ½ to 1 teaspoonful every 15 to 20 minutes, according to the urgency of the case. It is also excellent in all throat and lung troubles originating from a cold.

This is an excellent remedy in lung trouble: Make a strong decoction of hoarhound herb and sweeten with honey. Take a teaspoonful 4 or 5 times a day.

HONEY ON FROSTBITES.—If your ears, fingers, or toes become frozen nothing will take the frost out of them sooner than if wrapped up in honey. The swelling is rapidly reduced, and no danger occurs.

HONEY AND CREAM FOR FRECKLES.—Have you tried a mixture of honey and cream—half and half—for freckles? Well, it's a good thing. If on the hands, wear gloves on going to bed.

DR. KNEIPP'S HONEY SALVE.—This is recommended as an excellent dressing for sores and boils. Take equal parts honey and flour, add a little water, and stir thoroughly. Don't make too thin. Then apply as usual.

SUMMER HONEY DRINK.—One spoonful of fruit juice and 1 spoonful honey in ½ glass water; stir in as much soda as will lie on a silver dime, and then stir in half as much tartaric acid, and drink at once.

DR. PEIRO'S HONEY SALVE—for boils and other diseases of a similar character—is made by thoroughly incorporating flour with honey until of a proper consistency to spread on cloth. Applied over the boil it hastens suppuration, and the early termination of the painful lesion.

HONEY AS A LAXATIVE.—In olden times the good effects of honey as a remedial agent were well known, but of late little use is made thereof. A great mistake, surely. Notably is honey valuable in constipation. Not as an immediate cure, like some medicines which momentarily give relief only to leave the case worse than ever afterward, but by its persistent use daily, bringing about a healthy condition of the bowels, enabling them to perform properly their functions. Many suffer daily from an irritable condition, calling themselves nervous, and all that sort of thing, not realizing that constipation is at the root of the matter, and that a faithful daily use of honey fairly persisted in would restore cheerfulness of mind and a healthy body.—*Le Progres Apicole*.

COUGHS, COLDS, WHOOPING COUGH, ETC.—Fill a bell-metal kettle with hoarhound leaves and soft water, letting it boil until the liquor becomes strong—then strain through a muslin cloth, adding as much honey as desired —then cook it in the same kettle until the water evaporates, when the candy may be poured into shallow vessels and remain until needed, or pulled like molasses candy until white.

INDEX.

ILLUSTRATIONS

A CATALOG OF SELECTED DOVER
BOOKS IN ALL FIELDS OF INTEREST

CONCERNING THE SPIRITUAL IN ART, Wassily Kandinsky. Pioneering work by father of abstract art. Thoughts on color theory, nature of art. Analysis of earlier masters. 12 illustrations. 80pp. of text. 5⅜ x 8½.   0-486-23411-8

CELTIC ART: The Methods of Construction, George Bain. Simple geometric techniques for making Celtic interlacements, spirals, Kells-type initials, animals, humans, etc. Over 500 illustrations. 160pp. 9 x 12. (Available in U.S. only.)   0-486-22923-8

AN ATLAS OF ANATOMY FOR ARTISTS, Fritz Schider. Most thorough reference work on art anatomy in the world. Hundreds of illustrations, including selections from works by Vesalius, Leonardo, Goya, Ingres, Michelangelo, others. 593 illustrations. 192pp. 7⅛ x 10¼.   0-486-20241-0

CELTIC HAND STROKE-BY-STROKE (Irish Half-Uncial from "The Book of Kells"): An Arthur Baker Calligraphy Manual, Arthur Baker. Complete guide to creating each letter of the alphabet in distinctive Celtic manner. Covers hand position, strokes, pens, inks, paper, more. Illustrated. 48pp. 8¼ x 11.   0-486-24336-2

EASY ORIGAMI, John Montroll. Charming collection of 32 projects (hat, cup, pelican, piano, swan, many more) specially designed for the novice origami hobbyist. Clearly illustrated easy-to-follow instructions insure that even beginning papercrafters will achieve successful results. 48pp. 8¼ x 11.   0-486-27298-2

BLOOMINGDALE'S ILLUSTRATED 1886 CATALOG: Fashions, Dry Goods and Housewares, Bloomingdale Brothers. Famed merchants' extremely rare catalog depicting about 1,700 products: clothing, housewares, firearms, dry goods, jewelry, more. Invaluable for dating, identifying vintage items. Also, copyright-free graphics for artists, designers. Co-published with Henry Ford Museum & Greenfield Village. 160pp. 8¼ x 11.   0-486-25780-0

THE ART OF WORLDLY WISDOM, Baltasar Gracian. "Think with the few and speak with the many," "Friends are a second existence," and "Be able to forget" are among this 1637 volume's 300 pithy maxims. A perfect source of mental and spiritual refreshment, it can be opened at random and appreciated either in brief or at length. 128pp. 5⅜ x 8½.   0-486-44034-6

JOHNSON'S DICTIONARY: A Modern Selection, Samuel Johnson (E. L. McAdam and George Milne, eds.). This modern version reduces the original 1755 edition's 2,300 pages of definitions and literary examples to a more manageable length, retaining the verbal pleasure and historical curiosity of the original. 480pp. 5³⁄₁₆ x 8¼.   0-486-44089-3

ADVENTURES OF HUCKLEBERRY FINN, Mark Twain, Illustrated by E. W. Kemble. A work of eternal richness and complexity, a source of ongoing critical debate, and a literary landmark, Twain's 1885 masterpiece about a barefoot boy's journey of self-discovery has enthralled readers around the world. This handsome clothbound reproduction of the first edition features all 174 of the original black-and-white illustrations. 368pp. 5⅜ x 8½.   0-486-44322-1

STICKLEY CRAFTSMAN FURNITURE CATALOGS, Gustav Stickley and L. & J. G. Stickley. Beautiful, functional furniture in two authentic catalogs from 1910. 594 illustrations, including 277 photos, show settles, rockers, armchairs, reclining chairs, bookcases, desks, tables. 183pp. 6½ x 9¼.   0-486-23838-5

AMERICAN LOCOMOTIVES IN HISTORIC PHOTOGRAPHS: 1858 to 1949, Ron Ziel (ed.). A rare collection of 126 meticulously detailed official photographs, called "builder portraits," of American locomotives that majestically chronicle the rise of steam locomotive power in America. Introduction. Detailed captions. xi+ 129pp. 9 x 12.   0-486-27393-8

AMERICA'S LIGHTHOUSES: An Illustrated History, Francis Ross Holland, Jr. Delightfully written, profusely illustrated fact-filled survey of over 200 American lighthouses since 1716. History, anecdotes, technological advances, more. 240pp. 8 x 10¾.
0-486-25576-X

TOWARDS A NEW ARCHITECTURE, Le Corbusier. Pioneering manifesto by founder of "International School." Technical and aesthetic theories, views of industry, economics, relation of form to function, "mass-production split" and much more. Profusely illustrated. 320pp. 6⅛ x 9¼. (Available in U.S. only.)   0-486-25023-7

HOW THE OTHER HALF LIVES, Jacob Riis. Famous journalistic record, exposing poverty and degradation of New York slums around 1900, by major social reformer. 100 striking and influential photographs. 233pp. 10 x 7⅞.   0-486-22012-5

FRUIT KEY AND TWIG KEY TO TREES AND SHRUBS, William M. Harlow. One of the handiest and most widely used identification aids. Fruit key covers 120 deciduous and evergreen species; twig key 160 deciduous species. Easily used. Over 300 photographs. 126pp. 5⅜ x 8½.   0-486-20511-8

COMMON BIRD SONGS, Dr. Donald J. Borror. Songs of 60 most common U.S. birds: robins, sparrows, cardinals, bluejays, finches, more–arranged in order of increasing complexity. Up to 9 variations of songs of each species.
Cassette and manual 0-486-99911-4

ORCHIDS AS HOUSE PLANTS, Rebecca Tyson Northen. Grow cattleyas and many other kinds of orchids–in a window, in a case, or under artificial light. 63 illustrations. 148pp. 5⅜ x 8½.   0-486-23261-1

MONSTER MAZES, Dave Phillips. Masterful mazes at four levels of difficulty. Avoid deadly perils and evil creatures to find magical treasures. Solutions for all 32 exciting illustrated puzzles. 48pp. 8¼ x 11.   0-486-26005-4

MOZART'S DON GIOVANNI (DOVER OPERA LIBRETTO SERIES), Wolfgang Amadeus Mozart. Introduced and translated by Ellen H. Bleiler. Standard Italian libretto, with complete English translation. Convenient and thoroughly portable–an ideal companion for reading along with a recording or the performance itself. Introduction. List of characters. Plot summary. 121pp. 5¼ x 8½. 0-486-24944-1

FRANK LLOYD WRIGHT'S DANA HOUSE, Donald Hoffmann. Pictorial essay of residential masterpiece with over 160 interior and exterior photos, plans, elevations, sketches and studies. 128pp. 9¹/₄ x 10¾.   0-486-29120-0

THE CLARINET AND CLARINET PLAYING, David Pino. Lively, comprehensive work features suggestions about technique, musicianship, and musical interpretation, as well as guidelines for teaching, making your own reeds, and preparing for public performance. Includes an intriguing look at clarinet history. "A godsend," *The Clarinet,* Journal of the International Clarinet Society. Appendixes. 7 illus. 320pp. 5⅜ x 8½. 0-486-40270-3

HOLLYWOOD GLAMOR PORTRAITS, John Kobal (ed.). 145 photos from 1926-49. Harlow, Gable, Bogart, Bacall; 94 stars in all. Full background on photographers, technical aspects. 160pp. 8⅜ x 11¼. 0-486-23352-9

THE RAVEN AND OTHER FAVORITE POEMS, Edgar Allan Poe. Over 40 of the author's most memorable poems: "The Bells," "Ulalume," "Israfel," "To Helen," "The Conqueror Worm," "Eldorado," "Annabel Lee," many more. Alphabetic lists of titles and first lines. 64pp. 5 3/16 x 8¼. 0-486-26685-0

PERSONAL MEMOIRS OF U. S. GRANT, Ulysses Simpson Grant. Intelligent, deeply moving firsthand account of Civil War campaigns, considered by many the finest military memoirs ever written. Includes letters, historic photographs, maps and more. 528pp. 6⅛ x 9¼. 0-486-28587-1

ANCIENT EGYPTIAN MATERIALS AND INDUSTRIES, A. Lucas and J. Harris. Fascinating, comprehensive, thoroughly documented text describes this ancient civilization's vast resources and the processes that incorporated them in daily life, including the use of animal products, building materials, cosmetics, perfumes and incense, fibers, glazed ware, glass and its manufacture, materials used in the mummification process, and much more. 544pp. 6⅛ x 9¼. (Available in U.S. only.) 0-486-40446-3

RUSSIAN STORIES/RUSSKIE RASSKAZY: A Dual-Language Book, edited by Gleb Struve. Twelve tales by such masters as Chekhov, Tolstoy, Dostoevsky, Pushkin, others. Excellent word-for-word English translations on facing pages, plus teaching and study aids, Russian/English vocabulary, biographical/critical introductions, more. 416pp. 5⅜ x 8½. 0-486-26244-8

PHILADELPHIA THEN AND NOW: 60 Sites Photographed in the Past and Present, Kenneth Finkel and Susan Oyama. Rare photographs of City Hall, Logan Square, Independence Hall, Betsy Ross House, other landmarks juxtaposed with contemporary views. Captures changing face of historic city. Introduction. Captions. 128pp. 8¼ x 11. 0-486-25790-8

NORTH AMERICAN INDIAN LIFE: Customs and Traditions of 23 Tribes, Elsie Clews Parsons (ed.). 27 fictionalized essays by noted anthropologists examine religion, customs, government, additional facets of life among the Winnebago, Crow, Zuni, Eskimo, other tribes. 480pp. 6⅛ x 9¼. 0-486-27377-6

TECHNICAL MANUAL AND DICTIONARY OF CLASSICAL BALLET, Gail Grant. Defines, explains, comments on steps, movements, poses and concepts. 15-page pictorial section. Basic book for student, viewer. 127pp. 5⅜ x 8½. 0-486-21843-0

THE MALE AND FEMALE FIGURE IN MOTION: 60 Classic Photographic Sequences, Eadweard Muybridge. 60 true-action photographs of men and women walking, running, climbing, bending, turning, etc., reproduced from rare 19th-century masterpiece. vi + 121pp. 9 x 12. 0-486-24745-7

LIGHT AND SHADE: A Classic Approach to Three-Dimensional Drawing, Mrs. Mary P. Merrifield. Handy reference clearly demonstrates principles of light and shade by revealing effects of common daylight, sunshine, and candle or artificial light on geometrical solids. 13 plates. 64pp. 5⅜ x 8½. 0-486-44143-1

ASTROLOGY AND ASTRONOMY: A Pictorial Archive of Signs and Symbols, Ernst and Johanna Lehner. Treasure trove of stories, lore, and myth, accompanied by more than 300 rare illustrations of planets, the Milky Way, signs of the zodiac, comets, meteors, and other astronomical phenomena. 192pp. 8⅜ x 11. 0-486-43981-X

JEWELRY MAKING: Techniques for Metal, Tim McCreight. Easy-to-follow instructions and carefully executed illustrations describe tools and techniques, use of gems and enamels, wire inlay, casting, and other topics. 72 line illustrations and diagrams. 176pp. 8¼ x 10⅞. 0-486-44043-5

MAKING BIRDHOUSES: Easy and Advanced Projects, Gladstone Califf. Easy-to-follow instructions include diagrams for everything from a one-room house for bluebirds to a forty-two-room structure for purple martins. 56 plates; 4 figures. 80pp. 8¾ x 6⅜. 0-486-44183-0

LITTLE BOOK OF LOG CABINS: How to Build and Furnish Them, William S. Wicks. Handy how-to manual, with instructions and illustrations for building cabins in the Adirondack style, fireplaces, stairways, furniture, beamed ceilings, and more. 102 line drawings. 96pp. 8¾ x 6⅜. 0-486-44259-4

THE SEASONS OF AMERICA PAST, Eric Sloane. From "sugaring time" and strawberry picking to Indian summer and fall harvest, a whole year's activities described in charming prose and enhanced with 79 of the author's own illustrations. 160pp. 8¼ x 11. 0-486-44220-9

THE METROPOLIS OF TOMORROW, Hugh Ferriss. Generous, prophetic vision of the metropolis of the future, as perceived in 1929. Powerful illustrations of towering structures, wide avenues, and rooftop parks–all features in many of today's modern cities. 59 illustrations. 144pp. 8¼ x 11. 0-486-43727-2

THE PATH TO ROME, Hilaire Belloc. This 1902 memoir abounds in lively vignettes from a vanished time, recounting a pilgrimage on foot across the Alps and Apennines in order to "see all Europe which the Christian Faith has saved." 77 of the author's original line drawings complement his sparkling prose. 272pp. 5⅜ x 8½. 0-486-44001-X

THE HISTORY OF RASSELAS: Prince of Abissinia, Samuel Johnson. Distinguished English writer attacks eighteenth-century optimism and man's unrealistic estimates of what life has to offer. 112pp. 5⅜ x 8½. 0-486-44094-X

A VOYAGE TO ARCTURUS, David Lindsay. A brilliant flight of pure fancy, where wild creatures crowd the fantastic landscape and demented torturers dominate victims with their bizarre mental powers. 272pp. 5⅜ x 8½. 0-486-44198-9

Paperbound unless otherwise indicated. Available at your book dealer, online at **www.doverpublications.com**, or by writing to Dept. GI, Dover Publications, Inc., 31 East 2nd Street, Mineola, NY 11501. For current price information or for free catalogs (please indicate field of interest), write to Dover Publications or log on to **www.doverpublications.com** and see every Dover book in print. Dover publishes more than 500 books each year on science, elementary and advanced mathematics, biology, music, art, literary history, social sciences, and other areas.